Religion and Politics in Interwar Yugoslavia

Religion and Politics in Interwar Yugoslavia

Serbian Nationalism and East Orthodox Christianity

Maria Falina

BLOOMSBURY ACADEMIC
LONDON • NEW YORK • OXFORD • NEW DELHI • SYDNEY

BLOOMSBURY ACADEMIC
Bloomsbury Publishing Plc
50 Bedford Square, London, WC1B 3DP, UK
1385 Broadway, New York, NY 10018, USA
29 Earlsfort Terrace, Dublin 2, Ireland

BLOOMSBURY, BLOOMSBURY ACADEMIC and the Diana logo are trademarks of
Bloomsbury Publishing Plc

First published in Great Britain 2023
Paperback edition first published 2024

Copyright © Maria Falina, 2023

Maria Falina has asserted their right under the Copyright, Designs and Patents Act, 1988,
to be identified as Author of this work.

For legal purposes the Acknowledgements on p. ix constitute an extension
of this copyright page.

Cover image: Funeral of Alexander I of Yugoslavia
(© ullstein bild Dtl. / Contributor / Getty Images)

All rights reserved. No part of this publication may be reproduced or transmitted in
any form or by any means, electronic or mechanical, including photocopying,
recording, or any information storage or retrieval system, without prior
permission in writing from the publishers.

Bloomsbury Publishing Plc does not have any control over, or responsibility for,
any third-party websites referred to or in this book. All internet addresses given in this
book were correct at the time of going to press. The author and publisher regret any
inconvenience caused if addresses have changed or sites have ceased to exist,
but can accept no responsibility for any such changes.

Every effort has been made to trace copyright holders and to obtain their
permissions for the use of copyright material. The publisher apologizes for any
errors or omissions and would be grateful if notified of any corrections that should be
incorporated in future reprints or editions of this book.

A catalogue record for this book is available from the British Library.

A catalog record for this book is available from the Library of Congress.

ISBN: HB: 978-1-3502-8203-2
PB: 978-1-3502-8207-0
ePDF: 978-1-3502-8204-9
eBook: 978-1-3502-8205-6

Typeset by Newgen KnowledgeWorks Pvt. Ltd., Chennai, India

To find out more about our authors and books visit www.bloomsbury.com
and sign up for our newsletters.

To my parents

Contents

Acknowledgements	ix
Introduction	1
Religion, modernity and secularization	4
Religion and nationalism	7
Historiographical overview	12
1 Religion and Serbian state- and nation-building before 1918	19
Before the nation-state: Serbs under Habsburg and Ottoman rule	20
Working together: Church and state in independent Serbia	26
The Serbian Church and Serbian nationalism before the	
First World War	29
2 New Church for the new state: 'Liberation and unification' of lands,	
people and institutions	41
The new state	41
Where does faith come in? Yugoslavism and religion	41
Incomplete separation: Regulation of religious life and legal	
status of religious communities	45
Unification of the Serbian Orthodox Church and	
(re-)establishment of the Serbian Patriarchate	51
A happy coexistence? The Yugoslav state and the Serbian nation in	
the view of the Serbian Orthodox Church: 1918–mid-1920s	56
Community of the Church and nation	56
Reform movement from the outside and from within	62
The Serbian Orthodox Church and symbolic legitimization	
of power	65
3 The Serbian Orthodox Church faces the challenge of modernity	71
Royal dictatorship and integral Yugoslavism	73
Responses to new challenges	82
How to operate in a religiously diverse society	91
4 Climax: The Serbian Orthodox Church enters politics	101
Political Orthodoxism	102
After the assassination	104

1935–7: The Concordat crisis	107
1939–41: The breakup	114
Theorizing the nation	118
The national-religious synthesis	122
Epilogue: The war	135
The memory of the Second World War	136
The end of the Kingdom of Yugoslavia	137
Resistance or collaboration? The continuation of the interwar Serbian Orthodox political thought in the war	141
After the war	147
Notes	151
Bibliography	181
Index	201

Acknowledgements

I have always considered myself lucky to have met and enjoyed the company of many extraordinary people who have been sources of inspiration, intellectual challenge, comfort, and friendship. This book would have never been written without their generous support. This book started as a doctoral dissertation, and my deepest gratitude goes to my supervisor, Balázs Trencsényi, who has always believed in me, shared his endless knowledge, introduced me to colleagues across Europe and always pushed me to do better. I would like to thank the faculty and students of the History Department at Central European University (CEU), Budapest, where I conducted my dissertation research. Sadly, the university has been forced to abandon its home in Budapest and relocate to Vienna. CEU was my home for almost a decade, and I could not have wished for a better place to get my degree. I owe a debt of gratitude to many colleagues and friends whom I have met there, and whose advice and friendship continue to sustain me long after I graduated. I thank Jana Bacevic, Simina Badica, Bogdan Iacob, Michal Kopeček, Ksenia Krimer, Ferenc Laczó, Uku Lember, Zsófia Lóránd, Anna Mazanik, Katalin Stráner and many others for their friendship.

Two people have helped above and beyond while I was doing research in Belgrade. Radmila Radić generously shared her knowledge of the history of the Serbian Church and helped me find my way around people and books. Vladimir Petrović, a perfect host, guide, colleague and dearest friend at CEU and beyond, made my visits to Belgrade not only productive but truly joyful. I would also like to thank the staff of the Library of the Serbian Patriarchate in Belgrade for their assistance. I am grateful for their patience and the many cups of coffee.

Johannes Wischmeyer guided me through the intricacies of German historiography, and I benefited a lot from our discussions at the Institute for European History in Mainz. A postdoctoral fellowship by the Irish Research Council gave me the time and space I needed to thoroughly rethink the conceptual framework of the dissertation, conduct additional research and turn it into a book. I thank my host and mentor at University College Dublin, Robert Gerwarth, for his support and encouragement. A special thanks goes to my Dublin colleagues Susan Grant, John Paul Newman, Mercedes Peñalba-Sotorrío, Dmitar Tasić and Jennifer Wellington, who have read and commented on more drafts than I ever thought was possible. My colleagues at my current institutional home, the School of History and Geography at Dublin City University, offered their support and friendship that made the completion of this book possible while managing a full-time academic position during the pandemic. This book received financial support from the Faculty of Humanities and Social Sciences Book Publication Scheme at Dublin City University.

Sarah McArthur, with whom I have shared part of my academic journey, opened her London home to me, which allowed me to spend much-needed time at the British Library. Many thanks also go to my friends in Moscow, Olga Dieva, Tatiana Fazio, Tamara Dondurey, Anastasia Mityushina and Mur Soboleva, who always believed that my work is worth the effort despite all the challenges and precarity of academic life.

I am fortunate to have my husband, Ernst Visser, by my side. He has for years put up patiently with all the ups and downs of the book-writing process and taken care of our daughter Sonja, who is delightful but requires undivided attention, incompatible with completing the manuscript. During the last year of work on this book, I have found a fantastic and indispensable peer group of fellow academic mamas online, whom I have never met in person, but who have supported me virtually in a myriad of ways. Without their understanding, acceptance and encouragement, I would have never finished this book.

And last but not least, nothing would have been possible without the love and support of my parents, Irina and Anatoly, who always stand by me, even from thousands of kilometres away. I dedicate this book to them.

Introduction

The first time I visited Serbia in the early 2000s, I was an undergraduate student of history at Moscow State University. I flew to Belgrade to join a summer youth volunteer camp near the town of Valjevo in central Serbia, where we were meant to help the villagers restore an old house. Volunteering seemed like the best way to get to know the country, which was about to become the focal point of my degree for the next three years. More than two decades passed since then, and the interest has not waned.

That summer, the programme funding ran out. Our group of international youths ended up doing what I have since learnt people do in the summer in the Balkans – we ate way too much food and enjoyed the fantastic hospitality of our hosts, who were incredibly generous with their time and let us paint their fences, taught us to bake bread, grill meat, showed us around and shared their life stories. One of the camp visitors led a local archaeological dig of a Byzantine villa nearby. We started talking about the Byzantine heritage and the role of Christianity in Serbian history and culture. That day I knew that I had found the research theme for my undergraduate thesis.

Even during that first visit, when I barely spoke the language and didn't know much about the country, I was struck by the apparent importance of East Orthodox Christianity for the Serbian national identity. And yet, it looked so different compared to Russia, where religion was stately, imperial and splendid. The Serbian version of East Orthodox Christianity felt more intimate, more immediate and somehow omnipresent. It permeated every legend and story told by the villagers. People were proud of their religious heritage but also utterly disinterested in religious teaching and the values it preached. Our shared religion seemed to open many doors for me but also marked me as an outsider. It appeared that religion and faith were situational. They were invoked when talking about the past or differences with the neighbouring countries, but they didn't guide everyday life. During my subsequent visits, when I spent time in

Belgrade, Dubrovnik and Vukovar, I saw a different side of it – buildings marked by bullet traces and religious slogans indicating hatred and intolerance – the unmistakable signs of war and conflict. I was puzzled and intrigued.

Back in Moscow, my undergraduate thesis advisor recommended I focus my research on the late nineteenth century and the links between state-building and church institutions. That set me on a research path, which eventually led to this book. By the time I entered the doctoral programme at Central European University in Budapest, I was interested in nationalism as much as in studying religion. My dissertation was finished in 2011 and formed the basis of this book. In the ten years since, I have revisited some of my original assumptions, conducted additional archival research and reframed the story told here to make it grounded in Yugoslav interwar history rather than in Serbian national narratives.

***

This book has three narrative lines that intertwine and affect one another, coming to the fore in different moments – the relationship between religion and Serbian nationalism, the relationship between Yugoslav state- and nation-building and religion, and finally, the relationship between the Serbian Orthodox religious community and modernity. Taking the case of the Serbian Orthodox Church as an example, this book historicizes the widely held assumption that the bond between religion and nationalism in the Balkans, especially violent nationalism, is a natural one or that this bond has been historically inevitable.

This book brings together religion, nationalism, politics, state-building, secularization, and modernity and tells a complex yet coherent story of how East Orthodox Christianity came to be at the core of one version of Serbian nationalism. It also tells a story of the failed Yugoslav nation-building in the interwar period, as the two are intimately linked. The position of the Serbian Orthodox Church in society and in relation to other Yugoslav religious communities and the Church's political vision are the focal points of analysis. The book explores how this political vision emerged in reaction to and in interaction with the challenges posed by political modernity – the establishment of the modern multinational and multireligious Yugoslav state, the ideology of Yugoslavism, the fear of secularization, as well as the rise of communism and fascism in Europe. The most important Serbian religious thinkers of the period criticized and rejected certain parts of modernity. But through the very act of engagement with modernity, the Serbian Orthodox Church became part of it. Even the most anti-modernist, anti-democratic and anti-Western views of the

Serbian Orthodox clerics were an inherent part of European modernity. The book takes issue with the notion that Eastern Orthodox Christianity is essentially prone to anti-modernism. Instead, it tells a story of the dynamic interaction between the intellectual options contained in the Serbian Orthodox community and external factors, such as political changes, the presence of conservative émigré groups and the actions of other religious communities.

The book argues that far from being an organic one or being predetermined by the natural proclivity of East Orthodox Christianity, the bond between the Serbian nation, Serbian nationalism and religion was imagined, created and debated in the early twentieth century by various actors. It shows the complexity of the intellectual constructions made by the interwar East Orthodox clergy and lay thinkers, demonstrates the ambiguities and the self-contradictory character of this bond and argues that it is precisely this complexity that allowed for its later simplification and radical political uses.

The book is organized chronologically from the first chapter exploring the relationship between religion and Serbian state- and nation-building in the late nineteenth and the early twentieth century to the epilogue covering the years of the Second World War. It traces how the political vision of the Serbian Orthodox Church emerged and evolved in this period. In 1918, the Serbian Orthodox Church embraced and enthusiastically supported the new multinational and religiously diverse Yugoslav state. In March 1941, the Patriarch of the Serbian Orthodox Church, together with other important hierarchs, supported the coup-d'état, which led to the dissolution of the Yugoslav state.

Similarly to other post–First World War contexts in the region, with the creation of the Kingdom of Serbs, Croats and Slovenes, the Serbian elite and the Serbian clergy, who conceived of themselves as part of the national elite, suddenly had to operate in a new multinational and religiously heterogeneous environment. It took the Serbian Orthodox Church almost a decade to adapt to the new setting institutionally, but as Chapters 3 and 4 demonstrate, it has failed to adapt mentally. It continued to think of itself as, at best, 'primus inter pares' and, at worst, the only legitimate spiritual leader of the people. Since the mid-1920s, the Serbian Orthodox leaders began to think about and plan for a more active and engaged political position in response to the challenges of modern life. The royal dictatorship of 1929 gave the Yugoslav religious communities new incentives to turn political, as they constituted one of the few ways to assert national identity, different from the integral Yugoslav one. This meant new possibilities for mass mobilization. This combination of factors led to a gradual marginalization and rejection of those voices within the Serbian Orthodox community that did not accentuate the national dimension. The original idea of evangelical and social work of the God Worshipper movement was replaced by the national rhetoric of Nikolaj Velimirović. Weak attempts to include the values of the political left did not develop into anything significant. From the mid-1930s to 1941, the political vision and a 'plan for action' formulated by the Serbian Orthodox Church contributed to cementing the association of East Orthodox Christianity with Serbian nationalism. It was underpinned by new theoretical justifications for both open political participation and association with the national cause. The grand celebration of St Sava in 1935 was a direct result and a culmination of these developments. During the year of festivities devoted to the glorification of the main Serbian saint and a patron of the nation, the ideology of Svetosavlje was articulated and presented to the public. The Concordat crisis of 1937, often seen as a singular event in the history of church-state relations, originated from the same notion that it was time for the Serbian Orthodox Church to take an independent political stance even if it meant confrontation with the government. In 1941, the Serbian Orthodox Church sided with the Serbian national cause and against the Yugoslav state.

Religion, modernity and secularization

This book is about the role and place of religion in Yugoslav and Serbian history. My thinking about it is based on several broad theoretical assumptions about the role of religion in modern Europe, understanding nationalism as a modern political and sociocultural phenomenon, and the importance of ideas for political outcomes. Although this study is primarily limited to analysing one national case, it has been informed by my training as a comparativist. I hope that the outcome is that students of Yugoslav, Balkan and European history will find it interesting, informative and, ultimately, relatable. Below, I outline some of these theoretical foundations and where this book stands regarding the state of the art in Serbian, Yugoslav and Balkan historiography.

This book places religion, religious communities and actors at the centre of analysis. Religion here is understood as a set of beliefs, ideas and practices as they were articulated, understood and performed by people. It is not a religion in a sociological sense; there is no analysis of quantifiable measures of religiosity, although there is much talk about secularization and the loss of faith. If someone declared themselves a believer, I choose to take that at face value and focus my analysis on understanding the subjective meaning of their belief. When claims of secularization are made, I analyse the claims, not the sociocultural patterns that may have led to it. This is, first and foremost, a study in the history of ideas. However, this is not a theological study. It deals with the political aspects of religious thought and the impact of secular politics on religious communities and institutions.

Methodologically, I draw on the tradition of the Cambridge school in the history of political thought, which emphasizes the need to take the language of politics seriously and interpret it in relation to where and how arguments are made.[1] Sensitivity to context also comes from Roger Woods, who in his analysis of the conservative revolution in Weimar Germany called for political thought 'to be examined not as a static ideology but rather as ideas worked out in response to a series of conflicting pressures, as ideas which cannot simply be portrayed as if they were a political program, but rather an expression of tension'.[2] Attention to concepts, their formation and usage derives from the methods of German Begriffsgeschichte.[3]

One of the challenges was to apply these approaches to religious thought and religious actors, to truly place them in the centre of my analysis. I came to understand that the only way to make sense of what the protagonists of my story were saying, thinking and doing was to take their claims about religion and faith seriously, to take religion seriously. As Brian Porter-Szűcs argued, it is essential that we 'pay attention to how people describe their religious worlds, acknowledging that the actual substance of a particular faith has a significance that transcends the social function of religion'.[4] As this book demonstrates, deviations from the official position of religious institutions become crucial if we are to capture the rich intellectual worlds of religious actors. As Hartmut Lehman pointed out, to limit the research to the officially approved religious positions is to 'fail to perceive how in coping with the contingencies of life people may have used and did indeed use a variety of religious approaches'.[5]

This brings us to the question of agency and actors. Once religious thought and religiously informed narratives are taken seriously, it becomes impossible to treat their authors as secondary or somehow subjugated to secular actors. It has been generally accepted that 'intellectuals create different ideologies of national identity within a larger discursive universe of available materials. They do the imaginative ideological labour that brings together disparate cultural elements, selected historical memories, and interpretations of experiences, all the while silencing the inconvenient, the unheroic, and the anomalous'.[6] The protagonists of this book do the same. They may speak for the institutions of the Serbian Orthodox Church, on behalf of religious communities, or as individual actors, public intellectuals, religious thinkers and secular politicians, who explicitly or implicitly dealt with religion and faith in their work. These people and communities interacted with each other and lived together in the dynamic and challenging world of political modernity.

For a long time, scholars in the humanities and social sciences accepted the so-called secularization thesis, according to which religion gradually loses its central place in political, social and cultural life as modernity advances.[7] Modernization and secularization theories implied that once this process is complete, religion ceases to be a meaningful object of scholarly analysis other than in the framework of its waning significance. As Jeffrey Cox has put it, 'There certainly are many sociologists, not to mention historians, anthropologists, economists, clergy and journalists, who believe that religion in the modern world will survive only in forms that are sectarian and therefore marginal, fundamentalist and menacing, or internally secularized and therefore "not really religious".'[8]

Philosophers and sociologists of religion successfully challenged the notion that modernity must be secular. Talal Asad argued convincingly that secularism is not a neutral option,[9] Charles Taylor demonstrated how North-west European understanding of self is at the same time secular and profoundly Christian,[10] and Jose Casanova wrote of the secularization thesis as a self-fulfilling prophecy, which has its roots in the Enlightenment period when Europeans learned to think of religion and faith in secular ways.[11] A radical re-evaluation of the secularization theory that has taken place in the sociology of religion and religious studies is by now having an impact on historical research. This book is one such example.

This book is based on the understanding that the master narrative of secularization should be taken seriously precisely because it proved to be so pervasive. It should not be used as a heuristic tool. It should be scrutinized historically to help us understand the complex relationship between religion and political modernity, including nationalism, which is one of the book's subjects. This book takes up the research agenda suggested by Mark Edward Ruff, who argued that

> narratives of secularisation and religious decline often served as a way to create religious identity, defining it against a hostile outside world ... The fact that secularisation was so widely used as a concept in the past, means that it cannot simply be suddenly brushed aside. Historians must examine precisely why for nearly two centuries so many churchmen believed it to be critical to elevate

religious decline to a master narrative and how they shaped their own discourses and program for renewal around this phenomenon.[12]

To deliver on this ambitious task, I focused my research on the ideas more so than on the institutional histories, which form an important background against which these ideas are developed. As Renato Moro noted, an exclusive focus on church-state relations, political powers and religious institutions is, by design, quite limited and cannot adequately explain the ways and the forms in which religious actors, movements and institutions expressed themselves.[13] Analysis of the Serbian clergy and religious thinkers' response to the perceived threat of secularization forms an important part of the story this book tells. Without taking this reasoning into account it is impossible to understand the inner logic and driving forces behind much of the Serbian Orthodox Church's political vision.

Religion and nationalism

Both 'religion' and 'nationalism' are highly contested concepts. This book is based on the understanding that nations are a modern phenomenon, a product of modernity, and one of the formative components of the modern world, an axis around which a significant part of modern political life is organized. It is also understood that the nation is a social, political and cultural construction and that nationalism encompasses a variety of political and cultural ideologies and practices. This book explores how national identities are imagined and debated by looking at how historical and cultural narratives of a nation, the Serbian nation, developed. In this, I follow Homi Bhabha's argument about the importance of textuality and the value of close reading of texts about the nation.[14] This approach also embraces Craig Calhoun's notion that 'nations are constituted … by the way of talking and thinking and acting that relies on [claims about the nation] to produce collective identity, to mobilise people for collective projects'.[15]

The secularization theory had a significant impact on the study of nationalism, especially on studying the relationship between religion and nationalism. Rogers Brubaker classified the scholarship on the relationship between religion and nationalism into four categories: scholars in the first category treat religion and nationalism as analogous phenomena; in the second, they specify how religion helps explain things about nationalism; in the third, religion is treated as part of nationalism, and in the fourth, scholars examine distinctively religious forms of nationalism.[16] This is a helpful way to think about an extensive research field and is a testament that much has changed since the early 2000s when George Th. Mavrogordatos complained that 'despite the prolific literature on nationalism, and the growing literature on religion, there seems to be no general theoretical framework or systematic discussion focusing specifically on the linkage between the two ... Most [scholars], apparently, regard this linkage as given, or as incidental'.[17]

Many students of nationalism argued that nationalism should be interpreted as a 'secular', 'political', 'civil' or 'ersatz' religion. George Mosse famously pointed out structural similarities between the national movements in nineteenth- and early twentieth-century Germany and religion.[18] Unlike some of the more radical proponents of the idea that nationalism replaced traditional religion, Mosse acknowledged that the connection between Christianity and the cults, rites and symbols of nationalism was not limited to a formal resemblance. He agreed that 'the de-Christianization of the worship of people was never to become an accomplished fact' and underlined the importance of German Pietism for the development of the German national movement.[19] Since then, both historians and sociologists have argued that the relationship between religion and nationalism cannot be reduced to simple substitution. Talal Asad argued passionately that 'to insist that nationalism should be seen as religion, or even as having been shaped by religion, is ... to miss the nature and consequence of the revolution brought about by the Enlightenment doctrine of secularism'. He agreed that modern nationalism was, to an extent, based on 'preexisting languages and practices – including those that we call "religious" but did not accept that religion necessarily forms nationalism'.[20]

The importance of religious roots of nationalism and the incorporation of religious language and symbols by modern nationalism has been well documented and extensively theorized. Anthony D. Smith argued that religion and ethnicity constituted 'two of the nation's most important cultural resources and traditions'.[21] Smith located the role of religion on three distinct levels: the 'official level' of regimes, leaders and elites; the 'popular' level of religious beliefs and practices; and the 'basic' level of the sacred foundations of the nation constituted by community, territory, history, and destiny.[22]

Adrian Hastings offered a highly useable way to explore the multifaceted interaction between religion and nationalism by looking at the nation's foundational myths – the sanctification of the imagined birth of a nation and the commemoration of the greatest threats to a nation's survival.[23] This approach has been successfully applied to Eastern Europe, where the myths of victimhood and martyrdom are prominent. In a region where territories and population groups often become contested, these myths give an advantage as they 'invest the identity boundary with a moral significance: those who are down-trodden are morally superior to their oppressors'.[24] Examples of martyrdom myths include 'crucified Poland', 'Serbian Golgotha' and the Kosovo epic cycle. Even when religious vocabulary is not central, as is the case in the Jasenovac myth in Serbia, the idea of sacred suffering introduces a religious dimension into the political conversation about the nation.

Hastings, Smith and others have explored the link between the perception of the nation's uniqueness, usually expressed in its glorious past and extraordinary future, and the biblical idea of 'the chosen people of Israel'. While national particularity can be coined through other means, for example, racial thinking or national characterology grounded in anthropology, religious concepts and themes often do play an important role in the process of inventing and *justifying* the nation.[25] The recurrent use of biblical themes may be interpreted as proof that nationalism acquired certain religious characteristics and is structurally analogous to religion. On the other hand, it has been suggested that the use of religious language can be more productively analysed through the lens of the sacralization of the nation, that is, elevating the nation to the level of a sacred entity. Religious concepts and symbols can be powerful mobilization tools, which explains their widespread use by political actors. Friedrich Wilhelm Graf suggested that religious semantics of modern nationalism serve the purpose of strengthening the emotional binding of the individual to the nation at the deepest level of one's soul and the stabilization of national community as a comprehensive, innerly binding *Heilsgemeinschaft*.[26] With the common usage of concepts such as 'New Israel', 'God's people' and the like the nation starts to represent 'Heaven on Earth', the place of collective longing, an ideal of a harmonious community.[27] This does not have to be a subjugated relationship, in which secular actors (ab)use religion. As Mary Anne Perkins claimed, the 'language of nationhood offered a way for the traditional Christian symbols to be transformed, re-empowered and to remain relevant in the face of advancing secularisation'.[28] The resurgence of the idea of a national patron saint in twentieth-century Eastern Europe, which has happened with the direct involvement of clergy and other religious actors, suggests the validity of this claim.[29] The role of the clergy and, broadly speaking, of religious institutions in nation-building has been well documented, albeit not always critically reflected upon.[30] The positive accounts focus on the production of vernacular literature in the absence of secular national elites, educational activities and other social and political work of the national churches (*autocephalous* in the case of East Orthodox Christianity). This rather narrow view on the interaction between religion and nationalism has been dominant in Serbian and other East European historiographies and is common in the accounts of minority identity-building, especially when an ethnic group finds itself in a minority position with religion as a differentiating factor.[31]

Despite prolific theoretical research on the relationship between religion and nationalism, for a long time scholars who address this question using modern European examples tended to assume that religion is a 'social force available for nationalist manipulation'.[32] A critical re-evaluation of the secularization thesis and acknowledgement that it may not be universally applicable encouraged historians to pay closer attention to religion as an inherent part of European modernity.[33]

Students of German nationalism and German-speaking academics more generally have been especially prolific in addressing the questions: How did religion and nationalism interact historically? How was this relationship structured? What factors influenced it?[34] They focus on the intertwining of religious and national discourses rather than on religious roots of nationalism, or the role of institutionalized religion in nation-building and successfully employ notions such as 'sacralisation of the nation' and 'nationalisation of religion' in their analysis.

Martin Schulze Wessel defined 'sacralisation of the nation' as the transfer of functions and forms of display from religion to the nation, which results in a structural analogy between nation and religion.[35] 'Nationalization of religion' describes an adjustment process, during which religious people and communities incorporate national values into their thought and actions. Importantly, the aim of this process is not to secularize society or diminish the importance of religion. On the contrary, it is to find new reasons for religion to retain its significance.[36] Some scholars prefer to use 'politicisation of religion' to describe the same phenomenon, when 'as a consequence of an unexpected turning point in history, cults and religious symbols acquire definite political meanings'.[37] This notion is criticized by those who argue that in Europe Christianity has always had an important political dimension to it and thus has never been free of politics. Lastly, 'sacralisation of politics' is also used to make sense of the intertwining between modern politics, nationalism and religion. This concept originates from the debate on political religion and in contrast to 'nationalisation of religion', it 'does not refer to the political mobilisation of traditional religions, but to the modern political ideologies and movements which adapted religious habits to secular ends'.[38] In contrast to 'politicisation of religion', it is argued that through sacralization of politics the political sphere acquires religious character, but remains autonomous from traditional religion and can be hostile to it.[39] It is often a question of perspective and whether the agency is ascribed to secular or religious actors that make scholars choose one term over the other.

Finally, the longstanding debate among the scholars of Early Modern Europe over the confessionalization paradigm was creatively re-thought for the nineteenth and twentieth centuries. Originally coined by Heinz Schilling and Wolfgang Reinhard, it was used to describe the process of 'a fundamental social transformation that includes ecclesiastical religious and psychological cultural changes as well as political and social ones'.[40] It emphasized the simultaneous formation of the early-modern state and new church structures – confessions – that took place across Western and Central Europe from the sixteenth to the eighteenth century. As Reinhard put it, 'advanced state-building favored effective confessionalisation just as confessionalisation favored state-building'.[41] An important part of confessionalization was the churches' striving for the new groups to be as homogeneous as possible, that is, for the 'confessionalisation' of the subjects. The goal was achieved through close control over the educational system, press, migration policies and so on. When applied to the modern period, the idea of confessionalization of politics or nation is used to capture the emergence of competitive narratives about the nation and society by different religious actors.[42] This has been applied fruitfully to German nineteenth-century history, where Protestants 'quarrelled with the Catholics less about theology than about moral life and custom; less about the meaning of Christian ritual than the fate of national culture; less about God than the inner life of nations. In short, they quarrelled with Catholics about history'.[43] The rivalry between these narratives could eventually lead to their radicalization. Helmut Walser Smith concludes that German political Protestantism had the potential for radical nationalism:

> Indeed, for some German Protestants, nationalism was not an ersatz for, but part of religious belief ... religious belief supported national identity, provisioning it with memory, myth and tradition. In its ultramontane inflection, Protestantism not only reinforced national identity but equally important, radicalized the discourse of German nationalism.[44]

Students of Eastern Europe will recognize this pattern. Should one exchange 'German' for 'Serbian' and 'Protestant' for 'East Orthodox', the statement would be accurate. On the methodological level, such approaches underline the importance of the analysis of national narratives articulated by religious actors in religiously diverse societies such as Germany, Switzerland, Ukraine or Yugoslavia. It also sensitizes scholars to religious dimensions of national narratives even in religiously homogenous cultures, as religious mobilization could be triggered not only by the threat of or the competition with another religious group but also by the perceived or real threat of secularization. In such cases, the clergy and concerned lay members of the religious community use the secularization narrative as a justification for the active involvement of religion in public and political life.

Historiographical overview

The historical link between the Serbian nation and East Orthodox Christianity and, by extension, the institution of the Serbian Orthodox Church has been nearly universally accepted as organic by academics, politicians and the Serbian public. The idea that the two must remain inseparable has met more criticism but is widespread. This link is often thought of as existent 'since times immemorial' or at the very least since the Slavic tribes of the Balkan Peninsula converted to Christianity in the Middle Ages and is rarely analysed from a critical historical perspective. The notion that 'the Serbian Orthodox Church was a cultural and quasi-political institution, which embodied and expressed the ethos of the Serbian people to such a degree that nationality and religion fused into a distinct "Serbian faith". This role of the Serbian church had little to do with religion either as theology or as a set of personal beliefs and convictions' has become commonplace in professional historiography and public discourse.[45] This book takes issue with this approach and instead historicizes this link without denying the importance of the Church institution or East Orthodox Christianity in Serbian and Yugoslav history. On the contrary, it is through questioning the organic nature of the connection between the church and the nation, religion and nationalism, that the power and significance of the East Orthodox religious community are possible to analyse. My thinking about the role and place of religion in interwar Yugoslavia and Serbian history has benefitted from the research done by generations of scholars, not least because it gave me something to disagree with and forced me to formulate more clearly why a different perspective may be productive. Below, I outline briefly how religion and church history are treated in Balkan, Yugoslav and Serbian national historiographies of the modern period.

The growth of academic and public interest in the religious landscape of South-eastern Europe has been fuelled by the tragic events of the wars of Yugoslav succession in the 1990s and the Kosovo conflict of the early 2000s on the one hand, and the growing concern of Europeans with Islam in Europe on the other.[46] This politically driven interest was coupled with broader research need to explore and account for the rise of religiosity in post-communist Eastern and Central Europe.[47] The fate of religious communities and institutions under communism occupies a prominent place in the research agenda in most countries of the region and continues to fuel political debates. In stark contrast, the history of the long nineteenth century is far less charged politically and emotionally.

As Lucian Leustean has summarized,

> Throughout the nineteenth century, Orthodox churches remained at the core of nation-building processes by supporting both the elite and faithful in the construction of the nation. Through religious ceremonies and jurisdictional organisation, the churches reminded the faithful of the Byzantine model of church and state. Myths, religious symbols, and liturgical ceremonials continued to bring the Orthodox people together, even if they were subjects of different political authorities.[48]

Those living in the Ottoman Empire and, to an extent, the subjects of the Habsburg Empire found themselves in a situation when religious authorities took over the tasks of civil administration. Since the eighteenth century, a wide range of affairs, including family and marriage, commercial and criminal cases involving Christians only fell under the church authorities' jurisdiction. In the Ottoman Empire, the population was organized into five *millets* along religious lines. The millet system established the custom of using the leaders of religious communities for government functions. The East Orthodox Patriarch based in Istanbul (Constantinople) was the head of the *Rum millet* and had the authority and responsibility for all East Orthodox population of the Ottoman Empire.[49]

As nationalism took hold and Balkan Christians began to seek independence from the Ottoman Empire, a parallel process of establishing autonomous national or autocephalous churches took place within the larger East Orthodox religious community. The establishment of church structures independent from the Ecumenical Patriarchate and semi-independent states reinforced each other. This process is seen mainly as unproblematic throughout the region, with a notable exception of Greece, where already in the nineteenth century some religious actors perceived the association of East Orthodox Christianity with nationalism as contradictory to the universal nature of Christianity.[50] This was partly because the Ecumenical Patriarchate was controlled by the Greeks and partly because of the uneasy relationship between Christianity and Classical Hellenic heritage.[51]

Besides fulfilling the quasi-state functions, the East Orthodox churches in the Balkans fulfilled other essential tasks. Religious rituals helped keep the memories of the glorious past alive through the centuries of foreign rule. Clergy and monastic scholars preserved and expanded the knowledge of the history that eventually formed the basis of the secular school curriculum. Peter F. Sugar, after Emanuel Turczynski, called this close interaction of ethnic and religious consciousness *nation-confession* – 'the stage in historical development in which the national church-state identification descended from the political realm of the elites to the popular level, under the influence of modern nationalism, creating a new identification of nation with church membership on a somewhat vague purely folk religious emotional level'.[52] Towards the end of the nineteenth century, religious East Orthodox self-identification gave place to a new secular national identity strongly influenced by European liberalism. The clergy adapted to this new development by promoting the notion of the national church as the saviour of the nation, which, of course, increased the symbolic value of religion and the church institutions within the framework of an independent national state.

Historical accounts of the twentieth century are scarcer. Sabrina Pedro Ramet's volume on Eastern Christianity and twentieth-century politics is by today dated in many respects. Still, it remains the only one that covers the region in totality.[53] The more recent volume edited by Ramet addresses the post-communist period and has a narrow focus on conservatism and intolerance of the East Orthodox churches.[54] There is a striking lack of comparative regional and transnational research, although calls for such studies are made, and new initiatives begin to appear.[55] There have been several edited collections of national case studies, analysing the relationship between nationalism and religion in South-eastern Europe,[56] issues of European integration and EU level politics,[57] and broader issues of modernity in Eastern Europe.[58] Hopefully, they will pave the way for future comparative and transnational research. As Brian Porter-Szűcs remarked, this new history should 'avoid entirely the misleading question of whether the region does or does not fit some imagined normative pattern of secularization. Instead, our histories should explain the choices made and the constraints faced by Poles, Hungarians, Bulgarians, and others as they simultaneously constructed and responded to their own particular versions of modernity'.[59]

In Serbian national historiography, accepting the importance of religion and religious institutions for state- and nation-building did not produce critical historical research. Discussion of religion has been generally limited to the history of church institutions, the church's positive contribution to the national liberation struggle and the role of the clergy in education and other nation-building activities. A typical example includes Vasa Čubrilović asserting the close connection between the Serbian Orthodox Church and the people, the former being 'in service of the people and its struggle' against the Ottoman Empire, which resulted in the great suffering of the Church and the eventual abolishment of the Peć Patriarchate in 1766.[60] As Chapter 1 will demonstrate, this narrative became widely accepted by the end of the nineteenth century due to a conscious effort of the clergy. Not challenged often, the claim that the Serbian Orthodox Church had always supported national liberation is less straightforward if the Serbs of the Habsburg Empire are included in the picture.[61] Exceptional in this sense are the works of Bojan Aleksov and Yuriy Kostyashov. They examine aspects of the church–state relationship and religious life in Vojvodina from the 1600s to the breakup of the Habsburg Empire.[62]

Despite the vital place religion and church are given in the national narrative, there is only one comprehensive history of the Serbian Orthodox Church. The three-volume 'History of the Serbian Orthodox Church' was written by Djoko Slijepčević, a Serbian émigré cleric, who was once close to the circle of Nikolaj Velimirović and Dimitrije Najdanović.[63] His book appeared for the first time in Munich in the 1980s, was republished in Belgrade in 1991 and remains the most detailed account of the history of the Serbian Orthodox Church, although not free from subjective partisan opinions.[64] Slijepčević focuses almost exclusively on the history of institutions: administrative, educational and political.

The history of the Serbian Church and religion in Serbia in the twentieth century has received relatively little attention. For the interwar period, the researchers focused on the 'Concordat crisis', a political crisis caused by the refusal of the Serbian Orthodox Church to accept the terms of the agreement signed between the Yugoslav government and the Vatican in 1935–7. Leaving aside the sensationalist and conspiracy theory publications about the mysterious death of Patriarch Varnava, which happened on the night of the largest clergy-led street demonstration in Belgrade, most authors analyse the crisis through the lens of the strained Serbo-Croatian relationship and political difficulties the government faced at the time. For Serbian nationalist-minded authors, it was a perfect proof that the Croats were primarily responsible for the failure of interwar Yugoslavia.[65] The most comprehensive account of the crisis based on meticulous archival research is authored by Miloš Mišović, who emphasizes that 'the interests of distinct churches and national bourgeoisies were so much entangled that they were not to be easily separated'.[66]

Of all the research on religious topics, the work of Radmila Radić stands out in its depth, critical perspectives and use of archival material.[67] Although the main timeframe of her research is post-1945, she provides a valuable overview of the social structures of the Yugoslav religious communities in the earlier periods. The same could be said about the comparative study by Klaus Buchenau.[68] Buchenau, together with Thomas Bremer, pioneered research on the theological thought and intellectual production of the Serbian clergy in the twentieth century when most research in Serbian church and religious history is focused on church–state relations and social history, rather than on the history of ideas.[69] Lack of methodological diversity, characteristic of Serbian historical writing during the communist period, plagues it up to this day. Methodological innovations in Serbian historiography mainly took place in social history and anthropology. The turn towards social history was also caused by the general disappointment in political history experienced within the historical profession in the years after the breakup of Yugoslavia.[70] Both Buchenau and Bremer place Nikolaj Velimirović and Justin Popović at the centre of their studies. Bremer's interest is in the analysis of the theological doctrine. In contrast, Buchenau's prime interest lies in anti-Western aspects of theology and their political implications.[71] Buchenau contextualizes intellectual developments that took place among Serbian clergy in the first half of the twentieth century within a wider tradition of Orthodox thought and reflections on political modernity, with an emphasis on Russian religious thought. This research is now picked up by younger scholars, who continue to explore the thought of Justin Popović.[72] Radovan Bigović analysed the philosophical views of Velimirović, including his stance on history, science and anthropology.[73] Since 2006, the Theology Department of the Belgrade University has been organizing conferences in the framework of the research project 'Serbian Theology in the twentieth century' and launched a publication under the same title, with the aim to go beyond the dominant positivistic approaches to historical research.

Velimirović was at the centre of a public controversy in the early 2000s caused by the 2003 decision of the Serbian Orthodox Church to canonize him as a saint in a culmination of a long debate about repatriating his remains from the United States. His brief internment at Dachau in 1944 emerged as one of the points of a charged discussion. The internment was used to construct his image as a martyr and a victim of Nazi persecution leading to an outcry from the critics on the left, who argued that this myth-making is taking place at the expense of minimizing his anti-Semitism and radical nationalism.⁷⁴ Saint or not, Velimirović and other thinkers of the interwar period continue to inspire the forces of the Christian right and post-Communist radical nationalism in present-day Serbia and South-eastern Europe. Religious thought and political visions of the interwar period are at the centre of the phenomenon known as Neo-Orthodoxism, which references the ideas of 'political Orthodoxism' of the 1930s and is coupled with the Orthodox Churches' tendency to present themselves as victims of the communist regime and true protectors of the nation against the dangerous influences of the 'liberal West'.⁷⁵

When it comes to the history of interwar Yugoslavia, religion has not been a top research priority. There seems to be little movement beyond the two positions articulated over three decades ago by two great historians of Yugoslavia, Ivo Banac and Milorad Ekmečić. Both were interested primarily in the national question, formation of national identities and national ideologies, and considered religion only for its role in the political crisis in interwar Yugoslavia. Ekmečić argued for religion and religious ideologies to be the main obstacles to the success of the interwar Yugoslav state and the main reason for the Serbo–Croat conflict.⁷⁶ Banac, in turn, claimed that religion did not have a prominent place in the national ideologies of the South Slav peoples and that the disputes between Serbs and Croats were a result of the clash between different political cultures.⁷⁷ There have been significant developments in the historiography of interwar Yugoslavia in other areas. Dejan Djokić successfully shifted the emphasis from the static characteristics of national ideologies to the interaction between them and other political actors.⁷⁸ Jovo Bakić provided the most detailed analysis of the dynamic evolution of the ideology of Yugoslavism.⁷⁹ John Paul Newman and Pieter Troch centred their studies on non-state actors and away from the high-level conflict of the political elites.⁸⁰ And very recently, Emily Greble placed the thought and experiences of Balkan Muslims in the centre of her historical narrative.⁸¹

Finally, a note on primary sources is necessary at this point. The research is based on a wide selection of published material and involves only a relatively small number of archival materials. On the one hand, analysing public positions and debates requires particular sources: newspapers and periodicals, published popular brochures, parliamentary debates and the like. On the other hand, the archives of the Serbian Orthodox Church are, unfortunately, extremely difficult to access for a researcher not affiliated with a religious institution. In an informal conversation, a librarian of the Library of the Serbian Patriarchate, which is open to the public, confirmed that even a special letter from an archbishop would not guarantee access to the archives. He also confessed that the use of the archives is complicated by the very poor state of the catalogues and archival aids. The archival material used in the book comes from several fonds of the Archive of Yugoslavia in Belgrade and while interesting and important its role in building my arguments is secondary. The list of the periodicals includes the official publications of the Serbian Orthodox Church, newspapers and journals run by various lay groups and societies, and the national press. A detailed list is available in the bibliography.

1

Religion and Serbian state- and nation-building before 1918

All Serbian towns are much alike. They have wide, clean streets; solid red-roofed little houses built of stone; a church, which is unlovely, for the modern Serb has no gift for church architecture; a school, which is often a handsome and very well-fitted building; a town hall, or something more or less equivalent to one; and a market-place.[1]

This description by Mary Edith Durham, an early twentieth-century English traveller in the Balkans, captured perfectly the central institutions of modern nation-building: education, church, and government. A capital city would also feature a theatre or even an opera house. Durham contrasted the handsomeness of school buildings with the ugliness of churches. However subjective, this juxtaposition offers a helpful metaphor for the perceived more comprehensive benefits of modern education over the outdated values of religion, especially for a society going through modernization. And yet every town had a church, which rarely stood empty. Durham did not, perhaps, fully appreciate the important place that religion continued to occupy in Serbian society. This chapter explores this theme and analyses the essential ways religion was intertwined with Serbian nation-building in the nineteenth and early twentieth century.

Ivo Banac, a required reading for students of Balkan history, argued that in the late nineteenth century 'the Serbs, because of the patriotic tradition of Serbian Orthodoxy, *naturally* looked upon their Church as a national institution. Even when they were totally irreligious, many of their intellectuals propagated Orthodoxy, much to the irritation of those who wished to establish pure linguistic Serbianism'.[2] This well-known and widely accepted argument contains several assumptions that require a closer look. What exactly is a national institution? The position that the Serbian Orthodox Church contributed a great deal to the preservation of the Serbian national identity under Ottoman rule and the establishment of independent Serbia in the nineteenth century has been widely accepted by historians and contemporary commentators. However, this position and the narrative of the contribution to the national cause were established in the nineteenth century and promoted by the Serbian church hierarchy to achieve specific goals. This position is accepted uncritically to a remarkable degree. This chapter explores how and why this narrative was established and traces the process that turned out to be far from linear or straightforward. It highlights the important consequences that the narrative and the process of its establishment had for the interplay of religion, Serbian nationalism and the Yugoslav state in the interwar period.

Banac is, of course, correct in that many Serbian political actors, except for the Social Democrats, perceived East Orthodox Christianity as an important part of the nation's cultural and spiritual heritage. The 1889 program of the Liberal Party stated that the Party would act 'in accordance with the traditions of the ancient Serbian state and the spirit of the Orthodox Church', implying that the two, if do not entirely overlap, at the very least do not contradict each other.[3] Banac also points out that using religion as the primary marker of ethnic identity was not the only option. Language, and broadly speaking culture, was the other one. The discussion of the tension between these two markers and its many consequences is at the core of this book. In the late nineteenth and early twentieth century, politicians did not foresee just how far-reaching these consequences would become. Their failure will become part of the problem.

Before the nation-state: Serbs under Habsburg and Ottoman rule

Once the last independent territories of medieval Serbian states fell under the military pressure of the Ottoman Empire in the fifteenth century and were incorporated into the Ottoman imperial framework, the majority of the East Orthodox, Slavic-speaking population of the Balkans found themselves the subjects of the Sultan. In the military, economic and diplomatic struggle that ensued, the now Austrian-Ottoman border shifted multiple times. Since the eighteenth century, the frontier mainly moved southwards, shrinking the Ottoman lands. This, combined with two major migration waves from southern Serbia (largely today's Kosovo) north across the Danube in the late seventeenth and the first third of the eighteenth centuries meant that the Serbs now lived on both sides of the border. This life across two jurisdictions and the differences between Habsburg and Ottoman administrations had a lasting impact on the formation of the modern Serbian national identity and Serbian statehood.[4] Both factors were often presented through the lens of overcoming the historical separation of a single national community. The imperial policies concerning the regulation of religious life also diverged significantly. As discussed in Chapter 2, these differences remained influential well into the 1920s.

Like other great empires of the time, the Ottoman Empire consisted of many ethnic and religious groups governed from the capital. Sultan residing in Istanbul towered over all subjects of the empire. Still, he ruled over them from a considerable distance by a system of indirect rule when local elites were charged with collecting taxes and maintaining order. The myriad ethnic, religious, linguistic and other groups formed the *reaya*, the ordinary people. Since the eighteenth century, the word *reaya* applied exclusively to non-Muslims to designate their inferior status compared to their fellow subjects of the Islamic faith. The Ottomans didn't engage in ethnic homogenization of the empire until late into the nineteenth century. Both Muslims and Christians referred to the period before the Balkan wars as the *belle époque* –when members of different religious communities lived side-by-side peacefully.[5] For a long time, the Ottoman Empire presented a case where the difference was seen as natural and unproblematic, even if it implied discrimination. Since the late nineteenth century, the Ottoman Empire witnessed a considerable rise in ethnic and religious violence. The *belle époque* existed in memory rather than reality, especially when contrasted with the early twentieth-century anti-Christian violence, Balkan wars and anti-Muslim violence in the Balkans and, finally, the havoc of the First World War.

A significant part of the Serb-populated lands belonged to the Ottomans until the Congress of Berlin (1878), even though the Belgrade *pashalik* had acquired a degree of autonomy earlier and was transformed into the Serbian principality after the two Serbian uprisings. This coincided with the start of the *Tanzimat* reforms (Reorganization), which heralded the beginning of the modernization of the Ottoman Empire. This process intensified in the early twentieth century culminating with the Young Turk revolution of 1908. Constitutional reforms of the Young Turks bridged some of the distance between the sultan and the common folk by introducing the European-style parliament with elected representatives. Political modernization also meant that the earlier equilibrium of different groups that were unequal yet had worked out an acceptable modus operandi of coexisting in their everyday activities was replaced by new ideas and institutions.

Traditionally, religion was the basis for the administrative division and governance. In the millet system, all peoples of the empire were divided into five large communities according to their religious affiliation: Muslim, East Orthodox Christian (Rum millet), Jewish, Armenian (Apostolic, Catholic and Evangelical) and Syriac Orthodox. The system evolved, and the Catholic millet was created during the *Tanzimat* reforms. The millets were 'imperial institutions, creations produced by the Ottoman state's policies of recognising difference and ruling its peoples through intermediaries'.[6] The Ottoman legal system had provisions for the separate courts pertaining to personal law under which minorities were allowed to rule themselves (in cases not involving any Muslim) with relatively little interference from the Ottoman government. Greek, Bulgarian and Serbian upper clergy represented their respective communities before the Ottoman authorities in the Rum millet. With the rise of national ideologies in the European part of the empire in the nineteenth century, the authority of religious leaders was gradually replaced with that of new secular actors. Millet system is routinely quoted as one of the bases for nation-building in the Balkans, even though the transition of power in some cases entailed a bitter conflict between the Greek-dominated Ecumenical Patriarchate and Slavic-speaking East Orthodox Balkan communities.[7] The traditional Serbian national narrative maintains that the Orthodox Church was the key institution that survived throughout the five centuries of Ottoman rule and preserved the national identity in the absence of a nation-state. The second part of this chapter details how the Serbian clergy instrumentalized this narrative to achieve their goals. In the territories remaining under Ottoman control, Islam continued to enjoy a privileged position, even though with the Young Turk Revolution and reforms that it entailed, equality of religions was accepted in principle. In practice, however, that was not always the case. The East Orthodox Christian population in Kosovo and Macedonia had reasons to seek better conditions. The transnational nature of the Ottoman religious communities persisted in the post-imperial setting, even though it was not always in the interest of either the clergy or secular political actors to emphasize it.

The Habsburg Empire was similarly ethnically and religiously diverse. Composed of a string of territories with few historical connections, it was gradually centralized in the second half of the eighteenth century through the reform efforts of Maria Theresa (1740–80) and Joseph II (1780–90). One of the lines of reforms was to bring the Roman Catholic Church under greater state control, although this was done gradually. As a devout Catholic, Maria Theresa did not support the radically secular logic pursued by her sons Joseph II and

Leopold II and opposed the principle of religious toleration for Protestant or Eastern Orthodox sects, or Jews.[8] At the same time, the Habsburgs populated the border territories with the Ottoman Empire in Transylvania, Southern Hungary and Croatia with predominantly Eastern Orthodox Christian refugees from the Balkans and granted them a set of tax and administrative privileges, including religious autonomy.

In 1690, about 30–40,000 Serbs were led by the Patriarch Arsenije III Čarnojević [Crnojević] to seek refuge in Hungary in what came to be known as 'the Great Migration' (*Velika seoba Srba*). The privileges granted by Leopold I included freedom of the Orthodox religion and internal autonomy, including education. The Patriarch, who settled in Sremski Karlovci, was regarded by the Viennese government as the head of the Serb population and was endowed with secular powers, such as particular judgement in civil disputes and the collection of feudal dues and disposal of heirless properties.[9] The clergy became the leaders of the Serb community within the Habsburg Empire. Regular national church councils (*narodno-crkveni sabor*) came to resemble national assemblies. Their official task was to elect bishops, heads of monasteries and the Patriarch; in practice, however, they also discussed 'general problems and matters of interest to the Serbian community'.[10] This peculiar situation is sometimes referred to by historians as 'the Habsburg version of millet'.[11] While negotiating the conditions in 1690, Leopold I mentioned the possibility of recognizing the Serbian military leader, the *vojvoda*, as the secular head of the community. That would have been Djordje Branković (1645–1711). This promise has never been fulfilled, but the region in southern Hungary became known as *Vojvodina*. Although Branković was given the title of Count of the Holy Roman Empire, he was held in Vienna and never allowed to execute his duties.[12] Some of these privileges were curtailed as part of the overall consolidation of the Habsburg rule. After the death of Patriarch Arsenije III in 1706, the next head of religious community held the title of the Metropolitan rather than Patriarch.[13] Towards the end of the century, in 1770 and 1777, the Metropolitan's secular powers were abolished. Finally, the Serbian schools were placed under government control in line with the education reform of 1774 (1777 in Hungary), which established the general education requirement for children of both sexes. This means that one- or two-class schools were established. 'Given the relatively modest goals of these schools, the use of the vernacular was deemed appropriate and necessary, since few children would have understood other languages'.[14] Most of the teachers in Serb communities and throughout the empire were priests, often the only members of the community literate and educated enough to teach. A series of further reforms implemented by Joseph II in the mid-1780s, on the one hand, made more resources available for primary education, and on the other, extended broader religious toleration to non-Catholic Christian and non-Christian communities.

Under these conditions, the cultural influence of the Orthodox Church became very strong in the Serbian community, which affected the way ethnic identity was preserved and developed. When the Ottomans abolished the Patriarchate of Peć (in present-day Kosovo) in 1776, the centre of Serb spiritual life had already long moved to Hungary and, as Ivo Banac pointed out, 'by that time the Habsburg Serbs were increasingly adjusting themselves to the cultural climate of Central Europe'.[15] This climate included emphasis on literacy and education, secularization and the importance of history to develop a national community. Vienna, Pest, Novi Sad and Sremski Karlovci were the main centres of Serbian cultural and intellectual life by the early nineteenth century. They retained this position until well into the nineteenth century.[16] The Enlightenment intellectual and political tradition, which included anti-clericalism, also took root in the Serbian intellectual community, however small it was, as seen in the work of Dositej Obradović, a former Orthodox monk, the first minister of education in the semi-independent Serbian Principality, and the most significant author of the Serbian Enlightenment.[17] As Ljubinka Trgovčević observed, Habsburg religious tolerance and the new anti-clericalism helped the Orthodox Serbs 'liberate themselves from the strong traditionalist impact of their church. Both education and a new awareness of their own rights strengthened national consciousness, eventually leading to the creation of a nation-state and modern national culture'.[18] People and ideas moved freely across the Danube, but the existence of two centres of gravity meant tension. A distinct in Habsburg-based Serbian tradition of thinking about the nation and statehood was visible throughout the period and well into the twentieth century.

Another territory that came under Habsburg control was Bosnia. The Congress of Berlin of 1878 placed Ottoman Bosnia under Austrian jurisdiction, and the territory was formally annexed in 1908. One of the most religiously and ethnically diverse parts of the Balkans, Bosnia will occupy an important place in the plans of the Serbian clergy, as well as Serbian and Yugoslav political actors. The terms of the 1878 treaty stated clearly that Muslims were 'assured full liberty in relations with their spiritual leaders', that is, the Sultan and the Great Mufti in Istanbul.[19] Despite the Bosnian Muslim leaders' declaration of loyalty to Austria-Hungary, the Viennese administration continuously pursued limiting the possibilities of ties with Istanbul. They feared that spiritual guidance went hand in hand with political influence. In 1909, after the formal annexation of Bosnia, religious and cultural autonomy was finally granted to the Bosnian Muslims, establishing a separate Bosnian Islamic community, an institution that had not existed under the Ottoman rule, where the Muslim community across the empire did not have institutionalized national/ethnic divisions – a post-Ottoman 'millet system in reverse' with Islam now in the minority position. Habsburg's "civilising mission" in the Balkans altered the balance of power on the ground and brought many administrative changes. It also placed the Christian Catholic community in a more privileged position, while the Orthodox community in Bosnia continued to feel constrained. At the same time, the Serbs now had an opportunity to capitalize on independent Serbia across the border to the east.

The modern Serbian state emerged in the course of the military struggle with the Ottomans and with the diplomatic and military aid of the Russian Empire. It fashioned itself rhetorically in opposition to the Ottomans. This applied to both language and religion – the two identity markers pointed out by Banac. Although generally friendly, its relationship with Slavic-speaking and East Orthodox Russia was not always straightforward. By the early twentieth century (and before the Balkan wars of 1912–13), Serbia was uniquely homogenous in its linguistic and religious composition, with over 95 per cent of the population members of the Serbian Orthodox Church. However, this resulted from the demographic change that took place gradually over the course of the nineteenth century. Muslims and 'Turks' were pushed out by peaceful and violent means from the new Christian state.[20] Serbian statesmen and national 'awakeners' created and popularized the narrative of the Serbian suffering under the Turkish yoke and 'glorified the fight against the Turks as a political duty of Serbian patriots'.[21] As long as the Serbian territories remained religiously and linguistically homogenous, there was no pressing need to decide whether language or religion should be seen as *the* national marker. However, the complexity of the imperial settings discussed above will come back with the renewed force after the First World War, once the religiously, ethnically and culturally diverse kingdom of Yugoslavia was established.

The transformation of political and cultural spaces from imperial to nation-state settings ran parallel with the changes in the life of religious communities, including the Serbian East Orthodox one. These changes were part of the more extensive process of the coming of modernity, of which the emergence of nationalism and nation-states were only one aspect. Balkan religious communities and their leaders thus were faced with a variety of challenges. The most concerning were the fading authority of religious leaders and institutions, poor material conditions of the clergy and the low educational level of the peasantry. These were the circumstances in which the Serbian Orthodox Church established itself as a national institution.

Working together: Church and state in independent Serbia

Almost immediately after Serbia acquired a degree of political autonomy from the Ottomans in 1815, Prince Miloš Obrenović, the leader of the Second Serbian Uprising and the founder of one of the two Serbian ruling dynasties, started negotiating with both secular and religious authorities in Istanbul the re-establishment of an independent (autocephalous) Serbian Orthodox Church.[22] For the rest of the century, the Serbian Orthodox Church sought to become the national church in the sense of having autonomy from the Ecumenical Patriarchate on the one hand, and as an institution vital to the success of the emerging nation-state on the other. The two aspects were often intertwined and reinforced each other. In the words of Ramet, 'the establishment of national patriarchates in Bulgaria and Serbia, in particular, figured as part of the state-building process and was closely associated with the assertion of national identity'.[23] Ramet argues that 'Church autocephaly has been usually valued both as authentication of Christian culture/national identity and as an assurance of the exclusion of foreign clerical or even political influence'.[24] The former was in line with the anti-Ottoman and anti-Muslim sentiment and was also true for other Christian Balkan nations, such as Bulgaria and Greece. Foreign influence is more salient in the Bulgarian case, which saw a competition between Slavic- and Greek-speaking clergy. The Greek case itself is interesting as it featured an early critical debate on the desirability of modern nationalism and its challenges from the point of view of the Ecumenical Patriarchate, which the Greeks dominated.[25] In the case of Serbia, no such dispute took place.

The history of the Serbian Church in the nineteenth century is, by and large, a story of the transition from the millet system to the nation-state framework. Accompanied by many problems, this transformation sometimes was as complex as the life under the alleged Ottoman oppression. The lack of material and human resources was coupled with legal chaos and disunity. Separate dioceses existed in Serbia and Montenegro, both (semi)independent states, and in Bosnia and Southern Hungary, which belonged to the Ottoman and Habsburg imperial spheres. The administrative centre of the new church structures was in Belgrade – the centre of political power – but not all these territories were under the rule of the Metropolitan of Belgrade. The relationship between the two centres of religious authority, Belgrade and Sremski Karlovci, was not ideal. In 1901 the retired archpriest Aleksa Ilić revived an older periodical, *Christian Herald*, to bridge the many divides in the Serbian East Orthodox community and help fight off the common enemies: the Vatican and the neo-Protestant Nazarene sect. Ilić lamented the rivalry between Belgrade and Sremski Karlovci and was primarily concerned with the East Orthodox Christians living in Bosnia, who seemed to prefer their own ways.[26] Similar concerns and even bitterness were expressed by Archbishop Mojsej when discussing the 1881 crisis around the conflict of Metropolitan Mihailo and King Milan Obrenović. Mojsej accused the government of risking foreign, in this case, Austrian, influence in a deeply national affair: the election of a new Metropolitan by involving the Metropolitan of Sremski Karlovci. But he was also worried about the potential damage emanating from having two centres of authority: 'Did our government realise the threat to which it exposed the peace and order in the church of our nation and with that the basis of its survival and development in the national spirit?'[27]

Institutional complexity is often thought to be the chief reason for the Serbian Church's support of the Yugoslav cultural – and later political – project. The Serbian clergy saw a possibility for the unification of its numerous church jurisdictions in one legal entity, which would be easier to achieve in the framework of a common state, be it Greater Serbia or Yugoslavia. In fact, despite the seemingly complete overlap of interests, the church–state relationship in Serbia was often riddled with problems. One of the prime points of contention was the reluctance of some in the upper clergy to see the Church subjugated to secular political interests. They believed that 'the metamorphosis of Orthodoxy into an extension of the state, as the religious expression of the nation, weakened the church'.[28] While not all clergy felt that way, taking into account the opinions, thoughts and interests of the leaders and those who spoke on behalf of the East Orthodox religious community makes the position put forward by Banac and quoted in the opening of this chapter less straightforward than it appears at first glance. This chapter explores some of these tensions in the pre-1918 period.

From the Serbian Church's point of view, the history of the church–state relationship, from the moment the Church acquired formal independence in 1830, was the story of a gradual loss of the Church's autonomy within the nation-state framework. From the perspective of the young Serbian state, establishing the primacy of secular political authority and institutions was a vital part of the state- and nation-building. Given the past importance of religious institutions, it was essential to establish the structures of the secular state as the only source of legitimate power. To achieve this goal, the state did not hesitate to intervene in the internal affairs of the Church, and the Church gradually gave in. The removal of Metropolitan Mihailo in 1881 and his seven-year long exile is usually regarded as the perfect illustration of this process. The causes of the conflict between Mihailo and King Milan had little to do with religion and the Church. A prominent member of the Liberal Party and a close associate of Prime Minister Jovan Ristić, Mihailo disapproved of the anti-Russian foreign policy turn and the re-orientation of Serbia towards Austria taken by Milan after the Congress of Berlin. After Ristić resigned, Metropolitan Mihailo continued to publicly oppose the new government's foreign policy, now dominated by the Progressive Party. It took some months before Milan found a way to remove Mihailo, who was dismissed on the grounds of his and generally the clergy's opposition to the new taxation law, which introduced new payments for the clergy.

In the last two decades of the nineteenth century, the Serbian Parliament (the *Skupština*) passed several laws regulating various church-related procedures. Most crucial was the one on the electoral procedure for a new Metropolitan. The king could not forget how difficult it was to find a way to expel Mihailo in 1881. After the Metropolitan's return home from exile, a new law was passed that put the entire procedure under the control of the king. The council that elected the Metropolitan now included members of Parliament and ministers appointed by the king in addition to church hierarchs, thus creating a system in which secular authorities had the upper hand in the elections. It remained in effect until 1918, only to be reinstated in a slightly different format in the Kingdom of Yugoslavia after the First World War.

The material and financial state of the Serbian Church was remarkably poor throughout the nineteenth century. One of the most urgent and repeated requests concerned the issue of the fixed annual wage that the parish priests wanted to be paid by the state. The government repeatedly rejected the proposal. Meanwhile, parish priests had to engage in agricultural activities with their parishioners to survive. The money they got from the parish for their work and charitable contributions was not enough. Parish clergy argued that they could not perform all required activities under such conditions with the desired degree of commitment. Such difficulties made it challenging to ensure that every parish had a priest. Data shows that the number of priests per 1,000 citizens decreased continuously from 0.91 in 1846 to 0.6 in 1874 to 0.35 in 1914 and is often used to prove the story of decline.[29] These numbers and the underlying reality were well known to the contemporaries who interpreted them either as proof that urgent intervention was necessary or as a sign of religion's continuous and welcome decline. In the second half of the nineteenth century, most Church public communication concerned this issue in one way or another. However, the Orthodox Church in Serbia enjoyed many privileges and, as it often happens in religiously homogeneous and traditional societies, took most of them for granted. Under the 1903 Constitution (and under the previous Constitution from 1888), East Orthodox Christianity was recognized as the official state religion. All state national holidays were celebrated according to church rituals; religious instruction was compulsory.[30] Church–state separation was not implemented and was not on the agenda of any significant political actors. Interestingly enough, neither side saw it as an absolute necessity, as both hoped to benefit from the close relationship.

The Serbian Church and Serbian nationalism before the First World War

The close, intimate relationship between the Serbian Church and the Serbian state was not a novelty. Whoever wanted to emphasize that this was a well-established historical relationship often referred to the fact that medieval Serbian rulers were canonized as East Orthodox saints – the fact that later prompted scholars to talk about 'nation-confession'. The clergy used this fact as proof of their considerable contribution towards the preservation of the national memory and the national identity. Since the eighteenth century, religious cults of the medieval Nemanjić dynasty had been established across Serbian territories and quickly gained prominence in church rituals and public consciousness. One of the most important for contemporaries and future generations was the cult of Prince Lazar, the main protagonist of the Kosovo epic and myth. It has been noted that 'in popular perception Kosovo became a paradigm of a just struggle, self-sacrifice and dying on the "cross of honour" for a "golden freedom"'.[31] In the course of the nineteenth century, as a paradigm of collective self-understanding, 'Kosovo became intimately tied to the life of an entire people which was gradually becoming aware of itself as a nation in the context of other European nations and aspiring to define itself as one, in counter-distinction to the wretched "raja" (rayah) of the Ottoman Empire'.[32] In its capacity as a foundational myth, and a part of the nation-building process, the Kosovo epic has analogies in other European contexts.[33] However, the Kosovo myth could and should also be interpreted in the framework of the interaction between religious and secular actors. In this analytical framework, it can be seen as an important but not the singular instance of the sacralization of the nation. Should one opt for such an approach, the discursive practice of a religious community and religious institutions become as important as the discourse of 'mainstream' secular national actors. In this framework, the religious community is treated as an important actor, and the discourse it has created is taken on its terms.

This latter half of this chapter explores how the Serbian Orthodox Church reflected on modern politics and constructed a narrative of its importance for the survival and development of the nation in the two decades before the First World War. The story presented here adds nuance and complexity to a more conventional story told by the students of nationalism and politics discussed in the introduction, who accept uncritically the position articulated by the Church. The chapter shows that the motivations and reasons for constructing the link between religion and national identity were manifold and were part and parcel of the challenges of modernity.

One could reasonably expect the Serbian Orthodox Church, which considered itself an important national institution, to be an engaged public actor with an elaborate position on key issues of the time. However, until the early twentieth century, with rare exceptions such as Metropolitan Mihailo, most clerics were not conspicuous on the national level but did enjoy considerable authority in their local communities and often had a public standing there. This could be partially explained by the clergy's relatively low educational level on the one hand and their preoccupation with concerns and challenges of day-to-day life. The clergy did pay attention to significant political developments in the kingdom but often remained in the background and did not seek public prominence. This will slowly begin to change after the 1903 coup d'état and the change of the dynasty.

After the assassination of Alexander Obrenović and Queen Draga in June 1903 in a coup d'état orchestrated by the Serbian military, Petar Karadjordjević became the new Serbian king. Undoubtedly, the Serbian political elite perceived this event as opening a new period in national life. The modernizing, Western-orientated elite had high hopes for the new sovereign, who was raised in Western Europe, received excellent classical education and translated J. S. Mill's *On Liberty* into Serbian. They expected the new king to promote and strengthen democracy in Serbia. The religious elite, generally more conservative, in its turn also hoped that under the new king things would improve, that the 'new period [would] be inspired by the spirit of general renaissance, which [would] also help us, the clergy, to create from the people's heart a rich treasury of moral good'.[34] The hopes of the Serbian clergy, who 'waited impatiently for the new governmental program ... to see whether it will include in its agenda the question about the promotion of the Church and the clergy' remained unfulfilled. To their great disappointment, there was not a single word about the Church in the governmental address presented to the Parliament.[35] Dissatisfaction and frustration started to gain ground in the circles of the higher clergy.

One of the important changes stemmed from the coming to power of the Serbian Radical Party led by Nikola Pašić. The party had considerable support of the lower clergy, of whom many were members. Like elsewhere in rural Europe, it was a priest or a teacher who was the primary source of knowledge about the world, and to whom villagers often deferred for political opinion. Serbia's political landscape in 1903–14, the period which is often referred to as the 'golden era of democracy', was dominated by the Radicals, who controlled both the Parliament and the government.[36] Having the support of the clergy helped maintain their hold on power. It was not, however, entirely cynical. By then, Pašić developed a sophisticated vision of the Serbian political culture, which had East Orthodox Christianity as one of its pillars.[37]

Such active participation in public politics was actively debated, especially its partisan nature. Those in favour emphasized the right of priests as citizens to participate in political life, as enshrined in the Constitution (put forward by the Radicals). The Radicals themselves stressed the idea of civic duty – the clergy as a better-educated part of society was to guide the politically non-educated and immature population and make sure that they were not misled by political demagogues (read: political opponents of the Radicals). More importantly and more commonly, the assumption was that the presence of a critical mass of clergy in the Parliament could positively affect the work of the legislative body in the sense that it would pass laws required by the Church. Nikola D. Božić, the parish priest of the Belgrade Cathedral in the early twentieth century and the proto-presbyter of the Belgrade district, appealed on the pages of the monthly *Vesnik Srpske Crkve* ('Courier of the Serbian Church') to his fellow priests members of the Parliament to advance the Church question in parliamentary debates and to convince the deputies to pass the law on Church authorities, which got stuck in Parliament.[38] Church hierarchs perhaps somewhat naively believed that having politically active clergy would ensure a situation in which 'in all parties, there will be people filled by religious feeling, inclined to the Church and the clergy'.[39]

The hierarchs needed to have all the support they could gather. As the twentieth century progressed, they became increasingly more concerned about the prospects of their institution and more broadly about the direction in which the world developed. In the two decades before the First World War, they mounted sharp criticism of the present. The answer to the question 'Is it true that with every year our society falls further into moral deficit?' was always a 'Yes'.⁴⁰ The acute feeling of the coming crisis permeated most church publications. This crisis was strongly associated with the advance of modernity and technological progress. As one of the most prolific church publicists of the time, Miloš Andjelković, stated, 'one has to mourn the fact that in today's world, despite the progress and civilisation, there is less sincerity, fewer morals than there should be'.⁴¹ Of all the evils of modernity, it was atheism and materialism that the Church feared the most:

> More than 100 years have passed since the times of Rousseau. Science and education, culture and civilisation have made great progress and proceed with great steps from one year to another. But alongside this process, atheist and materialist theories are broadening and developing … The current state of moral order in society is based on a principle irreconcilable with Christian morals – it is based on crude egoism.⁴²

Based on the relatively limited number of available publications, it is hard to tell if this criticism of modernity was grounded in theological and/or philosophical thinking or whether it was political opportunism on behalf of the Serbian Church. Nikola Pašić and his colleagues in the Serbian Radical Party often used similar types of populist critique. They appealed to the national sense of collectivity, as opposed to either socialist class-based critique or the liberal emphasis on the value of each individual. It was a convenient way for the Serbian Church to justify its importance and continued relevance even in the modernizing world. Alongside the glorification of the past, which is discussed in the next section, this was one of the common strategies employed by the clerics when faced with the task to justify their existence and expenses.

Interestingly, the moral crisis and the clergy's political involvement could be linked differently. One of the regular contributors to the church periodicals, Mihajlović saw lasting damage where others saw the potential for improvement:

> When we return to sobriety from today's party drunkenness, when the party fire, whose flames have seized all the children of this land called Serbia, goes out, then we shall soberly notice even deeper wounds on the moral and religious side of our Fatherland, and shall feel even greater pains. Then we will come back to the question: How can they be soothed, and what is to be done so that the damaged and crumbling edifice of our people's religious and moral life can be restored, and we might be the same people in the future.⁴³

Mihajlović suggested that calmer, more focused work of the Church and the clergy was necessary instead of cynical party politics, he favoured private prayer in a monastic cell over a party rally:

> We hope that renewed monasticism, a new generation of monks will ... correct the mistakes of their predecessors and in their hidden monastic cells, with their sincere prayers for the happiness and progress of their people and their tribe, with great love and devotion, will work on the moral and cultural revival of their people and their Fatherland [44]

These two visions of a church as an active public and political actor versus a church that focused on spiritual work began to crystallize in the prewar decade. Around 1907–8, *Vesnik Srpske Crkve* started to regularly report on the parliamentary debates, especially when a priest gave a speech. A special section entitled 'From the National Parliament' was started, where some of the speeches were reproduced in full. Interestingly, most of them were concerned with the material/financial state of the parish priests. To legitimize their request for greater state support, the orators used the same arguments employed in most of the other church publications: the Serbian Orthodox Church contributed greatly to national progress; East Orthodox Christianity led the country into the community of cultured states and gave Serbia the right to remain within the circle of these civilized states.[45] It was a thoroughly historical narrative, albeit an uncritical one.

A critical transformation of the historical narrative occurred in 1909 during the parliamentary debate initiated by the elected representatives who were clerics. They introduced the case of a schoolteacher who was accused of propagating atheism outside the classroom. They argued that 'a teacher always remains a teacher, a priest remains a priest, and a professor remains a professor' to enlighten the environment in which he works by his personal example.[46] Naturally, the clergy found him guilty of spreading atheistic views and damaging society and wanted the rest of the deputies to share their condemnation and hold the teacher accountable. In his denunciatory speech, Archpriest Milan Djurić, a member of the Radical Party, extended the historicist argument into the present time. He claimed that East Orthodox Christianity was the foundation of the Serbian state. Hence it was the task of [the deputies/the people] to preserve this 'vivifying force, the force of persuasion for freedom, happiness, culture and progress of the Serbian people, for our freedom and its future'.[47] He mentioned Saint Sava and his great deeds concluding by saying that the Serbian Orthodox Church is one with the Serbian nation and 'the Serbian Church is the source of the Serbian people's vitality'.⁴⁸ Clearly, this kind of rhetoric was different from the then traditional historicist argument employed by the Church and anticipated the rhetoric of the Serbian Orthodox Church from the mid-1930s. There are sufficient reasons to claim that Djurić did not aim at the fusion of the Serbian national identity and East Orthodox Christianity and that there was no serious theoretical/theological thought behind it. He was well known for his oratory skills and the tendency towards patriotic style. Milan Stojadinović, Yugoslav minister of finance and prime minister in the 1930s, later recalled that Djurić had the habit of making references in his parliamentary speeches to 'the bones of the forefathers'. He also recalled that Djurić, who was the leader of the Radical Party in the town of Užice, spent more time at political meetings and conferences than he did in his parish church.⁴⁹ This was probably one of the earliest public discussions of the intimate links between religion and modern Serbian national identity. At the time, it still belonged to the margins of the public debate and few people engaged with it seriously. However, it does indicate that the origins of the discourse of Nikolaj Velimirović prominent in the late 1930s can be tentatively traced to the early twentieth century.

We have to be careful not to overstress the importance and prominence of Djurić's ideas and rhetoric. At the time, the language of nationalism permeated all public debates and shaped the political landscape in Serbia. The Serbian Orthodox Church learned to speak the language and developed an interpretation of its own position, which used references to the nation and its history. The key point was the assertion that the Serbian Orthodox Church defended and inspired the Serbian national identity in the past and continued to do so in the present. Church publicists underlined the clergy's contribution to the struggle for national liberation and highlighted the national character (*narodni karakter*) of the church's institution. 'It is the indisputable truth that the Serbian Orthodox priest as a *national* priest has always been a true friend of his nation', wrote Nikola Božić.⁵⁰ The common tropes used included national history, national development, freedom of the Serbian people, as well as references to the times when 'there was no ruler, no government, no nobility, but the priests, God's saints were with the people'.⁵¹

The bishop of Timok Milentije, in an article with a characteristic title, 'Historical contributions of the Serbian clergy in the service of Orthodoxy and its people', emphasized the Serbs' devotion to East Orthodox Christianity since the times of St Sava, which led them to prefer losing their political independence (on the Kosovo field) over changing their faith. He claimed that only those Serbs who retained their East Orthodox faith remained true Serbs, and those who converted to Islam or Catholicism lost their national identity. Furthermore, it was 'due to such a close rapprochement of Orthodoxy to the lives of the Serbs, and the nation to Orthodoxy, that the Serbs as an independent nation managed to survive'.[52] Milentije's goal here was to establish the significance and value of his Church in the nation-state framework. He did not necessarily aim to enter into a debate with the proponents of the linguistic/cultural definition of the Serbian national identity, which was dominant at the time. A similar position was expressed by others as well: 'Our Orthodox faith is closely linked to and united with Serbianness [srpstvo], since, simply by abandoning his Orthodox faith, a Serb abandons his nationality as well. That is why we cherish our Orthodoxy like the apple of our eye, as by preserving Orthodoxy, we preserve our nationality, our beloved Serbianness.'[53]

Such statements did not appear particularly problematic in the circumstance of a nearly perfectly religiously and ethnically homogeneous nation-state. Neither were they based on a solid theoretical foundation. Jevrem Bojović, a professor at Belgrade Theological Seminary, which offered the highest degree in theology awarded in Serbia, was one of the few authors who attempted to create a philosophical justification. His was rooted in the idea that a certain law of historical development required such a connection. He wrote,

> A fundamentally rational, ideal force maintains goodness, justice and truth as the norms by which the life of the people should develop – that is the historical law. It incorporates morals as its base; these morals [in their turn] are conditioned by belief in God. Hence, none of the peoples without belief can follow the historical law, as it will not have justice in its life.[54]

This, however, was not an argument about specifically Serbian nation and East Orthodox Christianity. Bojović's concern again was to explain the importance of the Church for the nation-state, as it was only the Church that was capable of preserving 'those moral forces without which no state or people can understand and fulfil their historical task'.[55] It seems that the Serbian clergy in the early twentieth century was not interested in defining the Serbian nation's precise boundaries or creating a refined intellectual construction to support their claims of the close link between East Orthodox Christianity and said national identity.

A rare exception in terms of originality of thought is presented by Čedomir Marjanović, one of the few Serbian clerics to receive higher-level theological training. Marjanović enrolled at the Old Catholic Theology Department at the University of Bern in 1903/4 (where Nikolaj Velimirović also studied several years later) after completing one semester in Leipzig. He successfully graduated from the University of Bern with a doctoral degree in theology in 1909 after defending a doctoral dissertation entitled 'Utilitarianism and Christianity'. Marjanović stood out from his colleagues in his education, international experience and political orientation. His sympathies lay broadly with the political left, but not with the internationalism of the Social Democrats and, most importantly, not with their materialism and atheism.[56] In 1905, while he was studying in Bern, Marjanović admitted the inevitable: 'We are now living in a period of transition from patriarchal culture to modern culture, in the time when our social conditions are far from what they should be.'[57] Marjanović's personal experience of living and studying in Switzerland and Germany allowed him to draw parallels and make comparisons very astutely. His conclusions were not favourable towards Serbian society. He lamented that 'this is when the vital traditions are not preserved; when even the thought of harmony between various social groups is remote'. A way to solve the problem, according to him, was to raise the social awareness of the people by placing the emphasis of school instruction 'not on practical education, but on social, humanitarian education'.[58] Marjanović argued for the promotion of 'social education', the foundation of which should be religious education, literature and history.[59] Marjanović likely witnessed the results of Catholic educational policy while studying in Bern and was rather impressed by it. Yet, as a student of the Old Catholic department, he was not uncritical of the official Catholic model, either. Marjanović claimed that cosmopolitan education did not correspond to the tasks facing Serbia. He insisted the school instruction needed to have a distinctly national character. This provided yet another justification for why more attention should be devoted to religion and history in school curricula.[60]

Some aspects of Marjanović's proposal were shared by another prolific although more conventional writer Milos Andjelković who repeatedly rephrased the quite simple idea that a 'nation is [only] truly educated and civilised [if] its morals [are] based on religious principles, [if its] morals are religious and not philosophical, not humanist'.[61] He emphasized the national aspect stronger than Marjanović did and dismissed the value or even desirability of social harmony built on anything other than religion. Andjelković also drew comparisons between Serbia and other countries:

> Everything shows that the decline of faith and religiosity in the nation is accompanied by the decline of morals, which has political decline as a natural consequence ... What makes modern-day Russia and England such strong states? Without a doubt, it is the religiosity and piety of the people. ... Both

states have religions as a motto and ideal of life. Policymaking itself and the entire state diplomacy are founded on the principle that 'religion is nationality'.[62]

The position presented and articulated by Andjelković was shared broadly by the hierarchy of the Serbian Orthodox Church and arguably to a much greater extent than the plan proposed by Marjanović. Andjelković made a successful career; he became a professor and archpriest and published actively until he died in 1931. Marjanović's life story was not as straightforward. Together with a group of young, well-trained theologians, he tried to implement his views in practice and took the initiative of publishing a textbook for the fourth grade of elementary school at his own expense. The book's second edition was banned by Metropolitan Dimitrije, who accused the author of propagating heresy. Marjanović tried to defend himself by arguing that his was only an alternative way of bringing Christianity to the masses. Still, the conflict escalated and eventually resulted in Marjanović being dismissed from his teaching position at the gymnasium.[63] Marjanović's dissatisfaction and disappointment in how church institutions developed themselves ran very deep. In fact, they were severe enough to make him join the quisling government of Milan Nedić in 1941 as minister of justice.

As demonstrated by these examples, towards the end of the nineteenth century, the Serbian clergy had reached a level of training and education that allowed it to keep track of intellectual and political developments abroad. The story of Marjanović's failure also demonstrates that new trends in social, political and religious thought made it to the Serbian Orthodox milieu but were not necessarily embraced by a large number of people. It has been assumed in the literature that Serbian students who went to study in Russian theological seminaries (the majority went to Kiev) brought back the spirit of Russian Orthodoxy, Dostoyevsky and a Russian–Serbian Slavic bond. However, recent research demonstrates that this was not the case. According to Klaus Buchenau, most Serbian students did not engage with theology or philosophy. Instead, they wrote on the 'ecclesiastical history of their home countries, for which they often lacked source material and which they usually interpreted in a shallow nationalist manner'.[64] They thus came back to Serbia more patriotic and nationally minded, rather than inspired by the depth of East Orthodox theology. In the early twentieth century, the prevailing attitude in Serbian clerical circles towards Russian theological education was rather critical, and preference was given to the secularized institutions of Western Europe. Thus, French and German intellectual sources were of importance.

Serbian clergy and religious writers may not have had a sophisticated theory behind the church's historical narratives and the link between religion and national identity. Still, they did have an acute interest in nationalism as a phenomenon of modern life and modern politics more broadly, including the main ideologies of the time – liberalism and socialism. The choice of readings with an impact in Serbian clerical circles seems arbitrary, but the tendencies are telling. For instance, the ideas on the relationship between Christianity and politics, social question, liberalism, tolerance and democracy put forward by Anatole Leroy-Beaulieu (1842–1912), a French publicist and a specialist in Russian and Balkan histories, found a friendly reception in Serbia.[65] In the preface to the Serbian translation, the editor complained about the contemporary attitude of the Serbian democrats to the clergy, whom they (the democrats) claimed to be an obstacle to the democratic development of the country.[66] Leroy-Beaulieu was presented as an alternative to such an attitude, a democrat who accepted patriotism. The editor probably selected the French scholar not because of the outstanding quality of his study but because his work on Russia and the Balkans was known locally in Belgrade.

The Church's interest in socialism, social issues and social work grew in the early twentieth century together with the growth of the Social Democracy and other left-wing ideologies in Europe and the Balkans, on the one hand, and with the rise of social work in the Roman Catholic Church on the other. This interest was critical and suspicious rather than open and embracing. However, it tentatively indicates that at least some part of the Serbian East Orthodox intellectual elite wanted to be seen as accepting of political modernity. Socialism, clearly, did not gain sympathy from the clergy, as secularization was one of its key messages. *Vesnik Srpske Crkve* published several very repetitive texts and translations, mainly from Russian, that blamed socialism and its adherents for being aggressively anti-religious and anti-clerical. Authors regretted that the socialist movement became part of Serbian political and social reality.[67]

The criticism was not limited to socialists alone. The Serbian political elite overall was often vilified for its lack of faith. One of the fundamental complaints by the clergy concerning the national elite was that educated people were not good parishioners and did not set a good example for the people. Some authors, such as Andjelković, believed that this was due to the influence of European philosophy, for instance, that of Schopenhauer and Feuerbach.[68] The fact that the Serbian elite, on average, followed the materialist trend of European thought makes Andjelković lament why they could not have followed Newton, Copernicus and Kant instead – they were religious or at least idealists in their philosophical constructions. Educated clergy in Serbia accepted the inevitability and benefits of modernity and technological progress. Still, they refused to accept that it must be accompanied by secularization: 'The Serbian nation is much more progressive from the point of view of its general cultural state that it used to be half a century ago, but from the point of view of religion and morals it shows poor results, far worse than it had before.'[69] Miloš Pantelić in exasperation compared Austrian and Serbian cases and clearly demonstrated that not all things 'Western' or 'European' were automatically rejected:

> Having seen how one of the enlightened nations, even its intelligentsia, respect its religion and how people go to churches and heartily pray there, it harmfully occurs to us that the situation in our country is different. We also have doctors, professors, scientists. We have intelligentsia. But how many of them receive communion annually? How many of them would ask the priest to pray for them to be united with Christ at the hour of their death? Not one![70]

Other voices were harsher in their assessment of the West and its impact on Serbian society. They talked of the 'contemporary evil' of the 'terrible universe of the West that devours its victims ... and threatens to destroy the culture and the most beautiful expressions of human heart and mentality' – all because it 'rejects anything religious and divine in a person's heart and soul'. And now to their horror, 'Apostles of this evil we find in our press, and unfortunately in our parliament.'[71]

Some of this judgement came as a reaction to the criticism and discussion of the Church's failures presented by the Serbian cultural and political establishment. The failures were manifold and difficult to overlook: monasteries were in decay, parish priests engaged in party politics, and Serbian peasants increasingly turned towards other sources of authority and spiritual guidance. Some clerics acknowledged the problematic nature of the situation but retorted to the historicist argument by saying that 'the intelligentsia should acknowledge previous work of the clergy and should try to understand the difficulties the Church faces today'.[72] In 1908 *Vesnik Srpske Crkve* initiated a new regular column in which the editor commented on the articles that appeared in the national press about the Church. As the secular press was critical towards the Serbian clergy and the Church, this part presents a continuous response to this criticism. As the pressure increased, the answer also radicalized, and the 'national card' was played more often and more forcefully. As an anonymous author observed, history cannot go backwards and 'Serbianness cannot be separated from Orthodoxy, clergy and the people'.[73]

We can see a variety of tendencies and opinions in the narratives articulated by Serbian clergy at the turn of the century. It is essential to underline that, firstly, the clergy's master legitimization strategy was based on a historicist argument about the contribution of the Serbian Orthodox Church to the national cause. It was later accompanied by the development of cults of national saints. Together, these two tendencies contributed to creating an image of the Serbian Church as, first and foremost, a national institution. Secondly, this discourse was in polemic with those who, like Marjanović, emphasized the social aspect of the Church's mission. But most importantly, it was directed towards the state to convince secular political actors of the indispensability of the Church as a resource for state-building. To a great extent, the Serbian Church was dependent on state support. This was primarily in financial terms but also applied to the Church's activities in Southern Serbia, Macedonia and Bosnia, where the interests of the Church coincided with the foreign interests of the Kingdom of Serbia. In these conditions, the leadership of the Serbian Church had neither the resources nor the interest to support and develop ideas of social work and social education.

2

New Church for the new state: 'Liberation and unification' of lands, people and institutions

The new state

Where does faith come in? Yugoslavism and religion

The previous chapter discussed the place of religion and religious institutions in modern Balkan nationalisms with a special focus on pre-1918 Serbia. It also demonstrated how the importance of religion and religious institutions for the national past was repeatedly emphasized by clerics and religious representatives on various occasions throughout the long nineteenth century, as well as how it has become an inherent part of national histories, mythologies and canons. In the period immediately after the First World War it was not essential anymore whether the Church's contribution had *really* (in the Rankean sense of the word) been that significant, for the link between Orthodox Christianity and the Serbian nation had been firmly established and was no longer questioned to any noticeable extent. However, in the context of establishing a multinational and a multireligious state, this strong association presented a number of challenges. Since interwar Yugoslavia was built around the supranational ideology of Yugoslavism, it is critical to examine what place it allocated to religion. After all, Jovan Dučić, a famous Serbian poet, who once said about Ivan Meštrović that it was possible either to be a Catholic sculptor or a Serb, but not both, was not alone in this thinking.[1] Dučić's remark reveals much about the destructive potential the bond between religion and national identity held for the multinational and multi-confessional Yugoslav state- and nation-building project. The question thus is: How did the proponents of Yugoslavism deal with the question of religion before and after the common state was established?

According to the official, government-sanctioned interpretation of Yugoslavism, the three separate South Slavic nations of Serbs, Croats and Slovenes, whose names featured in the name of the state, formed the so-called three-named people, that is, the Yugoslav nation. In this model, the mutual relationship of the constitutive nations resembled the Christian concept of the Holy Trinity. As Andrew Wachtel points out, 'This formulation must have seemed a stroke of genius to those who coined it, for whatever the doctrinal difference that separated Orthodox and Catholic Christians, the concept of the Trinity was familiar to all.'[2] It also indicates that from the outset Yugoslavia was imagined as a Christian state with little attention paid to the presence of significant non-Christian minorities.[3]

Scholarship on the role of religion in destabilizing the interwar Yugoslav state remains rather limited, despite the steadily growing number of studies on aspects of interwar Yugoslav history. The commonly accepted historiographical debate is best exemplified by the difference in opinion between the Yugoslav historian Milorad Ekmečić, who argued that religion and religious ideologies were the main obstacle to the creation of stable Yugoslavia and the main reason for the Serb–Croat conflict on the one hand,[4] and Ivo Banac on the other, who maintained that religion did not have a prominent place in the national ideologies of the South Slav peoples, and that the conflicts between the Serbs and Croats should rather be seen as the clash between different political cultures.[5] Josip Smodlaka, Croatian democrat and modernist,[6] would have agreed with Ekmečić. Back in 1922 he argued in favour of replacing the official name of the state 'The Kingdom of Serbs, Croats and Slovenes' with 'Yugoslavia'. He opposed the use of historic names of constitutive nations due to their powerful association with different religions, whereas behind this difference stood mutually incompatible histories and sociocultural traditions.[7]

Both Ekmečić's and Banac's positions share two important features. Firstly, they treat relationship between the Yugoslav state and its religious communities as a fixed one and do not account for the changes that occurred between the two World Wars. Secondly, they present each religion rather homogeneously and differentiate very little between the various positions articulated by religious actors. Before proceeding to the discussion of how East Orthodox Christianity, as represented by the Serbian Orthodox Church, interacted with and impacted the Yugoslav state, it is important to understand how the proponents of Yugoslavism understood the place and role of religion in relation to their political vision.

In the nineteenth and early twentieth centuries, ideologues of cultural Yugoslavism, who did not believe that they had a chance of actually living in a common South Slav state, could afford not to discuss religion in great detail. Curiously, solutions expressed in the cultural realm were much more creative in comparison to those provided by politicians. They emphasized the linguistic proximity of the South Slavic peoples and promoted linguistic nationalism. Nevertheless, many considered the potential threat to unity posed by religious difference if it were to be instrumentalized for political purposes. Ljudevit Gaj – together with Vuk Karadžić, one of the creators of the common Serbo-Croatian language and a central figure for the early stages of the Illyrian movement – denied any possibility for religion to be a prerequisite for Yugoslav unity.[8] Similarly, Jovan Skerlić, a great Serbian literary scholar, politician and public intellectual, argued at the turn of the century that a common Yugoslav political entity was possible only under the condition of the universal and total religious indifference of the people.[9] Such an expectation of religion being effectively removed from the public sphere will continue to form an important and powerful trend of political thought and will inform many state policies.

Jovan Djaja, one of the leaders of the Serbian Radical Party, fervently called for an absolute ban of religion from public politics, because the two were, in his opinion, irreconcilable. Djaja employed two typologically different arguments. In his normative, philosophical argument he insisted that for anyone claiming to belong to the modern educated world, 'there is no doubt that nationality does not depend on religion to any extent'.[10] In his more context-bound argument, he claimed that the existent irreconcilable religious differences and disputes among the South Slavs could be used by the enemies of Yugoslavia against it. Thus, religion should be eliminated from the field of public politics all together, as is fit to do in the modern state and society anyways.

Others, in contrast to Skerlić and Djaja, did not insist on the total secularization of national cultures and politics. Instead, they argued that religion could and should bring the brotherly nations together. Back in the mid-nineteenth century, in the context of the 1848 Revolution, the Croatian Ban Josip Jelačić declared that difference of faith and church was no longer a wall between the brothers.[11] In its address to 'the Slavs of the Roman faith', the Serbian Parliament in Sremski Karlovci assured its 'Catholic brothers' that political cooperation with the Serbs would by no means constitute a threat to their Church, and asked them to overcome the difference of religion for the sake of national brotherhood.[12] Without a doubt, it was the revolutionary context of the 1848 and the practical aims of the anti-Magyar cooperation that made the leaders of the two communities try to overcome or, one could say, neglect potential religious tensions. At least rhetorically and discursively the option was present.

However, there did exist a tradition of Yugoslavism compatible with religion. In 1877, one of the 'founding fathers' of Yugoslavism, the Archbishop Josip Juraj Strossmayer, underlined that by its very nature Christianity should draw Serbian and Croatian nations together and not estrange them; such a separation would be against the essence of the religious teachings of love and mutual understanding. Strossmayer argued that 'religion which would be able to sow discord between brothers would not be religion, but rather a sheer superstition; it would not be the God's truth, but a human delusion'.[13] However appealing this utopian vision of unity, Strossmayer articulated this very liberal, ecumenical understanding of religion and religious difference when the creation of the common Yugoslav state was more a matter of a dream than a realistic political prospect. Even though Strossmayer was a cleric himself and clearly aware of the political ambitions and importance of the Catholic Church, none of his or others' pre-1918 treatments of religion's role in the Yugoslav cultural and political project took religious institutions seriously as involved and important actors with their own aims and logic that do not fully overlap with the overarching Yugoslav idea.

This underestimating of the powerful agency of religious actors was evident during the talks that led to the signing of the Corfu Declaration in 1917, when both Serbian and Croatian representatives agreed that the formal introduction of the principle of religious equality would suffice to contain any potential threat coming from the strong association between religion and national identities on the one hand, and to harness the power of religion to make it work for the success of the Yugoslav experiment.[14] Most were quite optimistic about the prospects of the new Yugoslav nation, for they believed religion to be in decline and were expecting it to fairly soon be replaced by scientific rationality. This view was based among other things on the contemporary academic expertise, for instance, that of Vladimir Ćorović (1885–1941), one of the leading Serbian historians of the interwar decades, author of the monumental *History of the Serbian People*, rector of Belgrade University and a proponent of Yugoslavism.[15] These optimistic expectations were inspired by the increasing, albeit slowly, levels of social modernization and urbanization, which meant a considerable degree of secularization. They went hand in hand with the Enlightenment tradition of rationality, positivist belief in progress, the ability of science to explain the natural world and of social science to explain society.

Even such a short glance at some of the authoritative contemporary authors who dealt with the issue of religion in relation to the Yugoslav national project demonstrates that at the beginning of the 1920s there was very little critical understanding of the role of religion on the side of the secular political audience.

Once the new state was in place, its leaders had to deal with the religious issue in earnest, for it was now impossible to ignore it. The interwar period would see elements of both approaches – secular and Christian – combined to create a system that disadvantaged and marginalized individuals and organizations who advocated for religious interests, in particular the interests of non-Christian groups.

Incomplete separation: Regulation of religious life and legal status of religious communities

When it came to the practical day-to-day tasks of the state regulation of religious life, the very first challenge the government officials faced was to bring the legislation up to date to accommodate the new reality of life in a multireligious state. The change of the state borders in 1918 and the consequent demographic changes were of greatest significance. According to the census of 1921, Serbs made up a little less than 40 per cent of the total population of Yugoslavia, together with other Orthodox peoples (Macedonians, Bulgarians, Romanians and Vlachs) their numbers amounted to almost 45 per cent versus 39 per cent Catholics and 11 per cent Muslims.[16]

The establishment of a clear and satisfactory relationship between religious communities and the state suddenly went to the top of the government's priorities list. The key principles underpinning all state initiatives and policies at this time included the formal acknowledgement of religious diversity and the acceptance of the principle of religious equality, as well as the idea of the secular state as a neutral and impartial arbiter in case of an inter-communal conflict. It was expected that such a regulation of religious life can be achieved, which will safely limit the undermining potential of the established link between religious and pre-Yugoslav national identities on the one hand, and at the same time harness the social capital of religious institutions for the benefit of new Yugoslavia. In 1919, equality of all religions was granted by a special proclamation issued by Regent Aleksandar; the 1921 and 1931 Constitutions guaranteed freedom of conscience and stipulated that all religions recognized under the law would enjoy equal rights.[17] Despite the shared feeling of urgency, many secular political actors saw the task of guaranteeing religious equality as less daunting in comparison with managing national and ethnic diversity. This was partially due to the lack of detailed thinking on this question prior to 1918 discussed above.[18]

Interwar Yugoslavia guaranteed freedom of worship and organization to the so-called recognized religions, which included the three Christian confessions

(East Orthodox, Catholic and Lutheran) and Islam and Judaism. Other religious groups were categorized as sects and did not enjoy the same freedoms and protection. East Orthodox, Catholic and Muslim communities were numerically the most significant ones. Lutheran and Jewish communities were normally featured in the legislation as an afterthought. All five communities had significant financial support from the state. In return, they were expected to perform certain services, such as death and birth registrations, preparation of lists of army conscripts, but most importantly, clergy of all religious traditions was charged with the task of fostering the 'love and loyalty' to Yugoslavia and the king among the general public. They were asked to do so by delivering 'instructive moral sermons' on national holidays, and by acting together with the teachers as national educators 'on every possible occasion'.[19] In exchange for this service religious leaders expected not just financial, but also symbolic support, for instance, civil servants were asked to attend religious services not only on national holidays but also for religious celebrations, preferably weekly to show example to the public.

This illustrates that even though Yugoslavia did not have one state church, there was no complete church-state separation either. The government opted for an in-between option, which over time would become a source of many structural problems; for example, religious education in schools was first made optional (1921) but after repeated complaints from the Catholic community was reintroduced as a mandatory class (1929–33). Another noteworthy aspect of the relationship between the state and religious communities was the idea to mould them into specific *Yugoslav* one. While in itself the idea of nationalization of religion was not new, Europe did not see many examples when this was attempted in a multireligious setting *and* working against the backdrop of already existent ties between religion and nationalism. This task required a certain degree of state control over its religious communities, which increased over time and proved to be a source of discontent. Compared to 1921, the 1931 Constitution introduced a greater degree of state patronage over religious communities, but the tendency had been evident earlier.

In early December 1918, almost immediately after the Kingdom of Serbs, Croats and Slovenes had been created, the Ministry of Religions was established. It held supervisory powers and the highest administrative powers in all religio-political matters.[20] It will be abolished in 1929 and the Department for Religious Affairs will be established within the Justice Ministry. The Ministry of Religions was to serve as an impartial arbiter in any potential interreligious conflict, but the absence of up-to-date legislation made the job of the minister a nightmare, as technically his actions were to follow the 1921 Constitution as well as all separate legislations that governed religious communities prior to unification. It also fell to the Ministry to make sure that the overall Yugoslav character of religious communities becomes more visible over time. The details of the legislation in relation to East Orthodox Christianity as well as the Church's reaction are detailed in the next section. For the Roman Catholic and Muslim communities, the relationship with Yugoslav state took its own dynamic which reflected their earlier historic experience as well.

Throughout the nineteenth century the Catholic Church disliked radical nationalism, perceiving it as an ungodly offspring of the French Revolution. This began to change with the emergence of mass politics at the turn of the century, when the clergy felt obliged to follow the spirit of the times. Croatia and Slovenia, the two key Catholic majority territories in Yugoslavia, followed this broader European pattern. The leaders of the Catholic movement in Croatia, which now aimed to involve the masses, were divided on the question of primacy of religion over nationalism. As Mark Biondich put it, 'the conservative wing identified Catholicism with Croat nationality and emphasized the primacy of Catholic religious principles over Croat national precepts. The moderate wing operated in the liberal Strossmayerist tradition and downplayed the importance of religion in national identity.'[21] Or to use Ramet's distinction, the Catholics were split between 'the progressives, who favoured incorporating Croatia into a liberal Slavic state and expected union with Serbia along the lines envisioned by Strossmayer, and the conservatives, who preferred security of the union with Austria-Hungary, and who refused to amalgamate Catholic Croatia with Orthodox Serbia'.[22] The latter position is best exemplified by the words of Josip Stadler, the archbishop of Sarajevo, who brought religion and nationalism together: 'We are Croats and Catholics, and will stay so.' With the establishment of Yugoslavia in 1918, this more conservative strand was understandably perceived as dangerous by the secular authorities. This fear informed the decision-making process in relation to state policies and regulations.

The relationship with the Vatican presented an additional challenge. The older agreements (concordats signed between Serbia and the Vatican, and between Montenegro and Vatican, plus the laws of the Austro-Hungarian Monarchy) ceased to be valid as international regulations after 1918 and could serve only as domestic laws. The negotiations between the Yugoslav government and Vatican to sign a new Concordat went on until the mid-1930s, only to be met with the outrage of the Serbian Orthodox Church, who opposed the Concordat vehemently (more details on this will follow in Chapter 4). The

Concordat issue and the regulation of the relationship between the Roman Catholic Church and the Yugoslav state was the main preoccupation of the Catholic community till the late 1920s. While the Catholic higher clergy insisted on the signing of the new Concordat with the Holy See straight from the creation of Yugoslavia, governmental officials were reluctant to do so prior to the establishment of clear terms of church–state relations and the adoption of the Constitution.[23] The first draft of the new agreement was ready in 1922, but the negotiations with the Vatican started only in 1925 but stumbled over the issue of the use of Slavonic language and were suspended due to political opposition in the Parliament. From the Catholic perspective, the absence of the Concordat hindered ability of the community of believers to have a full and necessary relationship with its supreme institutional and spiritual authorities in Rome.

The fact that the supreme authority of the Yugoslav Catholics was located abroad did not make the matters easier, especially in light of the intention to create a distinctly Yugoslav Catholic community, or at least the one that was fully compatible with the interests of Yugoslavia. Although the suggestions for the Roman Catholic Church to emulate the autocephalous Serbian Orthodox Church and establish a Yugoslav Catholic Church independent from the Vatican remained marginal.[24] This was in addition to the long-held suspicion 'that some Croatian bishops could not reconcile themselves with the disappearance of the Dual Monarchy'.[25] It has been argued that the enthusiasm for Yugoslavia that the Catholic clergy may have displayed arose from the hope that Yugoslavia offered the best chance to protect the Dalmatian coast from Italian aspirations, as well as from the anticipation that the predominantly Catholic territories would enjoy a considerable degree of autonomy and that the state in general would be run by the Croats, hence the 'Catholic element would prevail'.[26] This support began to gradually wane starting in the mid-1920s, in part as a reaction against the ban on political activities of the clergy.

The Muslim community, the third largest in the country and possibly the most heterogeneous one, was subject to the most concerted effort to create a *Yugoslav* Muslim community. The first attempts to unify it failed and the government succeeded only after the introduction of royal dictatorship. In the 1920s, the Muslim community remained decentralized, as Yugoslav Muslims lived in three different regions centred around Sarajevo, Belgrade and Stari Bar, and the community was composed of six different ethnic groups: Bosnian Muslim Slavs, Muslim Albanians, Turks, Macedonian Muslim Slavs, Muslim Slavs from Sandžak and Montenegro, and Muslim Roma. Bosnian Muslims, who were a relative majority in the Muslim community, were also the most organized political force.

By 1918, those Yugoslav Muslims who remained in the country (many had chosen or were forced to move to Turkey) were generally loyal to Yugoslavia. This feeling, however, was weakened by the violence that Muslims in Bosnia, Kosovo and Macedonia experienced in 1917–19, primarily at the hands of the Orthodox population, as well as by the long tradition of the association of Islam with the Ottoman rule. Constant pressure on the Bosnian Muslim community from rivalling Croatian and Serbian political elites was a powerful factor that stimulated the formulation of a Muslim political agenda within Yugoslav politics.[27] The Yugoslav Muslim Organisation (JMO) was formed already in 1919, and since 1921 was headed by Mehmed Spaho. Although JMO was not a religious party, it was very much perceived by its supporters as such.[28] JMO aimed at representing all Muslims of the kingdom, but with growing political pressure it gradually turned into a Bosnian centred party, and virtually ignored the position of non-Slavic Muslims in Kosovo and Macedonia.

The situation changed in 1929 with the creation of the Yugoslav Muslim Community (*Islamska Vjerska Zajednica*, IVZ). A completely artificial construction, it united all Yugoslav Muslims under the supreme authority of *reis-ul-ulema* and as such came closest to the ideal of a nationalized Yugoslav religious organization. In certain aspects it continued the pattern of the relationship set up by the Habsburg administration in Bosnia. The position of *reis-ul-ulema* had originally been invented by the Habsburg officials for the Muslim population in occupied Bosnia in the late nineteenth century. The terms of the Austrian occupation of Bosnia agreed upon in Berlin in 1878 included a guarantee of the 'full liberty in relations with their [Muslim] spiritual leaders'.[29] The spiritual leaders in question were the Sultan and the Great Mufti in Istanbul. Nonetheless, Austrian administration continuously pursued policy of limiting the ties with the Ottoman Empire fearing that spiritual guidance went hand in hand with political influence. Religious leaders of Bosnian Muslims declared loyalty to the new Austro-Hungarian authorities and concentrated their effort on securing autonomy for their community, establishing 'a post-Ottoman millet system in reverse' with Islam now in the position of a minority religion. In 1909, after the formal annexation of Bosnia by Austria-Hungary, religious and cultural autonomy was finally granted to the Bosnian Muslims, thus establishing a separate Bosnian Islamic community, an institution that had never existed under the Ottoman rule, and which was now inherited by Yugoslavia.

Until 1929, all Muslims of Bosnia-Herzegovina (and other ex-Habsburg territories) were placed under the supreme authority of the *reis-ul-ulema* in Sarajevo, while the Muslims of Serbia and Montenegro, including the territories acquired in 1912, were governed by the *grand mufti* in Belgrade. The newly established IVZ was based on the Bosnian model and was generally dominated by the Bosnian Muslims.[30] It also limited the autonomy and authority of religious leaders and made them directly accountable to the Justice Ministry. The longstanding *reis-ul-ulema* Mehmed Džemaludin Čaušević did not accept this increased state control, rejected his appointment as Yugoslav Reis ul-Ulema and was pensioned off.

The reasons for the disagreement included divergent interpretations of the separation of church and state, which he shared with the leaders of the Roman Catholic and East Orthodox Churches, even if there is no church in Islam in the same way as it exists in Christian confessions. Another factor was the continued marginalization of Muslims on all levels of state administration. This Christian character of Yugoslavia persisted since the unification period, as exemplified by Ante Trumbić saying in 1917: 'I believe that politically it would be a mistake to establish a full equality between Islam and Christianity' and the systemic underfunding in later years.[31]

The ambiguous situation in which there was neither a strict separation of church and state nor an official state religion, yet religious institutions were expected to actively support the idea of Yugoslav nation, was behind a major dispute between religious communities and the government. That was the issue of clerics' participation in political life. The 1921 Constitution forbade all confessions and their representatives from using their power to achieve political ends.[32] The latter was a heavily debated issue in the period between 1918 and 1921 and the regulation was adopted against the wishes of the majority of religious community representatives. Even after the inclusion of the regulation into the Constitution it remained unenforceable in practical terms, for there was no special law detailing legal procedures that the clergy would have had to go through should they violate the Constitution. An important clarification is necessary at this point. Similar to how religious equality was understood by the civil servants as equal subjugation of religious communities to the interests of the secular state, 'political activity' was qualified as such when it was construed to go against state priorities or interests. In the most simplistic version of this, whichever party held the government tried to dissuade or prevent clergy from campaigning for its opponents. This effect was most noticeable during the campaign before the February 1925 national elections.

The Serbian Orthodox Church and its Croatian counterpart had by and large the same concerns regarding the matter, as the governmental idea to limit priests' rights to 'talk politics' was a part of the larger struggle to keep religion and religious authorities out of political life. We have seen already that many politicians and intellectuals agreed that the complete secularization of politics was the only way to overcome problems created by the multireligious character of Yugoslavia. Religious leaders in their turn insisted that this limitation went against the nature of clergy's work. In the words of Dr Anton Korošec, churches took interest in some political issues, and it was only natural that priests should talk about them while performing their duties.[33] Political activities of all religious institutions remained a sensitive issue and a point of dispute throughout the existence of the interwar Yugoslav state.[34]

From the religious communities' point of view, these state policies were self-contradictory. On the one hand, the freedom to administer internal affairs was granted to all religious communities and institutions by both the Royal Proclamation and the Constitution, but on the other hand the Ministries of Religions and Justice had significant power over the church-related affairs, and on several occasions intervened in the internal matters, such as the election of the Patriarch. Radmila Radić, the leading authority in Serbian historiography on modern Serbian Church history, observed that misunderstandings and, one could argue, miscommunication between the state and the religious communities were caused by the government's attempt to put all religious communities under state control, such as by applying agrarian reform to church lands.[35] In these instances 'unsanctioned' political activity of religious communities increased.

Unification of the Serbian Orthodox Church and (re-)establishment of the Serbian Patriarchate

For the Serbian Orthodox Church, creation of Yugoslavia primarily meant that as of 1918 East Orthodox Christianity was no longer the dominant religion of the overwhelming majority of the population. Nor did the Church enjoy the privileged status of the official state religion anymore, at least not formally. And yet, new political reality offered exciting opportunities to the Serbian Orthodox Church.

'Liberation and unification' – the phrase widely used at the time to describe the political process encompassing the Balkan Wars and the First World War – applied not only to the new state and its people but to the Serbian Church as one of its central institutions as well. While the success of the Yugoslav state and national consolidation can be seen from today's perspective as limited to say the least, the success of the unification and strengthening of the Serbian Orthodox Church was indisputable. For the Serbian Orthodox Church, the foundation of Yugoslavia signified the unification of the Serbian lands in one political entity, which in turn meant that six previously loosely associated church jurisdictions could now be united in one administrative body – the Serbian Patriarchate.[36] The Patriarchate was officially established (historically minded contemporaries talked of the *re*-establishment of the old Patriarchate of Peć) in September 1920.

The unification of the Serbian Orthodox Church was long-awaited by the members of the church and was the result of several decades of longing and hope. Despite this history, it did not run entirely smoothly. The clergy of some previously autonomous church organizations, in particular those in Bosnia and Herzegovina and Sremski Karlovci, were unwilling to submit to the centralized system administered from Belgrade, for it contradicted their long tradition of 'national' autonomy and self-government.[37] That resulted in the delay in the creation of a functional and stable system of local eparchies.[38] As a sign of protest against centralization, the Montenegrin clergy abandoned their official duties at the end of 1920. The situation was so grave that the minister of religions had to ask local bishops to intervene and promised to improve the lot of the parish clergy.[39] One of the long-term consequences of these changes was the abolition in the early 1930s of the all-Serbian union of priests, which was very active before the Great War. This structural change, which gave more authority to the episcopates, was reflected in the difference of opinion displayed by both the higher and lower clergy.

In 1920 a new law on the centralization of executive and judicial power in the newly established Serbian Patriarchate was passed. It extended the basic principles of Church administration stipulated in the 1910 Law on the Serbian Orthodox Church (of the Serbian Kingdom) to all newly unified territories and structures. The law gave most of the power to the episcopate, whereas it neglected and virtually ruined the lower-level communities. Theoretically, the basis of Church administration should be formed from these communities. The clergy from the former Habsburg territories, where this law had not existed previously, protested quite harshly against the way in which Church legislature was homogenized.[40] The state extended most of the laws that previously regulated the relationship between the Serbian Kingdom and the Serbian Metropoly to the Kingdom of Serbs, Croats and Slovenes and the new Patriarchate. Curiously, there is a similarity between the discussions within the Church and the general political debates in interwar Yugoslavia – centralization and federalization were the key points in both cases. The differences that stemmed from the patterns of historical development of ecclesiastical institutions and traditions were neglected. Belgrade-based higher clergy legitimized its homogenizing policy by making references to the previously existing homogeneous structure of the Serbian Orthodox Church, that is, the Patriarchate of Peć, abolished by the Ottomans in the eighteenth century.[41]

According to the regulation of June 1921, which described the responsibilities of the Ministry of Religions, the Serbian Orthodox Church, similar to other religious institutions, was put under state control in 'all politico-religious matters that fall into the range of state affairs'.[42] Thus, the clergy and hierarchs of those church dioceses that were new to the Patriarchate had to resign themselves first to the loss of their independence and autonomy to the central church authorities in Belgrade, and second to the increased state control. The Ministry of Religions was aware of the mixed feelings in these areas and surveyed religious activities very carefully, with extra attention paid to the questions of loyalty to Yugoslavia.

The re-establishment of the Serbian Patriarchate was officially proclaimed in Sremski Karlovci on 12 September 1920 following an earlier regulation issued by the Regent Aleksandar Karadjordjević in June. Two weeks later, Dimitrije Pavlović, Metropolitan of Serbia and Archbishop of Belgrade, was elected Patriarch of the renewed Serbian Patriarchate.[43] His official title was 'Serbian Patriarch of the Orthodox Church of the Kingdom of Serbs, Croats and Slovenes'.

Nonetheless, the government insisted on a different electoral procedure, described in a special statute which, ten years later, was transformed into the Law on the Election of the Patriarch. According to the statute the new Patriarch was to be elected by a special council, which consisted of both clerics and state functionaries. The minister of religions was the key figure in the process. In this fashion, Dimitrije, already elected once, was re-elected as the Patriarch a few months later, this time with the full approval of the secular state. This governmental intrusion into church affairs was the first, but not the last, instance of state control over the Serbian Orthodox Church internal affairs.

Various official international recognitions of the Serbian Patriarchate from other national Churches and the Patriarch of Constantinople followed in the next two years. The final ceremony to mark the end of the unification process was the enthronement of Dimitrije in Peć, the place of the last seat of the medieval Serbian Patriarchs, took place in August 1924. The ceremony was attended by King Aleksandar, who brought Dimitrije to the throne of the medieval Patriarchs, and his wife.[44] Following the ceremony held at the Dećani monastery, a series of public festivities and celebrations took place in Peć, Skopje and Priština, which involved local choral and dance groups, as well as the army.

The unification of the Serbian Orthodox Church required more than simply the homogenization of the internal ecclesiastical regulations in all territories and dioceses. At the same time, there was an obvious need for new legislation that would apply to the newly united religious institution and community, determine its position within the state and regulate the relationship with the secular authorities. Such a law (or a series of laws) was a matter of serious debate within the Church, as well as between the Church and the government. While Church representatives tried to preserve a degree of autonomy and secure special status, which they regarded to be their natural right, the state was eager to exercise more control over the Church institutions. The *Church Statutes*, the supreme regulations of the church life, were not approved by the government ten years after the unification. It was only in November 1929 when the government passed the law securing the Church's autonomy in taking decisions concerning its internal affairs. Years of difficult negotiations about the position of the Church were marked by the increased appreciation by all sides of the mobilizing potential that the Church had as an important social and national institution.[45] The negotiation process between Serbian clergy and the government about Church legislation did not end with the establishment (or *re*-establishment) of the Serbian Patriarchate in 1924 and lasted up until 1930 when the 'Constitution' of the Serbian Orthodox Church was finally adopted.

The 1929 Law on the Serbian Orthodox Church officially separated Church and state, but the Orthodox hierarchs' understanding of it was rather superficial, as the secular authorities continued to exercise too much (in their view) control over internal Church affairs, including the curriculum taught in religious schools and, most importantly, the elections of the Patriarch.[46] Religious scholars and legal experts close to the Orthodox clerical circles regarded separation of church and state to be the reinforcement of the Church's independence, while the state's logic was rather different, emphasizing the limitation of the Church's sphere of influence and placing it on equal footing with other recognized religious communities and institutions in the country. As discussed briefly above, the Yugoslav Catholics shared some of the reservations, especially in regards the school curriculum. After a prolonged and bitter discussion in 1930 between the Catholic Episcopate and the government over the power to appoint teachers of religious education, a government minister summarized why the Episcopate's demands could and should not be met: It would mean that 'the state denies its sovereign functions, which would prove the capitulation of the state before the Church'.[47]

In order to understand the problematic nature of the relationship between the Serbian Orthodox Church and the Yugoslav state, one must pay attention to the specific Orthodox understanding of the ideal church–state relationship. Serbian Orthodox authors tirelessly maintained that this relationship is fundamentally different from the views of both the Roman Catholic and Protestant Churches. In Orthodox understanding, the Church does not impose its rules on state structures and institutions, nor does it subordinate itself to the state. They function in symbiosis, as they ideally have common aims in mind. At the same time, the Church has never abandoned its right to public presence and visibility and met any attempt to limit it with an outcry of fury and rage.

When Eastern Christianity had developed a teaching about the Christian state as an image of the Kingdom of God, it was about the nature of power and the balance of power between the Church and the emperor. 'Symphonia', an old and complex East Christian teaching about the church–state relationship supposed that ecclesiastical and temporal leaders ruled in harmony. John Meyendorf wrote that 'the great dream of Byzantine civilisation was a universal Christian society, administered by the emperor and spiritually guided by the Church'.[48] In this system there was no conflict between secular and religious authorities, because their aims coincided; the two types of authorities, although separated in function, existed in an intimate relationship with each other. One researcher summarized the core problematic issue of the symphonia tradition in relation to the modern church–state relationship by saying 'there is no interdependency, nor is there a complete separation. In fact, the major problem of the concept of symphonia is that the demarcation line between church and state remains unclear. For this reason, religious leaders could achieve strong political roles in society and political leaders could influence the church's position'.[49] One can argue safely that this particular aspect of the Byzantine political and ecclesiastical structure survived in the Balkans.

Overall, the main problems in the relationship between the state and the three major religious communities in the early years of the Kingdom of Serbs, Croats and Slovenes were caused by the unclear principles of church and state separation on the one hand, and multiple misunderstandings of the question of how secular and religious spheres should be separated – and what the balance between the two should be – on the other. Although all three religious communities and their respective institutions wholeheartedly supported the creation of the common

Yugoslav state, there was visible tension between them and the government already in the first few years after 1918.

A happy coexistence? The Yugoslav state and the Serbian nation in the view of the Serbian Orthodox Church: 1918–mid-1920s

The Serbian Orthodox Church had produced a well-articulated national narrative as early as the nineteenth century. One of the major challenges it had throughout the interwar period was reconciling the existing and widely accepted narrative and the program of action underpinned by it (discussed in Chapter 1) with new political realities. The layers of incompatibility included the church–state relationship briefly discussed above; an understanding of the overlap between national and religious communities; as well as the attitude towards the (idea of) a Yugoslav nation. Not all these problems, however, appeared as self-evident in the first years after the end of the First World War. This initial lack of serious conflict between the Serbian Church and the government was, first of all, due to the political chaos of the postwar years and the unclear vision of the political future of the new state structures. Similar to how state structures and other fundamental political decisions were debated in the period between 1918 and 1921 when the first (the so-called *Vidovdan*) Constitution was adopted, for the Serbian Orthodox Church the time between the end of the war and mid-1920s was characterized by discussions of a variety of options (real or imagined) available to it. This chaos was also partly responsible for the lack of coherence in the Serbian Orthodox public discourse and for its at times self-contradictory character.

Community of the Church and nation

In 1917, Serbian Metropolitan Dimitrije, anticipating the formal creation of a common Yugoslav state, wholeheartedly accepted 'the idea of brotherhood and unification, worked on by the brightest minds of our people' and underlined the Serbian Orthodox Church's tolerance towards other confessions and religions, implying that the Church is not only supportive of the plan but also fully compatible with it.[50] In a similar vein, the birth of the Kingdom of Serbs, Croats and Slovenes in 1918 was met most cheerfully by the Serbian Church. It was the end of the difficult and devastating war, and the opportunity for all Serbian lands to be united in one state. This, according to the Serbian Church, was reason enough for universal joy. At this stage, the Serbian clergy and Orthodox thinkers acknowledged the multireligious character of the new state but did not single it out as problematic. The Church focused its programme for the next few years on promoting 'social unity based on love and truth' in order to help solidify the Yugoslav nation, society and state, which was, as one of the Orthodox hierarchs put it, 'our great national home'.[51]

In his speech at the official enthronement ceremony in August 1924, Patriarch Dimitrije happily underlined that 'the long centuries of tribal and religious separation' had come to an end. He went on to say that 'in the common Motherland, which was blessed by God, it is the task for all of us to get to know each other better and to see that we are brothers who have been separated until this moment by evil fate'.[52] The optimism and euphoria displayed by the Serbian Church hierarchy in the first years of Yugoslavia suggests that there was no profound understanding of either the inbuilt weaknesses of the political compromise struck by the Serbian and Croatian political elites, or of what the ideology of integral Yugoslavism could mean for the 'brotherly nations' and the Serbian Orthodox Church as the patron of one of them.

In the first postwar years the Serbian Church was preoccupied not only with the legal unification, but also with the pressing matters of replacing missing priests, rebuilding ruined parish schools and so on. It was not until the early 1920s, when the most urgent tasks had been completed, that the Church turned its attention to other issues. These first of all had to do with the transformed political environment. It was then that Church's optimism of 1918 and 1919 started to vanish. Yugoslavism, now elevated to the level of state ideology, had to be dealt with, and, of course, the new state itself with its new structures and balance of power presented certain challenges as well.

Judging by the survey of the Church press, the leitmotif of the early 1920s had almost nothing to do with the new state per se. It was an old and familiar refrain of the 'liberation and unification' *of all Serbs*. One could argue that this choice of rhetoric speaks volumes about the political position of the Church. By consciously overlooking the multinational character of the kingdom and keeping its traditional national narrative, the Serbian Church underlined the Serbian component in the new state. Even the more inclusive slogan 'liberation and unification of *all South Slavs*' was in contradiction with the diverse experiences of people in various parts of the country, for example that of the soldiers. It elevated one type of experience, that of the victorious Serbian side, to the normative level, while many war veterans who fought in the Austro-Hungarian army were ambivalent about their identity as ex-soldiers and felt uneasy regarding the rhetoric of 'liberation and unification'. Even Serbian war veterans were not in agreement over what was lost and won in the war they had fought.[53] So far, it was easy and convenient for the Serbian Orthodox Church to embrace and support the official rhetoric, which also strongly emphasized the Serbian element.

The rhetoric of Church unification did not just echo that of national 'liberation and unification', but also in many ways continued it. The two processes were seen to be inseparable. 'Enchanting centuries-long dreams have turned into glorious and majestic reality. The Kingdom of Serbs, Croats and Slovenes is resurrected, and within it is resurrected the United Serbian Orthodox Church', read the editorial of the first issue of the renewed official periodical of the Serbian Church in 1920.[54]

This idea of 'double liberation' was also reinforced by the state, who once again embraced the idea of the Serbian Orthodox Church sharing the fate of the Serbian nation. King Petar I's order from 1920 about the re-establishment of the Serbian Patriarchate reads: 'The Serbian Orthodox Church has always shared the political destiny of the Serbian people. That is why the forced political separation [of the people] resulted as well in the forced separation of the church'.[55] The same was held true for the opposite process: the unification of the Serbian nation into one state automatically meant Church unification. The state and the Church were in complete mutual understanding and were drawing on each other's authority and symbolic capital. Retrospectively, this light-headed attitude of secular authorities might seem somewhat careless, especially given the suspicion towards political power of religion in general articulated by some proponents of Yugoslavism. The link between the Serbian nation and the Orthodox Church had not been broken, it even became strengthened during the two following decades. 'The Serbian national Orthodox Church of St Sava has been preserving our nationality throughout centuries, and the Patriarchate remained the symbol of national unity even when state unity fell to pieces, with one Serbian state replaced by many', King Petar proclaimed in 1920.[56] No conflicting interests have been displayed so far.

Another issue discussed at the time was the contribution of the Serbian Orthodox Church to the Yugoslav cause. Given the centrality of the Serbian political elites and Pašić's success in promoting Yugoslavia as the successor of the Kingdom of Serbia, it is not surprising that the contribution of the Serbian Church to Serbian nationalism was now being reframed as its contribution to Yugoslavia. The Serbian Church, as an institution that shared the national destiny of the Serbs through all its ups and downs, was entitled in the view of many to special treatment. It was common understanding among Serbian clerics and many lay members of the Church that, Serbian Orthodox clergy made a larger contribution to 'liberation and unification' and that its sacrifice was greater than of any other social group. They expected this to be taken into account as the position of Church was clarified and regulated.[57] This, of course, ran contrary to the principle of religious equality, which meant that no religious group is given preference.

The Church reported that it lost one-third of its rank-and-file clergy – 1,056 of the 3,000 priests registered in 1914 had died or were missing by the end of the war.[58] The great scale loss and suffering, as well as the general contribution of Orthodox clergy were publicly acknowledged by the state.[59] King Aleksandar's charter on the enthronement of Dimitrije in 1924 read: 'We are witnesses to the work of the Serbian Orthodox Church, who bore severe losses and sustained the strength of our nation to reach this liberation and unification.'[60]

Of all the symbols of the suffering of the Serbian people during the years of the First World War, the most famous and powerful one was the so-called Albanian Golgotha, also known as 'Serbia's Golgotha through the gorges of Albania' – the retreat of the Serbian troops to the island of Corfu in the winter of 1915–16 through the mountains of Kosovo, Montenegro and Albania.[61] The use of biblical symbols, common for all Christian cultures, made it easier for the Church to link the national community and religious institutions. It also allowed the Serbian Church to join in on the forging of the national martyrdom narrative. This narrative was seen by many in the following decades as the reason for Serbia's 'moral right' to dominance in the country. Those state functionaries who supported this course were naturally in favour of the Church's involvement as it clearly added weight and authority.

Whereas higher clergy had not generally questioned the idea of the three-named Yugoslav nation and followed the general line of cheering the new state and new nation,[62] dissenting opinions had been expressed as well, and some concerns had been raised. There was an interesting discrepancy between the official statements of the Patriarch and other higher clergy on the one hand, and what the lower clergy thought about the same issues on the other. While Dimitrije repeatedly talked of unification and the beneficial coexistence of different religions and nations in one state, others wrote of the impossibility of the absolute equality of religions. Miloš Andjelković, who belonged to the sceptics' camp, explained it fairly axiomatically by simply stating that Christianity is the most perfect faith among all.[63] This echoed some of the voices from the 1917 Corfu Conference, although Andjelković did not suggest that secularization was an acceptable solution to this. Rather, he did not conceptualize it as a problem at all.

The Serbian Orthodox Church mounted quite a resistance to the idea of secularization, as demonstrated by its reaction to the article by the Serbian historian Vladimir Ćorović published in the widely read *Serbian Literary Herald* in 1919. The Church understandably perceived the argument about the positive (in terms of state-building) effect of secularization as the biggest threat to its own existence, power and influence. To prove the other side wrong in its expectations of religious decline, it demonstrated countless examples of popular religiosity and grassroots religious movements. The clergy employed an old argument, which had previously proved to be successful, about the intrinsic connection between the Church and the nation, essentially claiming that they were one.[64] Once the argument about the link between the Serbian nation and the Serbian Orthodox Church had been taken from its original pre-1918 context of sustaining a nation in an ethnically homogeneous nation-state and applied to the *multinational* Yugoslav context, the problems so much feared by the Yugoslavists were about to reveal themselves. It would be a matter of speculation to guess whether those who employed this argument in the early-1920s were conscious of its destructive potential for the multinational state. Most clergy simply continued to use tried and tested strategy in their disputes with governmental officials. There is no evidence to suggest that the Serbian Orthodox Church deliberately sought in the immediate postwar period to weaken the Yugoslav political project. It is important to note, however, that once threatened, the Serbian Orthodox Church immediately turned to the idea of national-religious fusion.

The discussion of nation, national identity and East Orthodox Christianity had its own logic and a long history. There are at least three sets of issues relevant to the discussion here, in the context of Serbian Orthodox Church and its relationship to the Serbian nation and Yugoslav state. First is the way the Church is understood in Christianity, and in particular, in Eastern Christianity and especially the understanding of the Church as a *community of believers*. At the start of the twentieth century, Church doctrine was the centre of attention in all Christian theological traditions. Jaroslav Pelikan argues that it became 'as it had never quite been before, the bearer of the whole of the Christian message for the twentieth century, as well as the recapitulation of the entire doctrinal tradition from the preceding centuries'.[65] Second is the way authority is understood in Eastern Christianity. Here, separation between secular and sacred spheres and authorities plays an important role. These two themes have been a source of dialogue and debate between Eastern Greek and Western Latin, primarily Roman

Catholic, churches for a very long time. The third set of questions appeared with the rise of modern nationalism and was intimately linked to the permeation of nationalism and national feeling into a realm that had previously been confined to theology, law and philosophy.

In East Christian tradition the 'church' was predominantly perceived as a living organism. Although there is no single precise and strict definition of church in Eastern Christianity, there is a common agreement that apart from being the 'living body of mystical encounter with God' it is also 'a community in creation, with its own structure, form and manner of operation'.[66] In contrast to Western Christianity, Eastern Orthodoxy perceives Church not merely as an institution within the state, but as the body of faithful believers. All ecclesiological models in Eastern Christian tradition emphasize the conciliar nature of the church, that is, its hierarchical but not monadic structure.[67] In Slavonic languages this characteristic trait of the Eastern Christian church is usually described with the concept of *sobornost*, which alludes to the fact that the supreme administrative authority lays not in one single person, but in a communion: the *sobor/sabor*, or council. This concept has an interesting history and is of particular importance for Serbian political thought, as it was used by lay political thinkers as well as by theologians.[68] In the early twentieth century the term was borrowed by Western theologians, and as Pelikan observes, use of the Russian 'word "sobor" for church councils to which Eastern Orthodoxy assigned authority in the church helped to make the term a way of distinguishing Eastern ecclesiology from both the "papal monarchy" of Roman Catholicism and the "sola Scriptura" of Protestantism'.[69] The third set of issues centred on nationalism, nation and national community. The 1920s and 1930s in the history of the Serbian Church stand out for the intellectual complexity and sophistication of religious and secular thought produced by the clergy, intellectuals' and students' circles close to the Church institutions. One of the striking aspects of the intellectual handiwork these people created was their ability to incorporate nationalism into theology. Suddenly, a scholarly debate had a distinctive national touch to it.

Miloš Andjelković argued that the Serbian Church did not represent any terrestrial power, 'but [was] the embodiment of national individuality'.[70] The discursive link between the Church and national community is thus a natural consequence of a more complex and much older intellectual tradition of the necessary and inevitable tie between religion and the nation. Bringing nation into the discussion of the Church could also be read from the perspective of the renewed interest in the social aspects of Christian teaching, which in turn was in reaction to 'the deepening awareness throughout modern culture that individuals were never isolated from one another but always participated in various communities'.⁷¹

At the same time, the nation was starting to be seen as the totality of believers. Miloš Andjelković, an archpriest and a professor in Belgrade known for his not-too-radical views, stated that no religion and no church could exist without a distinguishing national feature, and that the Serbian Church complied perfectly with the definition of 'church' as 'the corpus of the members of the nation'.⁷² The powerful emphasis on the collective identity of religious community, which overlapped with national identity, was one of the major legacies in the Serbian Orthodox Church discourse from the preceding periods, and one of the seminal ideas of the interwar period. Later, it turned out to have important political implications, but as far as the first half of the 1920s is concerned, politics were mostly kept out of the debate, be it with the Roman Catholic Church or modern secularists.

Reform movement from the outside and from within

The birth of Yugoslavia did not affect the Serbian Church's belief in the absolute superiority of the national church over an a-national or transnational one. One of the longstanding 'others' in this dispute was the Roman Catholic Church, primarily as represented by its institutions and hierarchy in Croatia. Serbian Orthodox thinkers and writers juxtaposed the national character of the Serbian Church to the clerical nature of the Roman Catholic Church. However, in the postwar years a new rival appeared rather unexpectedly in the form of the numerous sects and sectarian movements. Combined, the presence of these two 'enemies' had a significant impact on how the conversation within the Serbian Orthodox Church on modernity, nationalism, secularism and possible responses to them was shaped. The reform movement, largely inspired by these challenges, found some support within the Serbian Church, but also divided the body of the Church. Some of the reform stimuli came from the 'enemy': Neo-Protestant sects of the Nazarenes that were widespread in Vojvodina. The sectarians had a complex ideological profile which combined Evangelical practices with anarchism.⁷³ Arguably it was the Evangelical aspect that attracted the Orthodox Serbian population who actively converted.⁷⁴

Some of the reform initiatives had a national dimension to them, as seen in a new wave of discussions about the continuous use of Church Slavonic in the liturgies in the 1920s. The debate, which started back in the nineteenth century, revolved around the question of whether the Church Slavonic in its heavily

Russified version should be replaced by either a Serbianized version of Church Slavonic or modern literary Serbian. The latter option won eventually and was codified in the 1931 Church Statutes.

The main incentive for the reform was the desire to make liturgy closer to the community of believers, to attract more people to the Church, and to prevent conversions from Orthodox Christianity and thus constituted a modernization attempt. Those in favour of the modern literary language employed, among other things, a political argument that emphasized the unity of the new Yugoslav nation. In their view, it was only right that the modern national language should be used during the service. In 1921, one enthusiast called for translating all liturgical books 'into the language which our single, but three-named nation speaks. Let one nation pray to God in one language'.[75] The author either forgot or did not care that the nation prayed to different Gods. Most likely, however, he along with many others only paid attention to the Christian majority.

This was not the first time that the use of Serbo-Croatian in religious ceremonies was highlighted. Already in the middle of the nineteenth century, Ljudevit Gaj expressed a hope that the last religious differences between the Croats and the Serbs (which he considered to be unimportant anyway) would be reduced once 'celibacy is abandoned, and the old law of the Croatian Catholic Church comes back, namely the [use of the] national language'.[76] Language was, however, neither the most contested, nor the most important component in what we can label the 'reform movement'. Its most significant dimension, which reached far beyond Serbian and Yugoslav national boundaries was the issue of ecumenism.

Despite its public image, East Orthodox Christianity was not necessarily distanced from modernism and secularism, which were associated with the European ecumenical movement. For a rather short period of time, some of the outstanding representatives of the Serbian Orthodox Church were actively engaging with it. On the other hand, East Orthodox Christianity in the first half of the twentieth century was reluctant to establish a productive ecumenical dialogue with other Christian churches. One of the reasons for this, as noted by Jaroslav Pelikan, derived from the fact that it 'had fixed the authority of tradition, represented (but by no means exhausted) by the actions of the first seven ecumenical councils, as the norm for the orthodox interpretation of Scripture, and had denied to any member of the episcopate ... the right to exercise authority apart from this tradition'.[77] In the eyes of those adhering to this tradition, the ecumenical dialogue meant doctrinal compromise, not opening up of new horizons.

Among the East Orthodox Churches, the first to partake in the ecumenical movement at the official level was the Patriarchate of Constantinople. This happened in January 1920, when the encyclical 'Unto the Churches of Christ Everywhere' appeared. At the very beginning of this encyclical it is said, 'rapprochement between the various Christian Churches and fellowship between them is not excluded by the doctrinal differences which exist between them'.[78] The outrage of Orthodox clergy in Europe was primarily caused by the use of 'churches' in plural and by the fact that the same word applied to what the clerics had previously referred to as sects.

As a first, practical step for 'attaining mutual trust and love', it was deemed necessary for the national autocephalous East Orthodox Churches to accept the new (Gregorian) Calendar, 'so that all the great Christian feasts can be celebrated by all the Churches at the same time'. This was quickly done by the Patriarchate of Constantinople and later by many other autocephalous East Orthodox Churches, who paid a price for this: an internal schism. The split in the Greek Orthodox Church, the most severe and longstanding one, over the introduction of new calendar happened in March 1924 when the Old Julian Calendar was replaced, not with the Gregorian Calendar used by the Roman Catholic Church, but by the Neo-Julian, or Milanković Calendar.[79] A fraction of clergy and lay believers did not accept the reform and established the so-called Greek Old Calendarist Orthodox Church.

In the Serbian Orthodox Church, the debates over the change of calendar were neither deep nor fierce. The reformers underlined primarily the fact that the secular calendar was changed in 1918 (to the Gregorian), thus it would be wise for the Church to follow suit. Those opposing the reform drew on the examples of neighbouring Greece and Romania and called attention to the possible negative consequences of public unrest and even schism. Arguably, the calendar reform did not find sufficient support because the majority of the believers did not find the issue worth much trouble or effort, as opposed to the more successful language reform, the significance of which was easier to argue for. The opponents of the calendar reform used traditional anti-Catholic and anti-Western discourse and pointed out that there was no ecclesiastical or theological necessity for the change.

However, it would not be true to say the Serbian Orthodox Church did not display any positive interest in the ecumenical initiative at all. The interest in ecumenism and the theology of other Christian confessions came primarily from those Serbian clerics who went to study abroad, especially those who pursued their studies at the Department of Old Catholic Theology of the

University of Bern in Switzerland. Among one of the first to travel to Bern was Nikolaj Velimirović, later the most praised and famous Serbian theologian of the twentieth century for some and a controversial figure for his affinity with the Serbian fascist movement and anti-Semitism for others. He successfully defended his doctorate "Faith in the Resurrection of Christ as the Foundation of the Dogma of the Apostolic Church" in 1908. In the following years Velimirović spent time in England and Russia where he devoted his time less to formal study and more to getting to know the culture and life of those nations. Jovan Byford, one of the most critical authors to write recently about him, underlines that

> [Velimirović] who belonged to the first generation of young, talented and well-educated clerics offered a promise of a better future for the Serbian Church and a break with a tradition of paucity of intellectual and spiritual leadership. What is more, at this early stage of his clerical career [1914], Velimirović was widely perceived as a progressive young theologian and a liberal force within the Serbian Orthodox Church.[80]

He spent the war-years in England in an official diplomatic capacity. There, he built up a close collegial friendship with prominent English clerics, including the archbishop of Canterbury.[81] In his numerous speeches and sermons, highly popular with local audiences, Velimirović concentrated on Serbian and South Slav history and tradition. He did not specify Orthodox Christianity as a characteristic trait of the Serbian national character; instead, he underlined the affinity of Eastern and Western Christianity.[82] By all accounts Velimirović's interest and sympathy towards ecumenism and Western Christianity evaporated by the middle of the 1920s. The vast majority of the Serbian Orthodox Church did not express much understanding or desire to cooperate along ecumenical lines.

Thus, from the late 1910s until the early 1920s, the modernizing initiatives that originated in the Serbian Orthodox Church did not find sufficient support from the Church leadership, who were absorbed in the issues of Church reform and unification. At the same time, one has to be careful to note that the reform agenda did not necessarily lead to an anti-national, or even a non-national position. These two dimensions could be easily combined.

The Serbian Orthodox Church and symbolic legitimization of power

One of the aspects of the incomplete church-state separation discussed earlier in this chapter was the active involvement of religious communities in various public ceremonies and festivities. The Yugoslav state relied heavily on its religious institutions when it came to the promotion and explanation of Yugoslavia to broad audiences. While all religious communities took part, there was an expectation (prominent especially among the Serbian civil servants working from Belgrade) that the Serbian Orthodox Church will naturally be the most cooperative and supportive. While this was not always true – Roman Catholics and Yugoslav Muslims displayed significant levels of support of Yugoslavia during the period from 1918 to mid-1920s – there were good reasons for people to think that the East Orthodox element was more visible in the public national festivities and celebrations compared to other Yugoslav religions.

By and large, the Serbian Orthodox Church hierarchs as well as rank-and-file clergy were happy to play their part. That is, as long as they were not asked to do anything that directly contradicted their religious beliefs, habits or political preferences. Not all Serbian clergy were of course equally obliging, for instance some disgruntled priests in Vojvodina, reportedly, did not display sufficient enthusiasm when celebrating the king as the head of state. Vojvodina, a newly acquired border region with a religiously and ethnically diverse population, was monitored by the authorities with extra attention. In 1919–20 there were single instances of Orthodox priests accused of undermining the state unity.[83] However, the situation did not improve over time, and by 1928 the Ministry of the Interior expressed grave concerns about the numerous reports it received about the Serbian Orthodox clergy in Vojvodina publicly insulting the king, especially in the towns and villages along the border.[84] It is hard to estimate the exact levels of support for Yugoslavia or lack thereof in the border regions. When confronted with the reports, the religious authorities normally denied all allegations and professed their love and loyalty to Yugoslavia and its king. What is possible to say with a degree of certainty is that some decisions taken by the Serbian Orthodox Synod had a destabilizing effect on the national unity and did not foster good relationships with other religious communities. During the prolonged debate over the singing of the national anthem during religious ceremonies, it was the instruction of the Serbian Orthodox authorities issued to all parish priests to only perform the Serbian element of the anthem that led to multiple instances of community conflict.[85]

There was an undeniable, although poorly reflected at the time, preference for Christianity and Christian symbols in all of state-commissioned and state-sanctioned ceremonies. The Serbian Orthodox Church together with the secular authorities displayed a degree of what may be called insensitivity towards other religious communities, but it hadn't amounted yet to the level of consistent or in any way radical policy. The Serbian Orthodox Church continued to do as it always did. In some instances, their actions did not fit well with the new political reality. In other instances, it remained relatively unproblematic. What follows is the brief discussion of two such examples: commemorations of the First World War and attempts at the re-appropriation of classic culture and literary figures.

Monuments to national heroes, mass commemorations and rallies have been the subject of historical analysis of nationalism pioneered by George L. Mosse who demonstrated the importance of national monuments and the debates about them for better understanding of nationalism: 'The national monument as a means of self-expression served to anchor the national myths and symbols in the consciousness of the people, and some have retained their effectiveness to the present day.'[86]

For a state born during the war, commemoration of fallen soldiers was of particular importance. The Yugoslav case was not an easy one in terms of the symbolic belonging of the fallen heroes: during the war future citizens of the common state often fought on different sides. After 1918, the new state had to devise a way of commemorating those who sacrificed their lives for national 'liberation and unification' without underlining this difference. To add to the complexity, for the Serbs the First World War was inseparable from the Balkan wars of 1912–13 – together they formed the 'Wars of National Liberation' – an experience that Croats, Slovenes or Bosnian Muslims did not share, and that the Albanians of the Kosovo region did not necessarily perceive as either liberating or unifying. As Melissa Bokovoy observed,

> The commemorative tradition in Serbia after the wars of national liberation does not have a single narrative thread of a single arbiter of commemorative good taste. Instead, the Serbian monarchy, national and local political elites, the military establishment, veterans, survivors, historians, intellectuals, artists, and individual men and women commemorated the war in vastly different ways and for vastly different purposes.[87]

Serbian commemorative practices and sites of remembrance dedicated to the Balkan Wars often evoke the myth and memories of the medieval Kosovo Polje battle, thus having a distinctly Serbian national character with a strong religious component. The First World War memorials, cemeteries and commemorations were much more diverse and had more complex structures. It was here that tensions were most apparent between, on the one hand, the symbols used by the Serbian national institutions (primarily the Church and the army) and attempts by the state to create a more inclusive *Yugoslav* symbolism, on the other.

Zeitinlik, a Serbian military cemetery in Thessaloniki, the biggest of its kind outside Yugoslavia, was designed by Aleksandar Vasić and Nikolaj Krasnov in 1926 and built between 1933 and 1936. The cemetery is marked by a mausoleum which consists of a chapel and an ossuary. The chapel of Archangel Michael, built in the neo-Byzantine style, recalls the medieval Serbian monastery of Kosovo and belongs to the same series of big public constructions as the Cathedral of St Mark in Belgrade. Four lines from a poem by V. J. Ilić written on the front wall of the mausoleum talk of the fallen Serbian soldiers and express the emotions shared by the entire nation:

Padali od zrna, od gladi i žedji,
Raspinjani na krst, na Golgote visu,
Ali čvrstu veru u pobedu krajnju
Nikada, na za časak, izgubili nisu.

They fell from bullets, from hunger and thirst,
Were crucified on the Golgotha heights,
But their strong faith in the final victory
They have never, not for a moment, lost.

The Zeitinlik memorial complex is dedicated to those who fell on the Thessaloniki front surviving the 1915 retreat from Serbia, a war episode central to the national memory of suffering and sacrifice. The Serbian cemetery is a part of a larger memorial complex which includes Russian, Italian, English and French cemeteries. It thus unites Serbian heroes and victims of the war with other allies. At the same time the monument excludes other South Slav but non-Serb soldiers who fought on the Thessaloniki front. The memorial had a distinctly Serbian and Orthodox character: All inscriptions were made using Cyrillic script, mosaics created by a Greek artist were made in the traditional Byzantine manner. One scholar rightly summarized the impression the site gave to the visitors: It 'refashioned the deaths of these soldiers into a sacred experience that elevated Serbian national sentiment to religious heights built upon the sacrifices of saints and heroes'.[88]

However important the memory of the war and its heroes was for the Yugoslav and Serbian public discourse after the war, it was not the only element of commemorative practices. The task to find middle ground between conflicting views and intentions was equally difficult when a commemorative project was dedicated to a hero who was claimed by multiple actors. That was exactly the case of Petar Petrović Njegoš, the Montenegrin archbishop and ruler, but most importantly a celebrated Romantic poet.

The fact that Njegoš was regarded as a (or may be even *the*) Serbian national poet, while at the same time the state-sponsored and state-supported initiatives to re-conceptualize him as a Yugoslav poet is an interesting story in itself.[89] To add to it, let us not forget that he was also an archbishop and the head of the Church and State of Montenegro. The combination of the spiritual and the national-political had never been a problem in Serbian nationalism; most of the medieval Serbian princes were canonized as Orthodox saints. What actually did create a problem in the mid-1920s was the difference in understanding of the Serbian Orthodox Church and King Aleksandar and the extent to which the Serbian (i.e. Orthodox) part of Njegoš's heritage and identity could be overshadowed by his alleged Yugoslavism. This difference became visible in the course of the preparations for Njegoš's reburial.[90] The discussions that accompanied it are quite illustrative of the balance of power and state of affairs in the first half of the 1920s.

For the Serbian Church and most of the Serbian political and cultural establishment, Njegoš was primarily the national poet, an important figure emblematic of the fight for national freedom and national (i.e. Serbian) unity. Nikola Pašić, prime minister at the time, in a conversation with Gavrilo Dožić (then Montenegrin archbishop and future Patriarch of Serbia) agreed that the reburial of Njegoš was a matter of national importance to which the government should pay close attention.[91] After several years of mostly financial difficulties, the enterprise was taken up by the king himself, who assured the representatives of the clergy that, being a blood relative to Njegoš himself, he felt it only natural if he financed the works from his private funds. A new chapel design was commissioned to Ivan Meštrović, a celebrated Yugoslav sculptor.

King Aleksandar took the chance to celebrate Njegoš not as a Serbian national poet, but to turn him into a unifying, all-Yugoslav figure. Meštrović, a well-known Yugoslavist, made a project for the chapel that was free of distinct national style, but also free of any indication of the fact that Njegoš was an Orthodox archbishop. All of this could not leave the representatives of the Orthodox Church, who initiated the entire process, unbothered. According to Dožić (who we can believe expressed the collective opinion of the Orthodox hierarchy) the proposed 'monument on Mount Lovćen resembled Egyptian pyramids or even the unwieldy monuments erected to certain kings in the East'. Such a monument did not conform to the ideas and ideals of Christianity, as it was in its essence 'more pagan than anything else'.[92] The Church thus strongly opposed the modernist and Yugoslavist design of the Mausoleum that Meštrović prepared and King Aleksandar supported.

The king, although personally in favour of the project and despite the fact that he privately financed the entire enterprise, agreed with the criticism voiced by the Church. Meštrović's project had to be rejected. The new chapel built on Mount Lovćen was in full accordance with Njegoš's will and the Serbian Church's ideas of how its hero should be commemorated. The case of the reburial of Njegoš demonstrates how the Serbian Orthodox Church defended its heroes from desacralization and their legacy from misinterpretation. This clash of opinions, which did not develop into a fully fledged conflict, was but one of the Serbian Church's attempts to regain cultural power and political influence from the secular forces.

The same pattern will be repeated in a more radical and complex way in the mid-1930s, when the debate about St Sava arose (analysed in detail in Chapter 4). Nevertheless, the early 1920s were also marked by some debate around this medieval hero and the main Serbian national saint. This time, however, contrary to Njegoš's case, the Serbian Orthodox Church tried to present St Sava not as a national Serbian saint, but as a figure who can be accepted by all brotherly Yugoslav tribes, regardless of their religious affiliation. In 1922 the government passed a regulation, which made the celebrations of St Sava mandatory in all Yugoslav schools. That caused a significant outrage from Croatian Catholics. It was in response to this that the Serbian Orthodox Church presented an argument about the possibility of St Sava being seen as a common Yugoslav figure, and indeed about the very natural character of this point of view. This position argued that the deeds of Sava transcended confessional divides to the point that there was no imaginable reason that he should not be acceptable for the Catholics.[93] As a matter of fact, the author went even further in his claim about Sava's universality, maintaining that 'the manner of his work shows so much understanding of the needs of the people, that even a Muslim, if he is nationally conscious, can find [in Sava] his source of the strength for the national work'.[94]

This interpretation of St Sava, who was the main national saint and the patron of the Serbian nation, together with the general unification rhetoric, may suggest that the Serbian Church indeed tried to contribute to the Yugoslav cause. Nevertheless, the situation in which this theory was put forward, suggests that it was mere lip service and that the aim instead was to justify the inclusion of a characteristically Serbian saint into countrywide school celebrations. Although the main part of the debate around Sava comes in only in the 1930s, it is quite curious to see that the seeds of discord had been already sown as early as 1922.

3

The Serbian Orthodox Church faces the challenge of modernity

In 1934 *Pravoslavlje* (East Orthodox Christianity), one of the many new theological journals that flourished in the 1930s presented a set of questions that bothered Serbian clergy:

> Now, after the great Wars of Liberation, and after national unity has been achieved, in this new situation, we, the East Orthodox people, are facing a new question: Will East Orthodox Christianity exercise an impact upon the building of our future culture and to what extent? Will our people continue to go on their way through history beneath the wing of East Orthodox Christianity? Will East Orthodox Christianity be a factor as crucial for the national future as it has been for the national past?[1]

If the Serbian Orthodox Church focused its energy on institutional reforms and general recovery in the first postwar years, by the late 1920s, with most necessary changes implemented, the Serbian Church discovered that it faced new tasks and challenges. A decade after the end of the war, the hierarchs and lower clergy got multiple confirmations of the mobilization potential of religion and their ability to reach out to the broader population outside Belgrade clubs and *kafanas*, something that the government and many politicians failed to do. The question was whether this potential would be used to strengthen the Serbian Orthodox Church and promote its views or serve secular political actors' interests. The Serbian Church was ready to voice independent opinions on political issues, even if that led to a confrontation with the government. As Gavrilo Dožić wrote, the Serbian Orthodox Church was ready, if need be, to go 'into the people' to uphold its views and rights.[2]

Dožić mentions in his memoirs that shortly after the imposition of the royal dictatorship the Prime Minister General Živković was concerned that some members of the opposition would use their close relationship with the Serbian

Patriarchate to undermine his government.³ This reveals that the government was also aware of the political potential of the Serbian Orthodox Church and did not necessarily trust it to back up the official line. It was Živković's successor Milan Stojadinović who felt the full power of the alliance of the anti-governmental forces and the Serbian Orthodox Church.

To become a powerful social and political actor, the Serbian Church had to overcome several hurdles. As Miloš Parenta pointed out, 'East Orthodox Christianity today finds itself between the hammer and the anvil: between atheism, godlessness, the materialistic direction in thought and life on the one hand, and the propaganda of various Christian churches and sects on the other'.⁴ In the minds and writings of Serbian Orthodox clerics these two threats often appeared as a single unit and were intrinsically liked to each other. In fact, not only were the two obviously separate but Yugoslav Catholics (who were almost always perceived by Orthodox clerical circles as their key rivals or enemies) were facing very similar problems. This chapter explores how the Serbian Orthodox Church approached these potential threats and what kind of solutions it suggested. The chapter does so by following several discussions from the mid-1920s–mid-1930s on what exactly the Church public agenda should include. By the mid-1930s, the Serbian Church was making claims that were more overtly political and more radical than ever before.

It is part of the argument of this book that the dictatorship unwillingly created new opportunities for religious communities' involvement in politics, which was visible, for instance, in the way youth movements developed in the post-1929 period. The limitations imposed on the public sphere pushed the Yugoslav religious communities to engage with the national question in new and more problematic ways. Coupled with the specific concerns of the Serbian Orthodox Church about its position in society in the face of the challenges of modern life, it resulted in laying foundations for the appearance of the new and original political ideas fusing nationalism and religion that will become popular in the late 1930s.

In the period under question the Serbian Church continued to see itself as a defender and rightful representative of the Serbian nation. Now it was compelled to have not just an opinion, but also a specific action plan to address the perceived threats to the Church and the nation. The clergy thought of themselves as servants of God, the nation and the people. In contrast to the preceding decade when most of the effort was directed inwards (on Church reforms, improving parish life, raising the educational level of clergy, etc.), now energy was directed as much inwards as outwards. The state, society and the nation became the primary objects of the Serbian Church's attention.

Royal dictatorship and integral Yugoslavism

'To cleanse the Augean stables of Yugoslav politics was a formidable task requiring heroic measures. It was this which faced King Alexander', wrote an American political scientist in 1929.[5] In early January 1929, Aleksandar Karadjordjević dismissed Parliament and proclaimed a royal dictatorship. His decision followed a gruesome shooting in Parliament on 20 June 1928, in which the leader of the Croatian Peasant Party, Stjepan Radić, was mortally wounded. The dictatorship was Aleksandar's answer to chaos and instability, which had become unmanageable. In the 'Proclamation' that introduced the new regime the king stated that his main aim was to protect the unity of the state and the nation, as well as safeguard order and discipline. The only way to do so was to eliminate any intermediary between the king and his people, this included the Parliament or any other elected representative body.[6] With this goal in mind, a series of laws suspended those articles of the Constitution in which the state was defined as 'constitutional' and 'parliamentary'. A special law suspended public political life and banned any political activities of societies, clubs and political parties organized according to national or religious principles. In addition to this, strict censorship was imposed.[7] The official name of the state was changed to the Kingdom of Yugoslavia to underline the unity of its people.

King Aleksandar went to tremendous lengths to make the idea of integral Yugoslavism work. The full strength of the repressive apparatus was used to impose the idea of national unity on all citizens. The dictatorship represented the highest point of integral Yugoslavism, characterized by historians as 'based on the fictitious idea of the ethnic unity of the nation. The proponents of integral Yugoslavism believed that the unification of the state and society could be achieved through the imposition of "decreed" Yugoslavism from above'.[8] During the years of dictatorship, the 'Yugoslav idea' stood not for the national synthesis which might come into being over time but morphed into a state-imposed dogma which had to be implemented immediately.[9] The new, so-called Octroyed Constitution (Serb.: *Oktroisani Ustav*), imposed by the king in 1931, stipulated strict regulations for societies, clubs, political parties and other public organizations similar to the Proclamation of 6 January 1929. In a 1931 interview the king proudly said that 'Yugoslav politics will never again be directed by religious, regional, or particularistic interests'.[10] 'Particularistic' here meant 'tribal', 'national' in any sense other than that of 'Yugoslav national'. The nationalisms of the constitutive nations (Serbs, Croats and Slovenes) were now seen as centrifugal forces damaging state interests.

The first reaction of the Serbian Church to the news of the dictatorship was positive and, according to the then Montenegrin Metropolitan Gavrilo Dožić, the Church fully understood and supported the new regime, as it saw the necessity of it in the given political circumstances.[11] The Serbian Church, like many other political actors, thought the dictatorship was the only way to stop the seemingly endless parliamentary crisis and poor party politics. This understanding did not, however, prevent the Serbian hierarch from sharply criticizing the new Prime Minister General Petar Živković, who 'spent all his life in the barracks and did not know the life of politics'.[12]

The attitude to the new regime changed over time. Among the hierarchs of the Serbian Orthodox Church, the complete spectrum of opinion was present. While Patriarch Varnava was a faithful ally of the king, Dožić was more critical. The roots of his criticism lay in the incompatibility of his rather strong ideas of Montenegrin nationalism and the ideology of integral Yugoslavism, as well as in his personal rivalry with the Patriarch. Dožić had once unsuccessfully run for the Patriarch in 1930 before he got elected and appointed in 1937. Throughout this period, he argued that over-centralization of the Serbian Church was ultimately damaging the Yugoslav cause as it degraded parts of the whole by not respecting the autonomy of historical regions. His concerns and numerous complaints focused on the poor financial and material state of the Montenegrin clergy and Church properties.

In 1930 Varnava (born Petar Rosić) became the new Serbian Patriarch to replace the late sitrije, the first Patriarch of the unified and enlarged Serbian Orthodox Church. His election, again, was a moment of dispute between higher clergy and the government. This time, Gavrilo Dožić, the Metropolitan of Montenegro and the head of the electoral council, believed the election results were invalid, as the election was conducted according to the new law which made it easier for the king and secular authorities to assure the success of their preferred candidate. But even under new rules, Varnava, a personal friend of the king, was elected by only a small margin (Varnava received forty-five votes, Gavrilo Dožić – thirty-six, Bosnian Metropolitan Petar Zimonjić – thirty-four and Nikolaj Velimirović only two).[13]

In a sense, the dictatorship did not bring radical changes to Yugoslav church–state relations: state policies towards the three major religious communities, Orthodox, Catholic and Muslim, remained the same as in the preceding decade, the main difference being that these policies could be implemented now more consistently and with more government oversight.[14] The immediate changes concerned the organizational structures, something that the successive Yugoslav governments struggled with since 1918. The Ministry of Religions ceased to exist on 31 March 1929, and its functions were transferred to the Department of Religions within the Ministry of Justice. Yugoslav religious communities lost a dedicated civil servant, who often tried to address their concerns and advocate for religious interests with other ministries, most notably the Ministry of Education. However, because of the dramatic change to the rules of public politics, the relationship between the state and religious communities was transformed over time. A variety of opportunities and challenges presented itself to the religious communities and their leaders. It is important to point out that the change in the religious field was neither envisioned nor desired by the king and came as 'collateral damage'.

In the spring of 1929 the last Minister of Religions, Dragiša Cvetković, stated that the government's biggest concern in relation to the Yugoslav religious communities was the missing law on the interconfessional relationship, which could be passed only after the legislation regulating the status of every religious community had been adopted.[15] The process of writing of the legislation regulating the religious communities' lives had begun in 1918 but did not progress to anyone's satisfaction. The new government continued the work of its predecessors but abandoned the idea of introducing a single overarching law that could regulate all religious life in the state. Prime Minister Živković regarded the church–state relationship important enough to be included in his end-of-year report.

The new *Law on the Serbian Orthodox Church* finally passed in 1929 did not introduce many changes to the already established practices but increased the state control over religious affairs.[16] The draft version of the *Law on the Serbian Orthodox Church* prepared by the Serbian Church Assembly in 1927 was not approved by the government and did not make it to the Parliament. Two years later, the minister of justice unilaterally introduced changes to the project without consulting the Assembly, provoking public protests from the Serbian clergy. The main opponent to the changes further limiting the autonomy of the Serbian Church was Gavrilo Dožić. After a round of consolations, the law was passed on 8 November 1929 in a compromised form that considered some of the minor criticisms.[17] Based on this law, the Serbian Orthodox Church was finally able to adopt its own Constitution (*Ustav Srpske Pravoslavne Crkve*) in 1931. With this, the reorganization of the Serbian Orthodox Church which started in 1918 was officially completed.

The Constitution confirmed new administrative practices of the united Serbian Patriarchate with their rather high level of centralization and standardization.

Varnava, one of the most active proponents of the centralization principle, effectively countered criticism and asserted the need for the unified principles of organization.[18] Varnava's position, which aligned closely with the king's idea on state reform, and his willingness to work with the government made him the preferred candidate for the Patriarch after Dimitrije's death in 1930.

In relation to the Roman Catholic Church, there was less progress. Negotiations with the Holy See about the Concordat started in 1925 but proved to be unsuccessful; they were resumed again in 1930 and the draft agreement was completed in 1934. Shortly before the death of Aleksandar, Varnava, who was otherwise very supportive of the king, reportedly said about the proposed Condordat that it was easier to be a Metropolitan under the Turks, than a Patriarch under the Karadjordjević dynasty.[19] The sudden death of King Aleksandar postponed the ratification of the agreement for a few more years.

Legislation regulating the life of Yugoslav Muslims was also adopted in 1929. It created a new legal and administrative entity – the Yugoslav Muslim Community (*Islamska Vjerska Zajednica*, IVZ). Previously the Muslims of former Habsburg territories were under the authority of the Sarajevo Reis-ul-ulema, while those living in Serbia and Montenegro were under the authority of the supreme mufti in Belgrade. There have also been differences across the country in regards to the work of the Shari'a courts. The newly established IVZ was based on the Bosnian model and was dominated by Bosnian Muslims.[20] Similarly to the regulation of the Serbian Orthodox Church, the new legislation limited the autonomy and authority of Muslim religious leaders and made them directly accountable to the minister of justice. The government used IVZ to underline the political power of Mehmet Spaho's Yugoslav Muslim Organization, which, according to Belgrade, emphasized Bosnian regional identity too strongly. Nielsen convincingly argues that the authorities in Belgrade showed a propensity to regard Islam as an obstacle to national consolidation.[21]

The attitude of the Serbian religious leaders to the new regime was complex. While no one objected to its anti-democratic nature, in fact the Church embraced the idea of order and stability and the end of the corrupt party politics, there was no unanimous acceptance of integral Yugoslavism. In some publications directed at the general public, Serbian clerics talked of patriotism and love of fatherland in patriarchal terms equating it to love of one's family. The king was the 'father of the nation'.[22] This continued the already established tradition of public celebration of the king on 1 December and on the day of the Royal birthday. The newly elected Patriarch Varnava seemed content with the new state policies and lent his full support to King Aleksandar. So much so, that

Svetozar Pribićević accused Varnava of acting solely in favour of the king and his integral nationalism instead of taking care of believers, and the Serbian Church of becoming an extension of the state.[23]

At the same time, other clerics opposed the imposition of the ideology of integral Yugoslavism from the start of the dictatorship. This will become one of the key points of contention between the Yugoslav state and the Serbian Orthodox Church in the 1930s. Gavrilo Dožić will emerge as one of the most prominent critics. In his memoirs written after the Second World War, Dožić claims to have said the following to Prime Minister Živković in 1930:

> Under these circumstances we, the Serbs, want to remain in the future who our ancestors were and what they fought for over centuries with the motto '*Za krst časni i slobodu zlatnu!*'[24] We cannot forget, General, what is born to our blood, what we have inherited from our ancestors with our mothers' milk …. I think that the Serbs cannot and should not denounce Serbdom in the name of Yugoslavdom, if the Croats and the Slovenes do not want to do the same.[25]

Dožić, according to his own account, then continued, 'Today it [Yugoslavism] is a utopia, with no real foundation. And now the Serbs alone, without the Croats, have to build and propagate Yugoslavism as a common state idea. For me that is a naïve aberration.'[26] Dožić, therefore, did not straight out reject the possibility or even desirability of a united Yugoslav nation. He did, however, object to the Serbs giving up their national identity alone and without support of other Yugoslav constitutive nations. Along similar lines in 1927, two years before the change of regime, Miloš Parenta expressed the general hope that 'in several generations the unity of cultural and state life' would make the three tribes truly one nation. But until then, they would remain distinct, albeit brotherly, nations.[27] Given that the article appeared in the official publication of the Patriarchate, one can safely assume that his was also the position the Serbian Church leadership.

Curiously, such open criticism by Dožić did not extend to the king himself. Dožić had proven his loyalty to the royal dynasty back in 1918, when he was the first to propose the overthrow of the old Montenegrin Petrović dynasty in favour of unification with Serbia under the rule of the Karadjordjević family.[28] While Dožić had his reservations about the centralization of the Serbian Orthodox Church and continued to take his Montenegrin position seriously, he should not be made into a Montenegrin nationalist. By and large, the Karadjordjević dynasty was in the eyes of the Serbian Orthodox Church a Serbian, not Yugoslav dynasty, and the clerics thought it only natural that the royal family should take care of its own nation first. Despite the best efforts of the Yugoslav state, this association was not broken. Even more problematically, it was shared by the Roman Catholics as well, who understandably were less enthusiastic about it.

To the same extent that Aleksandar was a Serbian king, the 'nation' (*narod*) in church rhetoric was the Serbian nation. In this sense the Serbian Church had never given up the rhetoric of 'liberation and unification', which emphasized the sacrifice of the Serbian nation to the common Yugoslav cause. The government of Petar Živković represented what the Serbian Church did not like about the new regime: integral Yugoslavism in action. Živković was repeatedly and unfavourably compared to Nikola Pasić, who was fondly remembered as the defender of East Orthodoxy Christianity and Serbian national interests.

As the time progressed, both secular and religious authorities became aware of the role religion played in keeping 'tribal differences' alive. If before 1918 it was possible for the proponents of Yugoslavism to disregard the issue of religious differences, after a decade of living in a religiously diverse state nobody could turn a blind eye to it. This realization dawned on both sides gradually, with the leaders of religious communities demonstrating more sensitivity. Parenta underlined the role of religion already in 1925: 'The blood is one, the language is one, the national spirit is one, but the cultural spirit is not. And in it the religious factor plays the most important role.'[29] It was in this context that the 1929 dictatorship changed the rules of 'public engagement' for the Yugoslav religious communities.

Whereas political organizations based on religious principle were now forbidden, the state could not close religious associations that operated as part of the officially recognized religious institutions and whose activities stayed away from public politics. In some cases, it was not a simple distinction to make. For example, the decision whether educational activities targeted at children and youth made a religious organization into a political one was difficult to make. The case in point is the transformation and re-branding of the Croatian Catholic youth organization Eagles – the pre-1929 competitor of the state-supported, Yugoslav-oriented *Sokol* – into the Crusaders. The Crusaders [*Križari*] were allowed to operate as a strictly religious association affiliated with the Jesuits. Not everyone however agreed that their activities remained outside of public politics, and the government hesitated whether they should be allowed to continue.[30] The Crusaders inherited the membership, structure and, to a large degree, the programme of the Eagles. Some observers interpreted the emphasis on the Christian upbringing of the youth in their official statements as a smokescreen and lip service to the requirements of the new regime. Ivan Protulipac, Croatian lawyer, Catholic activist and former president of the Eagles, admitted this much in a private letter: 'We will pretend as though we work as a church organisation, while in fact we will function in the same manner we used to.'³¹ Together with Ivan Merz, who was closely involved with the Catholic movement started by the bishop of Krk Mahnić before the First World War, they sought to counter the perceived threat of liberalism and secularism among the Croatian youth. Lay religious movements have become increasingly important for European Christian communities in the first half of the twentieth century. *Catholic Action* proclaimed in 1922 by Pope Pius XI in his encyclical 'Ubi arcano Dei' was of utmost importance in this respect. Ivan Merz took up this concept in order to create a number of Catholic youth societies whose ambition was 'to nurture, through discipline, spiritual guidance and promotion of group unity, a new generation that would bring victory to Catholicism over liberalism in Croatia'.³² The Serbian Orthodox Church on the one hand clearly saw the Catholic Action in Croatia as an example to be followed in their fight with secular liberalism and materialism, or to use Miloš Parenta's terminology 'false liberalism'. On the other hand, however, it perceived Catholic activism as a threat to its own position and influence in areas with mixed population, especially in Croatia and Bosnia. As Catholic movements became stronger, the hostility in the Serbian Orthodox Church's rhetoric vis-à-vis Roman Catholics increased. Serbian Orthodox initiatives at promoting its own lay religious movement are discussed in the last section of this chapter.

Another contentious field related to the question of Yugoslavism and public activities of religious communities was education. It specifically concerned the primary and secondary school curriculum and the question of whether religious education classes should be taught by clerics appointed by the respective religious authorities or by the government-appointed lay teachers. Education and the upbringing of the youth have always been important for religious communities, who traditionally oversaw it. The secular authorities, in their turn, paid attention to education because they considered nation-building to be one of its primary functions with all other considerations subjugated to this overarching goal. Thus, control over education was important for both the religious and secular authorities, who frequently clashed over it. The stumbling block was the question of how to balance the interests of state and national unity on the one hand and the interests of religious communities in a religiously diverse state on the other.³³ The dictatorship radicalized this issue further by introducing new educational policies, which placed all educational institutions under central authority and aimed to establish a uniform education system.³⁴ The renewed efforts at modernization and nationalization of education deepened whatever disagreements there had been prior to 1929.

In a 1926 parliamentary debate addressing the religion-education nexus, Dr Dimitrije Kirilović suggested that religious education be excluded from the curriculum and be replaced by a course in the history of religions.[35] In Kirilović's view, religious education in state-run schools was not advisable in a religiously diverse state because it encouraged the disintegration of the state instead of strengthening national unity. He thus advocated what can be labelled a 'secularisation policy for national interests', when national and hence state unity is put above the interests of religious communities. The Serbian Orthodox Church as well as Catholic and Muslim leaders interpreted such initiatives as aiming at 'total secularisation', that is, undermining of religion, and refused to see any other logic to them. Responding to Kirilović, Aleksandar Živanović, an Orthodox priest and professor, argued that the Serbian Orthodox clergy and the Serbian Orthodox Church as an institution supported Yugoslav national unity, but only insofar as 'political unity', did not lead to an absolute eradication of all differences between the constitutive nations, by which he meant differences of religion.[36] After 1929 this point of view was no longer acceptable. Živanović did not elaborate whether religious diversity weakens or strengthens the common state, but he made it clear that removing religious education from schools would have an overall negative impact by destroying the morals of the youth. The representatives of the Roman Catholic and Yugoslav Muslim communities agreed. Dr Jure Turić, a Catholic priest, seconded Živanović and called for a better and more profound confessional education. He believed that it was not necessary to silence religious differences, but instead, through a more thorough religious education, people would reach a level of knowledge and understanding that would help bridge confessional differences, thus making hate, defiance and intolerance impossible.[37] This sort of ecumenical reasoning reminiscent of the late-nineteenth-century arguments did not find significant support among state officials.

All three major Yugoslav religious communities demanded that the government make religious education in state-run primary and secondary schools a prerogative of clerics, in other words, bar laypeople from teaching it. In the former Habsburg territories this was the case prior to 1918, but not in the Kingdom of Serbia, where a mix of both options was in place, probably because the Serbian Church did not have enough priests to cover all schools. The Serbian Orthodox Church was happy to part with this tradition and supported the Roman Catholic Church and the Yugoslav Muslim community.

Protracted and difficult negotiations with the government were initially unsuccessful for the religious communities. In the case of the Serbian Orthodox

Church a strange compromise was reached, which did not satisfy either side. The 1929 Law on National Schools was the main piece of legislation and gave the Ministry of Education the upper hand over religious education classes. At the same time, the Law on the Serbian Orthodox Church guaranteed that the Church will be consulted in all matters relating to religious education. For example, article 17 of the 1929 Law on the Serbian Orthodox Church put religious instruction in primary and secondary schools under the general supervision of the Ministry of Education. The minister appointed teachers of religious education, but only from the list of priests and/or laypeople preapproved by local church authorities.[38] A special provision was made for parents, who in theory could opt their children out of religious education classes, although it doesn't seem that many did. Similarly, textbooks used to teach religious education in East Orthodox schools/classes must be in compliance with the Law on Textbooks and be approved by the Ministry of Education, but only after the Holy Synod of the Orthodox Church had approved them.[39]

Yugoslav religious communities persisted in their demands and succeeded to somewhat improve the situation. An amendment passed in July 1930 made religious education mandatory again, to be taught by clerics appointed by local religious authorities. Larger schools were to have teachers with training in Christian or Muslim theology.[40] At the same time, the Ministry of Education had the right to fire or reassign those teachers who did not comply with the general educational policies of the state, and actively used this right when a teacher was suspected to have anti-Yugoslav views. At the height of dictatorship one of its proponents somewhat naively argued that religious education teachers encourage religious tolerance and work for the goal of religious peace and consolidation of the Yugoslav nation.[41] While this may have been the intention of the state-approved curriculum, in real life religious tolerance was not actively encouraged. Another major success for the religious communities was that the 1930 edition of the law allowed membership of schoolchildren in religious organizations outside the school.[42] This was especially welcome by the Roman Catholics, who invested a great deal in youth movements.

Integral Yugoslavism meant that the state aggressively insisted on total levelling of ethnic and cultural differences between the three 'tribes', as seen in its desire to streamline regulation of religious life and to better control the education. In contrast to the previous decade, this time official policies and rhetoric were met with considerable hostility by the Serbian Orthodox Church. With ways of expressing nationalism other than Yugoslav nationalism restricted, religious institutions became natural bearers of 'tribal' identities. Political actors unhappy with this iteration of the Yugoslav idea were willing to use religious communities to counter some of the state propaganda and used religious language and symbols in their own mass mobilization campaigns. The religious communities, in their turn, as their dissatisfaction with the government grew by the mid-1930s, began to see benefits in this cooperation. In these circumstances the Serbian hierarchs decided it was time to create 'an Orthodox public opinion', which would help lobby the government and Parliament (once it was reinstated) for Church interests.

Responses to new challenges

However important the problem of Yugoslavism was, the Serbian Orthodox Church operated in a much broader context, which was not limited to issues of the Yugoslav state. Serbian Orthodox religious intellectuals and clerics as well as thinkers and writers from other Yugoslav religious communities were concerned with the changes they saw happening at home and elsewhere in Europe: the rise of scientific thinking, materialism, individualism and the associated decline of spirituality. All of these are the hallmarks of modernity. The East Orthodox theological and philosophical tradition is rarely read and interpreted through the lens of the discussion of modernity, it is routinely said to have been a conservative, traditionalist and anti-modern force throughout the twentieth century. However, as many scholars of modernity have observed, critique of modernity doesn't make one a-modern. On the contrary, 'being modern means taking a stand on these [modernity-related] issues, but what exactly the stand will be is always a subject to a concrete societal and historical elaboration'.[43] The spectrum of opinions articulated by Serbian Orthodox thinkers falls within the range of what Kristina Stöckl describes as 'philosophical–ontological critique' of modernity. This type of critical reflection is different from the criticism of, for instance, economic capitalism or the over-bureaucratization of the state, as it disputes the very underlying philosophical notions of modernity: rationalism and individualism.[44]

Rationalism and individualism, and the associated liberalism and secularization, indeed were the focal point of the critique mounted by the Serbian Orthodox Church. This critique often took the form of criticism of the generalized 'West' or Europe, and – within Yugoslavia – of the Catholic areas, which were historically associated with the Habsburg monarchy and 'Europe'.

A 1921 editorial preface to one of the first publications in the book series *Library of Contemporary Religious–Moral Questions* opened with the following passage worth quoting in full:

> The spiritual life of all of Europe is in a state of turbulence today. Old views of the world and life, expressed in the spirit of the Christian religion, are falling under the impact of science and scientific philosophy. The new [views] are being created in their place, which, as they have proved in practice, do not promise [us] anything good. Old ways of social life are also ruined, and attempts are made to create new structures. In one word, religion is yielding to science, spirituality to materialism, democracy to socialism and communism. But parallel to that one can feel the decline of idealism in favour of materialism, the decline of altruism in favour of egoism. In practice, more and more corruption, anarchy and nihilism are spreading, which are followed by assassinations, murders, dictatorship and the most brutal terror.[45]

The passage succinctly presents all keywords of the Orthodox critique of modernity and reveals concern for the decline of religiosity and morality. But it also demonstrates that the writer was acutely aware of the postwar social and political developments on the continent. 'Assassinations, murders, dictatorship and the most brutal terror' is most likely a reference to the Bolshevik Revolution in Russia, which occupied a prominent place in the Yugoslav and European press but could also be a general comment on the rise in postwar violence. It is characteristic of the Serbian Orthodox public discourse that not only communism but also socialism is juxtaposed to democracy. By the end of the decade, majority of Serbian clergy were disappointed in practical implementation of democracy and parliamentary politics in Yugoslavia, but this editorial from 1921 firmly places the Serbian Orthodox Church on the side of democratic politics. By the late 1920s Serbian Orthodox Church identified its main enemies or rivals, which could be individuals, political and social movements, or indeed historical processes.

By the mid-1920s the Serbian Church had completed most of its institutional reforms and while it still had to wait for up-to-date state legislation on the regulation of religious life, it now had some resources to spare. A key task was the creation of an 'Orthodox public' and consolidated 'Orthodox public opinion'. This public would have internalized the East Orthodox worldview and be immune to materialism, atheism, socialism, Marxism, communism and other contemporary evils and temptations. This conscious and self-aware public was to include elite and common folk. It was supposed to publicly advocate for the

Serbian Church in the struggle with its rivals, local or global, share its goals and wherever possible lobby for the Church interests as their own. An ambitious goal by all accounts, but the stakes were high. Increasingly, the clergy talked about the 'survival of the nation and the humankind'. A large-scale war required appropriate means of defence and offence. The Serbian Church therefore was taking up a fight against the zeitgeist, and by doing so it brought itself into the zeitgeist, for it was not alone in this struggle. Its Catholic and Muslim counterparts faced similar problems, as did many other European religious communities, for whom secularization accompanied by atheism and materialism had been a reason for concerns since the nineteenth century, if not earlier.

Russian émigré theologian Sergey Bulgakov, well known and well respected in Yugoslavia, suggested that Orthodox Churches should have a more active position in society in order to counterbalance the negative effect of secularization and the general modernization of life. According to Bulgakov, such an active engagement with the world was possible only for a Church that itself was modern. Some of the Serbian clergy and Orthodox thinkers agreed. However, this attitude was opposed by another school of thought, known as 'Neo-Patristic', which argued for the re-examination and re-assertion of the Byzantine theological tradition. Some prominent Russian representatives of this school settled in Sremski Karlovci in Vojvodina after they were forced to flee from Bolshevik Russia.[46] A competition between these two positions became visible in the Serbian Orthodox intellectual circles and had an impact on the Church's public discourse and political position for the duration of the interwar period.

In their critique of modernity, and in particular in their analysis of secularization, East Orthodox authors identified two distinct 'danger zones': the creation of less favourable conditions for the Serbian Orthodox Church and its activities in Yugoslavia; and the decline of spirituality and weakening of Christian values across various social groups en masse. The former mattered here and now and was a specific Yugoslav affair; the latter did not stop at the borders of Yugoslavia and extended to the rest of Europe and the world. One could have argued that the first was a part of the second, much larger problem, if it were not for the fact that interwar Yugoslavia was a religiously diverse state and policies limiting the power of the Serbian Orthodox Church often were aimed at maintaining religious equality and peace rather than at achieving secularization. Not all policies directed at the limitation of public visibility or curbing the power of religious institutions had the complete secularization of society as a goal. Some however did, and usually came as part of a more general stride towards modernization, which included the goal of secularization in the sense of limiting the public presence of religious institutions and confining religious life to the private sphere. In its most radical forms, calls for modernization and secularization suggested the complete elimination of religion. These however were rare in the Yugoslav context. One such proposal came in 1933 from a member of the Yugoslav National Party, Dr Nikola Kešeljević. Kešeljević proposed a complete separation of church and state in Yugoslavia as a necessary step in limiting the scale of the religious communities' public engagement. His proposal aimed at radically restricting social activities as well as cultural influence of religious institutions: the ownership and control over all hospitals, schools and other social institutions that belonged to any religious organization should be transferred to the state; civil marriage was to become mandatory, and clergy should be regarded as 'ordinary persons'.[47] Kešeljević's proposal was more radical compared to the official policies of the dictatorship. As a proponent of strict and complete separation of church and state, Kešeljević reacted to the rise in public presence of religion and the strengthening of the political position of Yugoslav religious institutions. Here, the ambivalent character of the state's policies towards religious communities becomes apparent: the king and his government did not cut religion out of the public sphere. On the contrary, under the conditions of restricted political life, religion came to the forefront of the political debate and was increasingly used as a national symbol.

The general strategy of the Serbian Church was to treat all attempts to limit its authority as universal promotion of secularization, even when suggested reforms clearly had in mind the interests of the unitary state and did not aim at the elimination of religion and did not promote materialism/atheism. In other words, the representatives of the Serbian Church provided answers to the institutional challenge as though it was ontological. An official comment on the draft of Kešeljević's law published in *Glasnik Srpske Pravoslavne Patrijaršije* compared it with the extreme militant atheist policies implemented in communist Russia: 'From such thunders fired at the church there is only one step to the communist order of the state and society.'[48] Given the openly hostile attitude towards the Bolsheviks, this was not a mere comparison, but a warning. Thus, the Church readily imagined that the weakening of the Church institutions led to structural damage of society. The Roman Catholic Church reacted to the initiative with similar outrage but linked the proposal to the Freemason conspiracy.[49]

In interwar Yugoslavia the vast majority of proposals and policies, that involved limitation of the public presence of religions, did not suggest that this limitation must be absolute. In its most common form such a stance on secularisation grew out of the fear that too much religion in the public sphere will undermine state and national unity. The proponents of integral Yugoslavism were the most enthusiastic supporters of the idea of eliminating religion from the public sphere, without imposing the values and norms of atheism and militant anti-clericalism. First and foremost, they hoped to diminish extant differences and pacify conflicts between the three 'tribes'.

Paradoxically, the idea that secularization will strengthen Yugoslav national unity was possible only if one acknowledges that the 'tribal' identities had a strong religious component and that religion could be used for political mass mobilization. Yugoslav nationalism, in theory was as supra-religious as it was supra-national, however in real life Yugoslavia remained primarily a Christian state. As discussed at length in Chapter 2, the ambiguity and problematic nature of such an intellectual and political construction was obvious to many contemporaries. The religious communities of the Kingdom of Yugoslavia were not the only one doubted its feasibility.

The Yugoslav state did not actively pursue the policy of secularization, but its attitude towards public use of religion was ambivalent. On the one hand, it did not trust religious actors and wanted to exercise a considerable degree of control over them; on the other, it had to rely on religious communities in its efforts to promote the Yugoslav cause, as described in Chapter 2. By and large, the state was interested in maintaining religious peace and to that end it was willing to facilitate coexistence of religious communities and sometimes even their cooperation at a local level, but the lack of trust often led to the separation of religious communities rather than encouragement of cooperation.

Very often though, this interreligious conversation was seen by the Serbian clergy as a competition and rivalry, not as a dialogue. While the clergy were rarely able to contribute meaningfully to the dialogue on religious equality and religious peace, state officials were equally unable to see the problem from the perspective of religious communities. The Serbian Church repeatedly argued and truly tirelessly communicated to the state officials and the general public that the very nature of East Orthodox Christianity meant that it could never and should not ever be confined to people's private lives. While the Church leadership wanted to retain autonomy in decision-making and arranging their affairs, it did not seek a separation from the state and the public sphere: the Serbian Orthodox Church 'cannot coalesce with the state and state life, nor can it completely disentangle itself from it'.[50] This fragile balance partially derived from the long tradition of *symphonia*, or the church–state relationship in the East Orthodox Byzantine realm.

Once again theology becomes important for the understanding of certain aspects of the Serbian Orthodox discourse. Jaroslav Pelikan argued convincingly that in the twentieth century 'one of the first and most vital tasks of any theological justification in the church – any church – for the attention to the redemption of society was to clarify its doctrinal legitimacy within the structures and traditional authority, whatever those might be for a particular church'.[51] Given the rising importance of social teaching in the Christian world, it is not surprising then, that the Serbian Orthodox Church starts to pay more attention to the justification of its authenticity and even superiority over its main rival on Yugoslav territory, the Roman Catholic Church. Many of the Serbian Orthodox clerics referred to the specific East Orthodox character of the Church as an institution that was not hostile to the state and society. Thus, arguments which involved references to the Church as a collective, a community of believers need to be contextualized both politically and theologically.

Miloš Parenta, a longstanding editor of *Glasnik Srpske Pravoslavne Patrijaršije*, reiterated on multiple occasions that 'clericalism' and 'false liberalism' were alien to the Serbian Church. Clericalism, in his understanding, was characteristic of the Roman Catholic Church, in which the episcopate and the hierarchy occupied a position superior to both the community of believers and the state. True liberalism, which was typical of the Orthodox Church, fought against these tendencies. 'False liberalism', however, tried to oust religion and the Church from the public sphere and allowed it to exist only as a matter of individual choice in one's private life.[52] Parenta emphasized that, due to the very character of East Orthodox Christianity and especially due to the nature of its Church institutions, neither clericalism, nor 'false liberalism', that is, secularism, was possible in Serbia and in the Serbian Orthodox Church. He thus achieved two goals: He argued for the right of the Serbian Church to advocate for public visibility while he simultaneously rejected all accusations of being involved in political life and partaking in the decision-making process on the issues not concerned with the Church. These two statements could easily be seen as self-contradictory, but for Parenta active public presence did not equal taking part in politics, which was understood as party politics.

An important source of new and/or familiar but revisited ideas was the rather large wave of Russian immigrants to the Balkans, with the centres in Sofia, Belgrade, and Istanbul (Constantinople). Although most Russian immigrants to Yugoslavia were army officers (the remains of the Russian General Wrangel, one of the commanders of the White Army, were moved to the Russian Trinity Church of the Moscow Patriarchate in Tašmajdan Park in Belgrade two years after Wrangel's death in Brussels), several hundred university professors and other people of 'free professions' found refuge there. Some of the immigrants made successful careers, such as jurist and philosopher Evgenii Spektorski who became a university professor in Belgrade and Ljubljana; or Vladimir Titov, a conservative Church historian, who became a professor in Belgrade; or Vladislav Maevski, who served as head librarian in the library of the Serbian Patriarchate and a personal secretary of Patriarch Varnava. The Serbian Church in particular was happy to employ Russian émigrés who were often better educated than Serbian graduates and at the same time were eager to get a job and were willing to be stationed in remote areas. With this, the Church secured a better level of teaching and made sure that newly acquired territories where the Church had yet to establish itself were taken care of.[53]

Russian scholars with a fairly conservative worldview played a role in the intellectual evolution of the Serbian Orthodox Church. As a matter of fact, Russian intellectual influence in religious circles had been strong before the 1917 Revolution. Despite the fact that Serbian clergy had been educated in the Russian Empire since the nineteenth century, first in Kiev and Odessa, and later on in Saint Petersburg, it was rather through reading and travelling that Serbian students of theology became Russophiles and adepts of the Russian religious philosophy of Khomiakov and Dostoevskiy.[54] Nonetheless, a tradition of sending students to Russian educational institutions in the pre-1917 period facilitated the initial incorporation of Russian émigrés into the Serbian Orthodox community. The same could not be said, though, of the religious institutions of the émigré community abroad, namely the Russian Orthodox Church, with its centre in Sremski Karlovci.

Whatever the institutional conflicts between Russian and Serbian Churches in Yugoslavia, Russian presence in the kingdom added to the idea that now, after the Russian Empire had collapsed and the Bolsheviks were pursuing radical anti-religious policies, it is up to the Serbian Orthodox Church to lead and protect East Orthodox Christianity not just at home but also abroad. This self-imposed burden of responsibility and world significance added a new dimension to the self-image of the Serbian Orthodox Church. Structurally, it was similar to the old *Antemurale Christianitatis* myth that had been present in all European national cultures in the modern period. The feeling of being the last bearer of East Orthodox Christianity, the only true Christianity, was one of the reasons behind the shift towards more active policies towards the external world, both at home and abroad. For now, it was up to the Serbian Church to take care of the 'entirety of the East Orthodox world' and to 'ensure the mission of East Orthodoxy Christianity in the World'.[55]

Having identified the problems, the Serbian Church came to the conclusion that the current state of affairs was not acceptable. Consequently, the hierarchy turned its attention to possible measures directed at the improvement of the situation. Church hierarchs and intellectuals singled out several areas where action needed to be taken in order to possibly stop secularizing tendencies, improve the position of the Church and prevent the loss of morals and Christian character in the Serbian nation in the future. National elites, education and mass (youth) movements, all of which could qualify as propaganda to a hostile observer, were the focus of attention.

Many Serbian religious authors saw the core of the problem in the character of the national elite, or rather the national intelligentsia. The hierarchs assumed that the chances to create a profoundly religious and Christian nation and society – not an easy task even in favourable conditions – were extremely low as long as the leading social strata were indifferent towards religion at best, or openly anti-clerical and anti-religious at worst. On the other hand, with a national elite who shares and supports an East Orthodox worldview, the Serbian Church would be able to exercise impact on wider circles of society. The task therefore was to 'first equip the East Orthodox intelligentsia with the East Orthodox worldview. Make sure that they accept it. And then make out of them a disciplined elite … that will defend church teaching and Orthodox culture'.[56] The ultimate goal was, according to the same writer, to create Orthodox public opinion.

Despite the Church's grievances about an a-religious national elite, supporters of secularism and Yugoslavism evaluated the situation quite differently. They saw the national elite to be too bound to their ethnicity, or 'tribal origins', and religion. What was even worse in the Yugoslavists' point of view was the unwillingness of national elites to give up their ethnic and confessional orientation, something that effectively hindered the development of the Yugoslav nation and threatened the state.[57] Similar to the debates around the school curriculum, it was a matter of perspective to view the leading social strata as overly secular or excessively religious. Another reason for this difference in opinions was that the Church judged the level of piety and religiosity, while secular intellectuals paid attention rather to the cultural connotations of one's religious affiliation. That is to say, that while the clergy were not satisfied with general lack of interest in the Church and Christianity, some Yugoslav-oriented politicians and intellectuals were unhappy with the ever strong public link between religion and nation. Both sides had their reasons. A foreign observer reported in the late 1920s: 'The Serbian peasant has nothing against Croats and *prečani* in general; on the contrary he talks of them as honest people, although often regards them – Catholics – to be "non-Christian" or "*Švabi*". At the beginning I did not understand what they meant by it, until I realised that it was about a different faith.'[58] Religion never ceased to be a differentiating factor (together with historical regions) inside the presumably unified 'Yugoslav nation'.

One of the ways to create religiously minded elite was to make the Church more attractive. To do so, it was wise to invest in religious education, both general and professional. To achieve this goal, it was necessary to open more seminaries (and indeed five were opened in the years after the unification of the Church)[59] and to finally have an institution of higher education in theology within the country. The theology faculty of Belgrade University was opened in 1920, although it had been planned as early as in 1905.[60] It was here that a group of young theology students started the journal *Svetosavlje*, which was to become the herald of new religious ideology in the late 1930s. In 1931, a decade after the faculty was opened, a monastic school was established in Rakovica; it was moved in the next year to the famous monastery of Visoki Dečani. According to Slijepčević, by the beginning of the Second World War the majority of Serbian Orthodox priests and hierarchs were educated at home, and not abroad, as had been the case in the early twentieth century. The generation of Irinej Djordjević, Justin Popović and Velimir Hadži-Arsić was the last one to go to the West European and Russian universities, just before and during the First World War, making it the last generation of Orthodox theologians to be educated primarily abroad.[61]

Educational policies promoted by the Serbian Orthodox Church paid out. This was true both for general education and for the professional education of clergy. *Svetosavlje* published both the writings of students and their professors from the Theological Faculty as well as other departments of Belgrade University. The journal was one of the few common intellectual forums for the clerics and lay contributors, and thus worked towards the familiar aim of garnering the Orthodox elite. The 'core group' of people involved featured Djoko Slijepčević, Vasilije Kostić and Vlajko Vlahović; the group was influenced by their older colleague, Dimitrije Najdanović, and through him by Nikolaj Velimirović, by then already a bishop and a well-respected theologian.[62] As can be easily seen from the journal title, the members of the editorial board subscribed to the idea of *Svetosavlje*, but in contrast to Velimirović and Najdanović, they highlighted the social role of the Church and the peculiarities of parish life. The editorial statement in the first issue of the journal noted, '*Svetosavlje* is our distinct, truly devoted service to man through Christ. And that is our unique goal'.[63] The journal, which was apparently launched with the idea of social work, evolved over time and drifted towards more nation-bound themes and topics.

Thus, the strategic goal of the Serbian Church was to find allies or when that was impossible – to create a social group, that would share and defend the Church's Christian spiritual and political values and would have the capacity to captivate and inspire large parts of society. The ways to fulfil the task were many, and the international examples were of great help. The task that the Serbian Church set up for itself was the task that virtually any other church in Europe had been taking on since the middle of the nineteenth century. Its closest neighbour, the Roman Catholic Church in Croatia and Slovenia, was one of the possible sources of 'inspiration' and an example to draw lessons from. Education, always an important issue for a religious community with aspirations to public visibility, became even more important during the years of the dictatorship.

How to operate in a religiously diverse society

Apart from adjusting to new political climate and facing the challenges of modernity, the Serbian Orthodox Church was also concerned with the rivalry with other religious institutions and communities – the Roman Catholic Church, which was the second-largest religious community in the country; the Muslim community in the South and in Bosnia; and the growing neo-Protestant sects and churches in the former Hungarian territories in the North and in East Bosnia. This competition originated from the availability of multiple religious offerings and became more pronounced in the religiously diverse state, which at least formally embraced the principle of religious equality, unlike the pre-1918 Serbian Kingdom, which favoured East Orthodox Christianity. The fear of losing members of community was a powerful factor, which prompted the Serbian Orthodox Church to actively engage in fostering the growth of a 'consciously East Orthodox public'.

The Roman Catholic Church was in many senses the arch-rival: it was numerically stronger than any other community, it was powerful, rich and well organized. Although the Serbian clergy paid lip service to the principle of religious equality and pledged its commitment to maintain good relationships with all legally recognized religious communities, it did not shy away from using very strong rhetoric in its criticism of the Roman Catholics. On the pages of *Glasnik Srpske Patrijaršije*, the official periodical of the Serbian Patriarchate where official announcements, news and programmatic statements were published, contributors often claimed that the Roman Catholic Church maintained the pretence of friendliness, while in fact it has never been a 'true Christian church'. The sincerity of the Serbian Church in the face of Catholic duplicity was a constant refrain:

> His Holiness Patriarch Varnava sensed the Judas kiss [of the Croatian Catholics], but did not ever start the battle against the Roman Catholics. We [the Serbian Church] are in the position of defence against the foreign/barbaric invasion and spiritual invasive tendencies of Rome.[64]

Despite repeated claims of having no intention to get involved in the 'unworthy business of mutual accusations',[65] *Glasnik* did publish an anonymous article calling the Croatian Roman Catholics 'the third horseman of the Apocalypse' because of their 'nationalist separatism'.[66] The first two horsemen were the bearers of materialism and bolshevism, both by-products of a-religious liberalism. Presumably, the anonymous author followed an interpretative tradition, which sees the first horseman on the white horse as the righteous one, leaving only three to bring evil and disaster.

Association with Croatian nationalism and separatism was the biggest 'crime' of the Roman Catholics, especially in the dictatorship period. This accusation was supposed to be the ultimate proof of the dangerous intentions of the Roman Catholic Church in Yugoslavia, who, according to the Serbian Orthodox authors, had never truly supported the common state. The fact that the 'founding fathers' of Yugoslavism, Franjo Rački and Josip Strossmayer, were not just Catholics but high-ranking members of the episcopate was consciously overlooked. On the other hand, there were multiple known cases of the Catholic clergy supporting and campaigning for the Croatian Peasant Party of Stjepan Radić. The Ministry of Religions received numerous reports and complaints during and immediately after the 1925 elections, when Radić directed the campaign from prison for a party, which was officially banned, yet allowed to participate in the elections.[67] Reports consistently mention that Catholic parish priests incited Croatian nationalism and campaigned for the Croatian Peasant Party in churches and schools.[68] A Catholic priest from B. [Beli?] Manastir reportedly urged his parishioners to vote for Radić, even though he himself voted for Pašić 'because only under this disguise [I] can campaign actively for Radić'.[69] Another clergyman from the Dalmatian hinterland collected donations explaining that it was 'better to give donations to Radić, who works to save the Catholic faith, than to pay taxes that only support Serbs in Belgrade'.[70] This echoes a widespread sentiment that the taxation system unjustly favoured Serbs and put undue hardship on the peasantry in Croatian and Slovenian lands. Perhaps, this clergyman was harder in his rejection of the Yugoslav state than most, as he was arrested shortly afterwards for hiding two army deserters.

The Serbian Orthodox clergy did not stay away from the elections either. But with the majority of rural clergy supporting the Radical Party, which was in government, that was not considered a dangerous or unwanted activity. A small proportion of the Serbian clergy lent their support to other political parties, and those who campaigned for the Republicans or the Democrats, faced consequences similarly to Radić's supporters. Picking up on this, the Catholic Church returned the accusation of nationalism, and emphasized the Serbian dimension of many, presumably strictly religious, activities of the East Orthodox Church in Yugoslavia. One such set of activities was the celebration of St Sava.

St Sava's Day marked on 27 January, was one of the most disputed celebrations, as it brought together concerns of Yugoslav educational policies and respect for religious diversity. Inclusion of what was essentially a religious holiday central to the Serbian Orthodox community in the national school calendar provoked harsh reactions from the Yugoslav Catholics and Muslims. Similarly to the debates about the national holidays and the fine line between national and religious character of the festivities, the Ministry of Education argued that the holiday was a 'day of general cultural-national school celebration' and as such was separate from the religious holiday marked by the Serbian Orthodox Church.[71] Early 1930s saw a litany of complaints from the Yugoslav Catholic and Muslim communities, who pointed out that the presumed separation of the national and religious celebration did not work in real life. This was especially true for the religiously and ethnically mixed areas. For instance, Catholic authorities in Savska Banovina complained that Catholic Croatian children were made to recite Orthodox and explicitly Serbian poems as a part of St Sava festivities at school.[72] The Ministry of Education reiterated that it never intended to offset the religious balance and clarified that Muslim and Catholic students were not expected to attend the religious part of the celebration. However, Antun Bauer, the Archbishop of Zagreb, questioned that such a distinction was indeed possible, and at the very least pointed out that the Serbian secular and religious authorities continuously ignored it.[73] The dispute escalated further in 1935, when the Serbian Orthodox Church held wide celebrations during the Year of St Sava. Under pressure, the Ministry for Education made it obligatory again for all students to attend the school commemorations. Both Catholic and Muslim communities fought back, and the Ministry conceded stating that no citizen can be forced to participate in religious festivities of other religions.[74] This, however, came only after the official end of the Year of St Sava. The centrality of St Sava to the national and political thinking of the Serbian Orthodox Church is discussed in detail in the following chapter.

Religious competition was not limited to the well-established religious communities. In a somewhat surprising turn of events one of the influential rivals of the Serbian Orthodox Church was a smaller neo-Protestant sect, the Nazarens. Its prime significance lies in the response it elicited from the East Orthodox community, making the impact indirect. The neo-Protestant sects and churches grew exponentially at the turn of the nineteenth century and in the first decades of the twentieth century throughout South-eastern Europe, including in Yugoslavia.[75] The key contribution of the Nazarens was the inspiration they provided to an original Serbian grassroots religious movement known as *Bogomoljački pokret*, or the God Worshipper movement.[76]

The origins of the God Worshipper movement are obscure, but the researchers and contemporary commentators agree that the roots can be found in late nineteenth century Vojvodina and Banat, then Austro-Hungarian territories.[77] The movement became better known during the First World War, with its members active in hospitals and at the front. Metropolitan Dimitrije talked in 1918 about the resemblance of the God Worshippers to the Nazarenes, and how at first the army was suspicious towards them, but it soon turned out that they were 'very honest people and consummate solders'.[78] Despite this praise, the clergy and the hierarchs often remained distrustful of the members of the movement and especially of the possibility of its turning into a sect similar to the Nazarenes and abandoning the Serbian nationality.[79]

In 1925, one of the founders of the movement, Milan Bozoljac, tried to defend the God Worshippers by explaining to the Serbian clergy the rules of the movement, which, according to him, was of strictly 'moral-religious character' with no political programme and no intention to acquire one.[80] Its main aim was to raise the level of piety which had sunk very low after the devastating 'wars of liberation'. Bozoljac's main concern was to convince parish clergy that the movement was not a sect (like the Nazarenes or Adventists) but belonged to the body of the Serbian Orthodox Church, had the blessing of the Patriarch and therefore was to be supported by the clergy. The reason why many clergymen believed the God Worshippers to be a sect was not so much their piety and church attendance, but the fact that the groups met regularly outside the church service to pray and read the scripture. Members of the movement would often criticize those priests and bishops whose behaviour they found un-Christian and whose knowledge of the New Testament was lacking, as it was because of their failures that the moral renewal of the nation through faith in God and evangelical work was needed.[81]

In the 1902s, the God Worshipper movement consisted of numerous uncoordinated local organizations with members counting between 100 and 300,000 in Vojvodina, Serbia proper and north-eastern Bosnia, the majority in rural areas.[82] Early attempts at coordination failed until the archbishop of Žiča, Nikolaj Velimirović took interest in the movement. With Patriarch Dimitrije's blessing and together with Bozoljac in 1921 he established a National Christian Community [*Narodna Hrišćanska zajednica*] in Kragujevac, an organization whose purpose was to serve as an overarching structure for the dispersed movement. Patriarch Dimitrije gave his blessing on the condition that further activities should take place with consent of local clergy.[83] The same year, in an article entitled 'Do not push them away', Velimirović urged the parish clergy to have a friendlier stance towards the movement. He wrote admiringly about this grassroots, sincere and naïve religious movement that had emerged from the Serbian countryside. At the same time, the archbishop would have preferred the movement to exist in urban as well as rural areas, as it was more likely that the countryside would imitate the town than the other way around.[84] Already in the early 1920s, ahead of many of his colleagues, Velimirović was trying to find a way to infuse East Orthodox Christianity into the secular intellectual circles and the national elite, hence his concern for the capacity to influence and engage.

The rest of the Serbian hierarchs began to pay consistent attention to the God Worshipper movement nearly a decade later. In 1931, at a regular meeting of the Assembly of Hierarchs, the movement occupied a prominent place on the agenda. An official missionaries' course was set up together with the special missionary fund (building on the already existent tradition of training lay preachers) to make sure that those in search of a more spiritual experience stay within the structures of the Serbian Orthodox Church and do not join the Nazarenes or other sects. The Serbian Orthodox Church recognized the potential and importance of the movement in maintaining East Orthodox values in the Serbian countryside and smaller towns. By that time Velimirović had been supervising the movement closely and leading its growth for ten years. Two popular periodicals with wide national circulation *Mali Misionar* and *Veliki Misionar* had been established.

The God Worshipper movement is the closest the Serbian Orthodox Church came to having its own popular religious movement. Apart from the poorly educated peasants and artisans, the membership also included some very prominent politicians, mostly those embracing Serbian nationalism infused with anti-modernism: anti-Semitism, criticism of Freemasonry and broad European values, as well as continued focus on peasant culture as 'true' Serbian culture. Slijepčević noted in this regard that 'the city degenerates and kills all great movements that are born among the people. And in our country, it was from the common people that all great movements and great men had come. The salvation of the country will also come from the people.'[85] Towards the end of the 1930s and especially during the years of the Second World War, the movement became associated with Dimitrije Ljotić and his fascist movement Zbor. While not all God Worshippers became 'Ljotićevci', the leadership of Zbor including Ljotić himself had been members. Among those with dual membership also were Dimitrije Najdanović and Djoko Slijepčević, theologians close to Velimirović both of whom actively published on religious and national issues. Their thought is discussed in more detail in the following chapters. While it would be inaccurate to claim that the God Worshipper movement in its entirety became nationalized and politicized, it is indicative of a broader pattern in interwar Yugoslavia that a movement which started out by emphasizing spirituality, piety and engagement in social work ultimately became associated with an anti-modern nationalist political agenda.

The link between popular religion and national identity was particularly prominent in religiously and ethnically mixed areas and in the borderlands. It was expressed there more consistently and earlier compared to the more homogenous parts of Yugoslavia. It was also these areas where Varnava chose to promote 'the Orthodox cause' more actively, for instance during the 'tour' he made through Bosnia and Dalmatia, including Dubrovnik, which was closely followed and reported in the press.

A Sarajevo-based journal called the attention of its readers to the fact that 'it was natural for the Balkan peoples to be East Orthodox and unnatural to be anything else'.[86] The argument was simple and simultaneously all-encompassing: It was natural for the Serbs, as well as other Balkan Slavs, to be Christians of the East Orthodox rite, because without it they do not have history. Consequently, 'an Orthodox person who converts to Islam abandons the history of his people. One who converts to another Christian confession falsifies his nation's history'.[87] This position exemplifies the fear of possible conversions from East Orthodox Christianity and demonstrates that by tying religious national identities together, the Orthodox thinkers and clergy sought to keep their community strong. It is no surprise then that it was Bosnia, one of the most heterogeneous regions of Yugoslavia, that gave birth to the Brotherhood of St Sava, a society established in Sarajevo whose main declared goal was to 'awaken the East Orthodox Christian consciousness', work towards the improvement of social relations in local communities and fight inequality.[88] At the same time the main publication of the Brotherhood, periodical *Bratstvo* [Serb. brotherhood], devoted many pages to discussing the dangers posed by the Adventists and the Nazarenes, demonstrating that the presence of neo-Protestant churches and sects in Bosnia was a concern. Unlike the God Worshipper movement, the Brotherhood of St Sava remained a relatively small organization with a greater focus on the nation and national rhetoric.

Interaction with other religious communities and institutions took place at the international level as well, where the forms ranged from regional East Orthodox alliances to the worldwide ecumenical movement. In an effort to find allies in its struggle, the Serbian Orthodox Church looked beyond the borders of Yugoslavia. There was a series of initiatives to organize a mobilization campaign of the East Orthodox community on national and international levels throughout the entire interwar period. These attempts varied from a genuine ecumenical movement in the early 1920s inspired by the Anglican Church to a plan to unify autocephalous East Orthodox Churches in the Balkans to a strictly ethno-national mobilization of the late 1930s. Both the ecumenical and the East Orthodox international ties were associated with Nikolaj Velimirović. In the early 1930s, he participated in the Pan-Orthodox Conference held at Vatopedi Monastery on the Holy Mountain of Athos. The next year he led an official delegation of the Serbian Orthodox Church to Bulgaria, visiting Sofia and Rila Monastery. In 1933 the Serbian Church took part in a Balkan regional conference held in Bucharest, and in 1936 in the Orthodox Theological Congress in Athens.

Miloš Parenta argued that the disorganisation of national churches and 'apathy of a great part of our world towards religious affairs [were] two primary internal threats to East Orthodox Christianity'.[89] To counter these dangers he suggested that a common Synod of autocephalous East Orthodox Churches could be set up to assist in mobilizing the public opinion and making the national elites appreciate the significance of religion in everyday life. Thus, international cooperation was guided by concerns similar to the ones influencing domestic decisions.

In May 1933 a conference of Balkan Orthodox Churches took place in Bucharest under the presidency of Romanian Patriarch Miron. The conference was a part of the global structure of the *World Alliance for International Peace through the Churches*. At the conference Romanian, Greek, Bulgarian and

Yugoslav delegations discussed a broad range of social issues that their institutions faced on daily basis. Similar to Parenta's suggestion a few years earlier, they sought to create a strategy for regional cooperation, which would help counter materialism, atheism and communism – all were identified as major threats to East Orthodox Christianity and society in general. As Radmila Radić observed, the 'representatives of the Serbian Church in the 1930s were more afraid of communism than of fascism, as the consequences of communism were clearer for the Church, while they could hardly imagine at that time what kind of evils fascism would bring'.[90] Such attitude was not limited to the Serbian Orthodox Church, as anti-communist feeling was widespread in Europe, but it could partially explain the inclination of a fraction of the clergy to support the anti-communist, anti-modernist fascist and para-fascist political movements, such as in the case of the Romanian Iron Guard.[91] Romanian religious philosopher and publicist Nichifor Crainic, while talking about the problem during the open discussion, 'insisted on the necessity for the [East Orthodox] church not to stay static, but to act dynamically' in order to cleanse the national education of communist influences.[92] He also called for the re-Christianization of society via intensive social work and especially via engagement with the youth.[93] Other suggestion by the delegates included the founding of an 'Orthodox League' that would bring East Orthodox Christianity to the fore in the public sphere and support of already established local 'Orthodox activism'.[94] The Serbian God Worshipper movement fit nicely into this loose programme of mobilization and creation of an 'Orthodox public opinion'. The final resolution of the conference and its recommendations to the participating national churches embraced anti-communism and a more active social and political engagement of the churches. However, the resolution also underlined that each individual church should remain independent of any political party but should cooperate with the state authorities. Given a poor democratic record of all participating countries, it is clear that the Balkan East Orthodox churches did not have democracy as one of their values or goals.

Back home, the language used to talk about the public engagement of the Serbian Orthodox Church gradually radicalized. New more ambitious goals of what was now referred to as 'Serbian Orthodox messianism' included the spiritual liberation of [Serbian] brothers from European cultural influences, from the vain, deadly *Kulturträger* and Western spleen, fiction and lies'.[95]

Thus, while denying a commitment of the Serbian Orthodox Church to any political party and opposing the very need for it, Najdanović and others argued for a need to establish a national belief system in which 'Orthodox values' would be dominant. This took the goal of establishing an East Orthodox elite or an East Orthodox public one step further and elevated it to the national level. Despite repeated claims that the Serbian Church did not participate in politics, Najdanović made a strong case in favour of 'Orthodox activism'. Among other things he maintained that the 'superiority of Orthodox thought, if it is not materialised into a force, a movement, a blow' will turn into something abstract and useless.[96] We can see therefore an open 'call for action' taking place in the middle of the 1930s. Many of these calls rhetorically emphasized the value of ancient tradition (which Orthodoxy, unlike Roman Catholicism or Protestantism, was said to have preserved), but ultimately, they form a new modern phenomenon in the East Orthodox world which had never been strong in missionary work.

To sum up, Serbian Orthodox clergy felt a strong need for action to safeguard the position of the Church in the face of the challenges presented by the Yugoslav state, most notably by integral nationalism, but perhaps even more importantly by the general spirit of the times. At the same time, because of the layout of the Yugoslav political field, the mobilization potential of religion was more readily recognized via its close association with nationality. Even if this recognition led to the introduction of policies hostile to religious institutions, it encouraged the representatives of religious communities to serve as spokesmen for their respective national communities. Attempts at theological justification will follow.

Vasić's presentation of the problem quoted at the opening of this chapter is illustrative of the concern for the nation and national progress being tied to and growing out of the concern for the broader societal development. The Serbian Orthodox Church had no doubts as to whether it was necessary to preserve religion as a central marker of Serbian national identity, nor did it intend to drop its own national character for the sake of Yugoslav national unity. It rejected with indignation the idea that the Serbian Orthodox Church should omit the word 'Serbian' from its name because it infringed upon Yugoslav unity. In rejecting this possibility, Dimitrije Najdanović built upon the already well-established narrative of the sacrifices the Serbian nation (and the Serbian Orthodox Church) had made for the common cause. Importantly, we can see in his argument the substitution of the martyrdom of the Serbian nation by the martyrdom of the Serbian Church: 'Any sacrifice by [the Serbian nation] is in the first place a sacrifice by the Orthodox Church, which has created and nurtured Serbdom, preserved it and filled it with the morality of Piedmont self-sacrifice.'[97] Najdanović pays lip service to the official understanding of Yugoslavism, saying that it is about 'the cultural synthesis of the healthiest elements of the experience, capacities and the spirit of the three peoples [Serbs, Croats and Slovenes], the apotheosis of their virtues'.[98] At the same time, he makes it quite clear, without stating it directly, that East Orthodox culture is superior to other cultures, and that it is the East Orthodox Church that should lead the national struggle.[99] Similar attitudes were behind the assumption that all Yugoslav school children should participate in the celebrations of St Sava – a Serbian Orthodox saint and a patron of national education.

Overall, in the period from the mid-1920s to the mid-1930s the Serbian Orthodox writers shift the focus of their attention from the Yugoslav *state* to Yugoslav *nationalism*. Once it was an ideology that had to be dealt with, a natural response was to create an alternative ideology or political programme that could be used to promote the interests of the East Orthodox community. Although the government was very much inclined towards secularization policies, the overall character of the Yugoslav state remained to be shaped by Christianity. Because the dynasty was Serbian Orthodox, politics were dominated by the Serbian element, and the Serbian Church started to have a more visible public presence, the overall impression of King Aleksandar's regime was that it favoured East Orthodox Christianity. In the eyes of the non-Orthodox members of the political establishment, especially if they already were in opposition to the government, that was yet another reason to work against the existing political regime. King Aleksandar was aware of the complications that arose from his belonging to the East Orthodox faith. Ivan Meštrović recalls in his memoirs, how the king commented that his position in matters of interreligious relationships was delicate not only because both [Roman Catholic and East Orthodox] churches had gained in political strength and had conflicting agendas, but also because of his being Orthodox.[100] The Serbian Orthodox Church also contributed to the strengthening of the link between religion and nation. New Orthodox churches were constructed throughout the country in the 1920s and 1930s. It was not only the fact of building a Church in a certain area (with a bigger or smaller East Orthodox population), arguably that was often necessary given the wartime destruction, but also a question of style. The Neo-Byzantine, or Serbo-Byzantine style was dominant in the 1920s and early 1930s in both Church and secular architecture. St Mark's cathedral in central Belgrade, designed by the Krstić brothers as an enlarged replica of a fourteenth-century church in the Gračanica monastery is one of the most telling examples.

4

Climax: The Serbian Orthodox Church enters politics

This chapter explores the period from the death of Aleksandar Karadjordjević to the start of the Second World War. In just a few years, the Serbian Orthodox Church made its final steps to enter the political arena as a force to be reckoned with. As the previous chapters have demonstrated, religion had been a part of political life in Yugoslavia since its inception. The critical difference was that now the Serbian Church advocated for itself, not supporting a secular state or a political party. It has indeed become an independent political actor. It has nearly completely withdrawn its support for the Yugoslav project and shifted the focus of its attention to the Serbian nation. It entered politics to defend itself against the perceived threats of religious competition, unfavourable state regulation of religious life and secularization. A prime example of this newly found independence is the Concordat crisis of 1935–7. Although perhaps the best known – and hence the most written about – instance of confrontation with the government, the crisis is illustrative of a more profound process.

To justify this engagement with politics, key East Orthodox thinkers and writers of the period pursued several lines of reasoning. This level of intellectual engagement was also new compared to the preceding decades. One approach dominated all others – *svetosavlje* – the ultimate fusion of Serbian nationalism and East Orthodox Christianity. Several factors had to come together to make this possible, among them the sudden death of Aleksandar Karadjordjević, relaxation of the rules guiding the public sphere and changes to the country's administrative structures. This chapter tells a story of the Serbian Orthodox Church presenting an ideological response to the challenges of modernity in the form of *svetosavlje* and of the marginalization of alternative pathways.

Political Orthodoxism

The new reality of the Serbian Orthodox Church's participation in public politics, together with the desire of the Church to define and impact public life underpinning its actions, could be termed 'political Orthodoxism'. The political stance of the Serbian Orthodox Church tended to be conservative, at times anti-modern, and often favouring Serbian interests. But none of these were predetermined or unchallenged. Political Orthodoxism as a category, is broader than 'clerical fascism' or even 'clerical nationalism', it does not limit the political participation of the clergy and other members of the East Orthodox community to a particular ideological option. Instead, it points at the fact of political involvement in general. It is a useful tool to make sense of the ideological trajectory of the Serbian Orthodox clergy in the late 1930s and 1940s. Political Orthodoxism evokes a parallel with political Catholicism. However, they relate to each other more as a metaphor rather than being structurally similar. The same applies to the relationship between 'Catholic action' and 'Orthodox action'. Political Orthodoxism was an expression of the East Orthodox community coming to terms with the modern world in all its complexity. The term was originally coined in interwar Romania, where Nichifor Crainic, a religious thinker with a theological background as well as editor of the important journal *Gindirea*, and Lucian Blaga, a poet and philosopher, worked towards the creation of a theory that would answer the challenges posed to Romanian society by modernity.[1]

By the second half of the 1930s Serbian religious elite had accumulated sufficient intellectual capital, the result of successful earlier efforts to improve educational level of the clergy, to reflect more consistently on the nature of modern public politics, and the role and place of religion in it. Dimitrije Najdanović, one of the leading theoreticians of the Serbian Orthodox Church in the 1930s, advocated the necessity of involvement in political life to advocate for itself and the impossibility of political impartiality for the church as an institution and a community. That represented a sharp contrast with the attitude articulated in the previous decade, when the Serbian Orthodox clergy justified their political involvement by claiming to work for the good of the secular state and by contributing to the general societal development.

Najdanović discussed the problem in abstract terms, without drawing examples from contemporary Yugoslav politics. His ideas were meant to be relevant universally. At home, his position was in line with Patriarch Varnava's views, who defended the right of Orthodox priests to take part in political life, when their community was threatened.[2]

Najdanović's argument was built on the assumption that ideas, including political ideas, are superior to any material substance, although the two form parts of the indivisible whole. Hence, any conflict between political actors, parties or states is only a reflection of a more fundamental struggle between ideas. Najdanović believed that Christianity – one of the fundamental ideas of the modern world – was now under attack and in need of defence. This is similar in essence to Catholic *Rerum Novarum*, in which the Pope called for the Catholics to defend their worldview and political opinions based on their religious beliefs. Najdanović used Carl Schmitt's notion of 'political theology' in support of his theory of Christian foundation of all modern politics. It was the proof of Christianity's superiority over any secular ideology.

He argued that modern political ideologies of Marxism, social democracy or liberalism are ultimately the same as traditional religion in their pathos and dogmatism. He came very close to characterizing them as 'political religion'. His interest, however, was not in the analysis of the functioning of modern ideologies, but in giving a theoretical justification to a politically independent position of the church. Going back to the well-established narrative of the dangers of secularization, Najdanović concluded that if Christianity and modern political ideologies operated in similar ways and competed on the same field, then any political struggle could be characterized as a 'war for religion' where the issue at stake was whether Christianity or some other 'religion' would win.[3] Consequently, it was necessary to create and/or support such a force in society that would promote Christian values and a Christian worldview. This again, was not a novel idea, but the systematic thinking behind it was new. It also released the Serbian Orthodox Church from any restraints that it may have felt regarding its loyalty to the secular Yugoslav state. If the Yugoslav government did not support the Serbian Church to an extent required by the struggle with other political ideologies, the Church was free to act against the state.

Najdanović articulated the theory underpinning the actions of the Serbian Orthodox Church in 1935–41, his own version of political Orthodoxism. Even when a question under scrutiny was of a pure institutional or administrative nature, the Church was guided by it. 'War for religion' was in the background of the debates on the national question as well. This chapter will demonstrate how the national question was used by clerical circles to create the basis on which clergy would build their politics, and how religious mobilization was attempted by appealing to national sentiment. Although during the Concordat crisis anti-government opposition made use of the crowds mobilized by the Serbian

Church, the relationship between the East Orthodox religious community and the secular political forces, including the government and the Crown, has changed compared to the earlier period. If in the 1920s the Serbian Church was generally happy to lend its support to the Yugoslav political project, by the late 1930s it no longer advocated for Yugoslav national unity or religious tolerance even nominally. As this chapter will show, the intertwining between East Orthodox Christianity and Serbian nationalism became the strongest in this period. The ultimate goal of the Church was not the promotion of Serbian nationalism per se (as many of its opponents and critics have suggested), but the victory over secular ideologies.

After the assassination

The death of King Aleksandar in 1934 came as a shock to the Yugoslav political establishment and citizens. While the state was paralysed by the news of the assassination and people rallied behind the legacy of the fallen monarch, backroom arrangements were conducted to secure the transition of power. The issue of the utmost importance was the office of the head of state. The king's eldest son, Petar, was an infant, and the Constitution provided for a regency. However, it gave no indication as to the composition of such a body. The scrutiny of the king's papers resulted in finding a hastily written last will, which suggested that the regents should be Prince Paul, the late king's cousin; Radenko Stanković, professor of medicine, physician, and former minister of education; and Ivo Perović, the former assistant minister of interior. The dispute that occurred over the authenticity of the document between Prime Minister Nikola Uzunović and General Petar Živković was a clear symptom of the weakness of the system established by the dictatorship.[4]

With the support of General Petar Živković, the dead king's trusted man in the military, Prince Paul successfully removed Uzunović and established himself as an unofficial head of the regency. The newly established government of Bogoljub Jevtić did not get the necessary support and was short-lived. The pro-governmental block headed by Jevtić received about 60 per cent of the vote in the (manipulated) elections of May 1935, while the united opposition block, headed by Maček, who was released from prison in December 1934, received 37 per cent. Prince Paul decided that a new figure was necessary and appointed Milan Stojadinović as prime minister. He stayed in this position until early 1939 when Cvetković took over.

Although Prince Paul repeatedly claimed that it was not in his powers to alter the Constitution, he considered revising it to bring back some form of parliamentary democracy and – probably – decentralization. In 1936, Prince Paul sought advice on this matter from Yugoslavia's four leading constitutional experts and was told that the proposed changes could indeed be made under the existing legislature.[5] Stojadinović, the new prime minister, was also in favour of the liberalization and, importantly, was not a staunch supporter of integral Yugoslavism.[6] He aspired to be a Serb counterpart to Maček, Korošec and Spaho, all of whom were recognized as leaders of their respective national communities.[7] During his premiership Stojadinović failed to unite the Serbian political elite due to its diversity, and importantly because he did not have the support of the Serbian Orthodox Church.

The Constitution remained unchanged, but important changes were introduced to the rules of public engagement. Most importantly for religious communities, censorship was, if not lifted, significantly liberalized. This almost immediately resulted in the growth of the number of religious periodicals (some short-lived, others with a longer presence) that took a critical stance towards the state and the regime and invested a lot of time and effort into discussing contemporary social and political issues. Among the most influential and intellectually important publications in the Serbian Orthodox community were *Hrišćanska misao: Časopis za Hrišćanska i društvena pitanja* (Christian Thought: A Journal for Christian and Social Issues), published in 1935–41 and edited by Djoko Slijepčević, who was close to Dožić and Velimirović; and *Svetosavlje: Organ studenata Pravoslavnog bogoslovskog fakulteta* (Svetosavlje: Publication of the Students of the Orthodox Theology Department), published in 1932–41. *Svetosavlje* turned more radical and nationally oriented (if not nationalist) around 1937. Both journals envisaged their audience to be comprised of educated theologians (lay and clerics), whose interests transcended narrow dogmatic issues. These and other publishing initiatives formed a platform for a more open and increasingly radical discussion on the role and place of religion in modern society, which was not possible before the death of Aleksandar.

Religion continued to be an important factor in the post-dictatorship political life, and some even suggested that the clergy should be represented in the regency. Once Prince Paul was confirmed as regent this possibility was dismissed. The Serbian Orthodox Church used the burial of King Aleksandar as an opportunity to affirm its importance to the stability of the shaken state. Envisaged as a spectacle of popular unity, the king's body was transported across the country, with the people paying their respects along the way. The culmination of the procession was the burial ceremony in Oplenac Church in Topola, attended by the era's crème de la crème of European statesmen showing solidarity. Footage of the assassination and the burial was widely screened in Yugoslav cinemas, showing inter alia the East Orthodox priests taking a prominent part in the ceremony. The official documentary in fact ended with the waving of censers in the church. The representatives of other congregations naturally attended, but the king was buried in accordance with East Orthodox ritual. At the same time, the Orthodox priests were very vocal in sermons dedicated to King Aleksandar, who posthumously became not only the 'Chivalrous King Unifier' but also the 'King-Martyr'.

The Orthodox Church contributed a great deal to the creation of the image of the King-Martyr and had always, regardless of its opinion on the Yugoslav state, held Aleksandar Karadjordjević and his memory in high esteem. In the years following his death, Aleksandar's martyrdom was at times elevated almost to the level of the martyrdom of Prince Lazar, one of the foundational mythical figures for Serbian national and religious imaginary. On the fifth anniversary of Aleksandar's assassination, a contributor to *Hrišćanska misao* wrote: 'October 9th is forever the day of our pain. But it is also the day of our glory. Suffering is catharsis.'[8] Suffering and catharsis are, of course, fundamental religious experiences in the eyes of the Christian Church. On the national level, 'catharsis was made into the first principle of history'. Thus, Aleksandar, although not a saint, was symbolically put in the same cohort of medieval Serbian rulers, most of whom were saints and national patrons.

In October 1939, the Serbian Church organized numerous ceremonies to commemorate the fifth anniversary of the heroic death of the king. Liturgies, services and the like took place all over the country, from Oplenac and Belgrade to the smallest countryside villages. It is symptomatic that, in the plentiful eulogies by the Orthodox clergy (which were often wholly or partially republished and thus made available to the broader public), Aleksandar Karadjordjević was praised not only for his achievements regarding 'liberation and unification', but also for being a truthful son of the Orthodox Church. Jovan, Bishop of Niš, gave a speech in the Oplenac Church in which he said the following:

> Our Church lost its prime faithful son, who loved his Church and religion and adhered to national traditions, but he also did not underrate other religions and churches in his Fatherland; and on the contrary, [he] respected them and protected, defended and helped them all equally.[9]

What on the surface seems like a continuation of the already familiar embrace of religious diversity, in 1939 was meant as a reprimand of Cvetković and Prince

Paul who were juxtaposed with the idealized image of Aleksandar. After the Concordat crisis and just after the Cvetković–Maček agreement such a statement was a thinly veiled criticism of the government's attempt to change the rules of the regulation of religious life, even though it was Aleksandar himself who initiated a new round of talks with the Vatican. It was symbolic of the drastic shift which was finalized in these years: from the overwhelming support of Yugoslav secular authorities to their sharp criticism.

1935–7: The Concordat crisis

One of the key events of the 1935–41 period was the Concordat crisis – it demonstrated with certainty that the Serbian Orthodox Church was able and willing to stand up to the government. The issue of relationship with the Vatican had persisted ever since the establishment of the new state. Although the first draft of the agreement was written in 1922, negotiations with the Vatican started only in 1925 and proved insufficient to resolve the difference over the use of the Slavonic language. At the same time, the proposed agreement was met with criticism by many domestic politicians, including the influential Croatian leader Stjepan Radić. The talks were suspended to be resumed only after the imposition of the dictatorship. In 1933, at the king's own initiative, the issue was put back on the agenda, mostly because the question was connected to relations with Italy. Complex negotiations were underway, but the king's assassination caused a delay of the contract, most of which had already been drawn up. One could speculate as to whether Aleksandar would have faced similar challenges as the ones his successors met in attempting to promote the Concordat and secure political support for its adoption. This issue had fallen on the shoulders of the regency and the newly appointed Prime Minister Milan Stojadinović.

In 1935, when Stojadinović contacted the Serbian Orthodox Church regarding the signing of the agreement, the Church voiced serious disagreements without yet making them public. The thirty-eight articles of the Concordat fixed the position of the Roman Catholic Church in Yugoslavia as equal to all other 'recognized religions' in the country, confirming the already existing national legislation; the bishops selected by the Catholic Church were to take an oath to the king upon assuming their offices. The state in turn secured financial help for the Catholic Church proportionate to the support provided to other religions. The Catholic Church also received financial compensation for the lands nationalized during the agrarian reform. Finally, religious education in majority Catholic schools was made compulsory under the supervision of the local catholic authorities. When the text of the agreement was submitted to Parliament in late 1936 for its ratification, the public debate almost immediately became very heated.

The Serbian Orthodox Church vehemently opposed the planned agreement. It saw the Concordat as granting the Catholic Church a more privileged position in contradiction to the principle of equality of religions guaranteed by the Constitution. Patriarch Varnava summarized the objections to the settlement in an open letter to Prime Minister Milan Stojadinović.[10] In addition to the alleged violation of the principle of equality of religions, he pointed out the fact that, according to the Concordat, the state would have surrendered part of its powers to an exterritorial institution (i.e. the Roman Catholic Church with the centre in the Vatican), and finally remarked on the financial arrangement working against state interests.

A comprehensive account of the discussions and debates among the hierarchs of the Serbian Orthodox Church and the impact these debates had on the fragile balance of power in the country remains to be written. It is nevertheless clear that the Serbian Church's unwillingness to accept the Concordat was used by opponents of the Stojadinović government. One could speculate indefinitely about the oppositional forces that wanted to change the regency to Queen Marija, General Vojislav Tomić and Patriarch Varnava (as was allegedly written in Aleksandar's 'real' testament) and whether Varnava and his closest associates acted independently or were manipulated.[11]

Either way, on 19 July 1937, Parliament started the ratification discussions and, that same day, the Orthodox Church organized an open-air liturgy in the centre of the capital to pray for the improvement of the Patriarch's health, who had fallen ill. Belgrade city authorities prohibited the passing of the procession through the city centre. There were clashes with the police and the demonstration increasingly gave the impression of being anti-Stojadinović, not just anti-Concordat. One of the priests leading the demonstrations, Bishop Simeon, was wounded and had to be taken to hospital. The talk of the injuries that he suffered was greatly exaggerated in the press; the publications were often accompanied by a series of pathos-inducing photographs. Mainly due to this fact, the event was labelled the 'Bloody Liturgy'. Some of the opposition forces joined the street processions, among them the supporters of Dimitrije Ljotić, General Živković and even the Communists, all of whom hoped to gain ground in this time of chaos and unrest. However, no major opposition parties sided openly with the Serbian Church in July 1937, although the Democrats had openly criticized the Concordat plans in 1936.

When Parliament voted in favour of the Concordat on 23 July, the Assembly of Hierarchs of the Serbian Orthodox Church pronounced an anathema against everyone who voted for it. That same night, Patriarch Varnava died. The ungrounded rumours that the Patriarch was poisoned spread through Belgrade and across the Serbian part of the country. That exacerbated the already unstable situation and further clashes took place outside the capital. The British newspaper *The Times*, which in general followed the conflict between the Yugoslav government and the Serbian Orthodox Church very closely, reported that a proclamation prepared by the Serbian Church on the occasion of the Patriarch's funeral was banned by the authorities since it compared Varnava to Aleksandar Karadjordjević both of whom 'died for their cause, at the time they were most needed by their people'.[12] Under pressure, Stojadinović had to back up and withdraw the Concordat agreement from Parliament. The crisis showed that the government, despite its somewhat brutal ways of dealing with the demonstration of public protest, was not very strong, and that made the opposition hopeful. By October 1937, an agreement was reached between the Croats and the Serbs, and the Bloc of the National Agreement was formed. Its members called for the restoration of a democratic regime and a solution to the Croatian question as the two key steps necessary for the stabilization of the situation.

In the latter part of 1937 both the Serbian Church and the regency tried to resolve the conflict and find ways to cooperate. Ultimately, 'the Concordat project' of Prince Paul and Milan Stojadinović failed, the document was withdrawn from Parliament and the Serbian Church post factum assured the state that its protest was not directed against the secular power per se, but personally against Prime Minister Milan Stojadinović. The status of the Catholic Church remained unclear. Prince Paul and Stojadinović regarded the agreement with the Holy See to be important both from an international perspective (because it would improve relations with Italy) and a domestic one (because it would help resolve the 'Croatian question'). Maček, who was aware of Stojadinović's plan to win over some of the Croatian sympathizers by signing the Concordat, never supported it. Maček's position demonstrates that he did not see the Croatian question in religious terms and believed that religion had no place in politics. Moreover, he insisted that the Croats 'are a catholic, not a clerical nation', thus presenting Catholicism as a cultural characteristic.[13] After 1937 Stojadinović was gradually pushed aside, with Dragiša Cvetković emerging as the person entrusted with power and Prince Paul's confidence. Despite a victory in December 1938 elections Stojadinović's government fell in February 1939.

Recent scholarship on interwar Yugoslavia suggests that next to the Serbo-Croatian conflict, which had been habitually cited as the main reason for the instability and eventual collapse of the state, there were equally important division lines within the main ethnic groups.[14] Going one step further, the interwar period is interpreted as a time of numerous attempts to work towards an agreement between the Croats and the Serbs, not only as their constant fight. In the Serbian case, the intra-ethnic rift is usually associated with the rise of Serbian nationalism and increasing dissatisfaction with integral Yugoslavism aggressively promoted during the dictatorship. The centralist solution adopted in 1918 and continuously supported by Aleksandar and the regency share the responsibility for the instability of the interwar state. The events of the summer of 1937 demonstrate that the Serbian Orthodox Church had become an important actor in the relationship with the Croats, as well as among the Serbian political establishment. Its new position makes it more difficult to clearly see the boundaries between religious life and secular politics. It is important to have this analytical distinction even for the period where day-to-day politics and religious life were closely intertwined to be able to see how the Serbian Church attempted and succeeded to win the public over.

Discussion and polemic about the Concordat are less interesting as far as the actual content of the agreement with the Vatican, but the articles of the document singled out for criticism and the style and rhetoric employed deserve attention. These debates, and opinions articulated in them, are interesting because of the additional meanings of which the authors were not necessarily aware. It is not the Concordat per se that is under scrutiny here, but the discursive field that was formed around it in the years 1935–7 and some of the political implications of the debate.

The reasons for the Serbian Orthodox Church's hostility towards the new Concordat are almost impossible to grasp from the debates alone. The opposition came from its inability to fully accept the reality of a religiously diverse state, in which the Serbian nation was not (de jure) the dominant one. Towards the end of the 1930s, the prevailing understanding in the Serbian Church's political imagination was that East Orthodox Christianity, the nation and the state form an indivisible whole. Finer points concerned the rules of engagement in the public sphere.

The Serbian Orthodox Church put effort and energy into making the Concordat issue as publicly visible as possible: It published an incredible number of brochures as well as articles; important overviews published in other periodicals were reproduced in Church-run publications. A recurring argument against the proposed agreement used by both secular and religious speakers referred to the ban on public discussion of the Concordat, including publications in the press. The authors suggested that the government had expected negative reactions to its initiative and thus tried to avoid potential complications: a populist though effective strike at the Cabinet. By drawing attention to the issue of political censorship, the Orthodox clergy made a point that appealed to the democratic opposition.

Another point often made by the Serbian Church concerned the agreement's possible negative impact on the state. Here, in line with the rhetoric used in the 1920s, the Serbian Church presented itself as a defender of the state (not of the Serbian nation). Serbian clergy argued that the Concordat would damage religious peace in the country by disturbing the current balance and insisted that this was its main point of contention.[15] They underlined the potential threat to the stability of Yugoslavia. Such a position reveals that despite its claims of respect to all religious communities, the Serbian clergy willingly ignored the complaints of other religious communities, when it was not convenient to engage with them.

One of the assumed dangers was Roman Catholic missionary activities, which were to be allowed throughout Yugoslavia with no restrictions. The fear of Catholic proselytizing was one of the main driving forces behind the Serbian Church's opposition, and as discussed in Chapter 3 it was a well-established trope. The way this fear was presented to the public is not very surprising: The emphasis was laid on state unity, as it was impossible for the clergy to make a meaningful argument on the grounds of fear of religious competition. The Serbian clergy drew upon opinions of legal experts who pointed at the possible conflicts between the Concordat and the Yugoslav Constitution.[16] The Serbian Church seconded secularists' appeal to the 'sovereignty of the state authority' and the supremacy of the rule of law. In reiterating this criticism, the Serbian Church concealed the fact that it was directed against the Orthodox Church as much as it was directed against the Catholic institutions and displayed remarkable intellectual agility (a few years prior a lot of effort went into dismantling the argument it now supported).

Ribar called for the 'depoliticisation of the clergy' of all confessions, not only the Catholics. A very similar position was articulated by a Slovenian secularist, supporter of integral Yugoslavism, who accused the government of making too many concessions to the Vatican, which would result in a creation of 'a state within the state'.[17] The anonymous author claimed that no other state had signed a Concordat so favourable towards the Holy See. Together with Ribar, he was concerned about clericalism in politics and the fact that schools might become religious again, a clear step backwards in his eyes. 'We will return back to the dark Middle Ages', he writes, 'should we accept the Concordat'.[18] He feared that the Yugoslav-orientated *Sokol* movement would have a harder time competing with the Catholic Action youth organizations.[19] The activities of Catholic youth organizations, some of which indeed were critical of Sokol, were limited by the dictatorship and the new Concordat would reverse that in a direct threat to national unity.[20]

It must be said that the Croatian clergy did not exactly embrace the proposed agreement either, although for different reasons. A part of the Croatian Catholic clergy was unhappy with the division of dioceses (some of the Croatian dioceses were to be under the rule of the Archbishop of Ljubljana). In a mirror reflection of the secularists' concerns, some Catholic clergy (albeit a minority) thought that the Roman Catholic Church had conceded too much to the demands of the state. At the same time, Vlatko Maček, the leader of the Croatian Peasant Party and anti-clericalist, reportedly said that, among Croatian peasants, the Concordat was met with certain distrust as it gave priority in matters regarding land disputes to the Catholic Church.[21]

The Catholic archbishops, led by the Archbishop of Zagreb Dr Antun Bauer, denied that there was any possibility of religious unrest because of the Concordat. On the contrary, they emphasized that it was the opposition from the Serbian clerics which could 'provoke the unwanted religious struggle'. The argument thus reached a deadlock when both religious communities accused each other of undermining state unity. The logical impasse did not stop the Serbian Orthodox clergy, as time went by the tone and the rhetoric became more violent and uncompromising.

Apart from the habitual allusions to the sacrifices the 'long-suffering Church' made for the good of Yugoslavia, there were also more radical statements. The Montenegrin clergy compared the Concordat to the Ottoman invasion and claimed that Montenegrin clergy and people had never in their entire history yielded to the enemy and they would not do so now.[22] The reasons to oppose the agreement were already familiar: the alleged danger to religious peace in the country and concerns for the sovereignty of the state. In contrast to the more cautious voices of the Serbian clergy in Belgrade, those from the margins of the Yugoslav East Orthodox territories openly stated that they opposed the Concordat to secure the 'centuries-old, historical position of the Serbian national Church in the Yugoslav state'.[23] The Montenegrin clergy did what those in Belgrade could not afford to – it stated openly what it really wanted: a privileged position for the Serbian Orthodox Church. By 1937 most of the lower clergy and some hierarchs have abandoned even the pretence of supporting the Yugoslav nation-building project and opposed the Concordat because it violated Serbo-Orthodox religious interests.[24]

Patriarch Varnava had to be more careful with his choice of words. In one of his wrathful speeches against the Concordat he avoids the distinction between the Yugoslav and the Serbian nations. In the following quote, 'the entire national organism' refers to Yugoslavia, while 'the national saint church' is the Serbian Orthodox Church:

> We are accused of bringing politics into the church! We do not bring in politics into the church, but those who have lost reason, patriotism and respect bring poison to the entire national organism ... Who else will tell the truth to the people if not the national saint [St Sava's] church?[25]

A clear populist touch in Varnava's speech demonstrates that the Church in its official institutional capacity aimed at attracting not only the believers, but also the entire national community, that is the people. Rhetorically though, it was Archbishop Nikolaj Velimirović who authored the most radical and most powerful speeches. He employed his considerable talent as a writer and public speaker to make the Concordat project fail:

> Raise three fingers Orthodox Serbs! This popular rebellion does not undermine, it will fortify our homeland. Down with all antinational elements: parasites and bloodsuckers, capitalists, godless and communists! The Serbian faith is awakened because it is hurt. Serbian national consciousness is awakened because it resists the attack from all internationalists and those who build bridges for the Pope of Rome and his Church – the oldest international, the oldest fascism, the oldest dictatorship in Europe![26]

Velimirović uses the same set of references here as in his texts on *svetosavlje*, but with a clear populist touch to them. In the Archbishop's value system 'international' was a qualification as bad as 'fascist'.

The Concordat crisis exposed an important shift in the position of the Serbian Orthodox Church – it demonstrated its readiness to go against the government. The combined efforts of the Serbian Orthodox Church and secular opposition led to the withdrawal of the Concordat from Parliament and eventually to the fall of the government and the prime minister ultimately contributing to the destabilization of the state. Throughout the crisis the Serbian Church continued to claim that it was committed to supporting Yugoslavia, but its actions revealed that the Serbian clergy's and government's understanding of what was good for Yugoslavia have diverged. The Serbian Church selectively embraced such criticism of the Concordat that was possible to twist into an anti-Catholic position. It thus demonstrated its ability to manoeuvre on the political scene and choose allies from the ranks of former enemies when needed. It was in these years that the Serbian national interests were openly juxtaposed to the interests of the Yugoslav state for the first time. For the time being this position was articulated from the margins of the Serbian Orthodox Church.

1939–41: The breakup

The first 1939 issue of *Glasnik Srpske Pravoslavne Patrijršije*, the official bi-weekly periodical of the Serbian Orthodox Church, contained a curious publication – an excerpt from Franklin Delano Roosevelt's speech before Congress on 4 January 1939. The publication ran under the title 'President of the United States of America Mr Roosevelt on freedom of religion' and included the following passage:

> There comes a time in the affairs of men when they must prepare to defend, not their homes alone, but the tenets of faith and humanity on which their churches, their governments and their very civilization are founded. The defence of religion, of democracy and of good faith among nations is all the same fight. To save one we must now make up our minds to save all.[27]

The excerpt was a preamble to an article discussing the difficulties experienced by the Serbian Orthodox Church and the need for a better state support. After the successful resistance to the signing of the Concordat, the Serbian clergy renewed its efforts to push for the official recognition of the Serbian Church's privileged position in the state and the guarantee of favourable conditions for East Orthodox Christianity and its institutions on the national level. In its quest to re-examine the principles of equality of religions and the rules of regulation of religious life, the Serbian Church borrowed from and creatively used a variety of sources. Even if it sometimes meant that these ideas were misrepresented to serve the goals of the Serbian Church. In this case, the Church drew on the authority of the American president who, in fact, spoke about the coming war in Europe, the supremacy of democracy over dictatorship and the need to safeguard American democracy. None of these issues interested the Serbian Orthodox Church.

Roosevelt started his address by underlining the importance of religion, democracy and 'international good faith' for America and the need to protect them. The main point of the speech, not included in the publication in *Glasnik*, was that the danger comes from the 'storms from abroad', from Nazi Germany. The Serbian Orthodox Church had no profound interest in democracy and did not speak out against the royal dictatorship while it was in place. It used the American president's words to drive home a different message – that religion was vital for political stability and world peace. In the Yugoslav context, it was suggested that the governmental recognition of the value of religion should be followed by giving more political power and privileges to religious communities. Given the Serbian Orthodox Church view that not all religious communities were equally good for Yugoslavia, it meant that more power should be given to the Serbian Orthodox Church at the expense of other religious communities and secular institutions of authority.

The persistence of the Serbian Orthodox Church (or at least the zeal expressed by some of its higher clergy) to continue the pressure on the government was met with criticism. A fraction of the Serbian Orthodox clergy (and of lay activists) who supported the idea of social work as exemplified by the God Worshipper movement in the 1920s continued to voice their concerns. They argued that political involvement of the Orthodox Church came at the expense of the attention needed to address the day-to-day problems of parishes, parishioners and priests. An anonymous author (most likely affiliated with the Agrarian Party in Montenegro) saw the reasons for the current crisis of the Serbian Church precisely in its too active political position as well as in its unwillingness to drop the fight around the Concordat, which, in the eyes of the author, came dangerously close to a 'fight to annihilation' (*borba do istrage*).[28] The lack of comprehensive national legislation on the regulation of religious life was seen as a problem. Curiously, the author blamed the Serbian Church for this, not the government of the Roman Catholics. At the source of the problem was the desire of the Serbian Church to secure for itself a hegemonic position in the new state and to become a 'powerful political factor' even though Yugoslavia was a religiously diverse state. His was a minority opinion, but the Serbian Orthodox community remained divided over the question of church-state separation in general and the relationship with the Yugoslav state in particular.[29]

In the short but intense period of 1939–41 the relationship between the Serbian Orthodox Church, now headed by the former Montenegrin Metropolitan Gavrilo Dožić, and the Yugoslav state (i.e. the government of Dragisa Cvetković and the regency of Prince Paul) became increasingly strained. Prince Paul complained that all Serbs were against him and that the Patriarch 'whom he had brought to power' and the Serbian Church in general did not support him.³⁰ Indeed, the higher clergy voiced its discontent with current governmental policies with increasing frequency. They were mostly concerned with the division of the Serbs (as a national and religious community) into multiple administrative entities. Given that in the previous two decades much of the Church's efforts were directed towards the creation and maintenance of a single Serbian national-religious community, their concerns are easy to understand.

According to the agreement signed between Maček and the Prime Minister Dragisa Cvetković in 1939, known under its Serbo-Croatian name *Sporazum*, the Croatian *banovina* was created. It comprised predominantly Croatian lands and had a considerable degree of autonomy. Under the agreement, the central government in Belgrade controlled defence, internal security, foreign affairs, trade and transport, but an elected Sabor and an appointee (*ban*) by the king were in charge of Croatian internal matters. There were rumours about giving the Croatian part more powers, even creating a separate currency, the kuna. As happened many times before, the reactions to the change were very much the reactions to rumours as well.

Irinej Djordjevic and Nikolaj Velimirović, the two figures of growing prominence and popularity, were among the most vocal critics of the Sporazum and came close to an open conflict with the government. The Assembly of the Hierarchs of the Serbian Orthodox Church fiercely debated the *Sporazum* and whether Orthodox clergy could and should take part in political life. Orthodox priests took an active part in a short-lived 'Pan-Serb movement' and were particularly active in Bosnia. The movement was created as a response to the inclusion of majority Serbian territories in the Croatian banovina and called for the secession of these areas. This movement known by its motto 'Serbs, rally together!' lost popularity by the mid-1940, once its supporters realized the new political arrangement was there to stay.

A few years before the Sporazum, in early 1937, an organization called the 'Serbian Cultural Club' (*Srpski Kulturni Klub*, SKK) was formed in Belgrade. It set for itself the task to define and defend Serbian interests in Yugoslavia. Of the seventy founding members of the Serbian Cultural Club, twenty-three were professors at Belgrade University and other educational centres, including five people who had been rectors of Belgrade University during the interwar period: Slobodan Jovanović, Pavle Popović, Vladimir Čorović, Dragoslav Jovanović and Petar Mićić.³¹ Among other members were high-ranking state functionaries, representatives of industrial and banking corporations, military generals and a number of well-known artists, architects and engineers.

Archimandrite Justin Popović joined the club few years after its foundation. There was no dictating members' political opinions; they belonged to a variety of political parties and held a range of political views. The idea to create such a society belonged to Slobodan Jovanović, a famous Serbian historian, intellectual and politician, who believed that some key Serbian national educational institutions were abandoned after the creation of Yugoslavia. Among them, he listed the Sarajevo-based *Prosveta*, *Matica Srpska* and church-school autonomies in the former Habsburg territories. This led to the neglect of the Serbs outside of Belgrade and central Serbian lands. Their best representatives were not members of a single government.[32]

The Serbian Cultural Club was conceived as a meeting place and forum for those who were interested in Serbian national culture, and according to Slobodan Jovanović's initial plan the organization had no immediate political goals.[33] Nevertheless, in the very first months of its existence the club presented itself and functioned as a platform for the negotiations between different Serbian political parties, as they were all concerned with the Serbian national question. Eventually it turned into an organization where Serbian national interests and demands were defined and formulated.[34]

The Serbian Cultural Club saw its aim as reworking Yugoslavism from an abstract ideology hostile towards any Serbian, Croatian or Slovenian national character into an organic unity of all national forces, which could maintain a sense of both their uniqueness and interconnectedness. This idyllic goal was supposed to be achieved through the gradual constructive work of the respective national elites. Jovanović underlined the difference between the Yugoslav state and the ideology of Yugoslavism, and therefore saw no contradiction in claiming to work towards the creation of the new Yugoslav identity and the fact that the two immediate tasks of the club were to preserve Serbdom and Yugoslav state unity.[35] Translated into the language of real-life policies it meant, first of all, opposition to increasingly aggressive Croatian nationalism. Orthodox priests, who were members of the club, did so as enthusiasts of the nationalist movement, not as religious workers.

Starting in mid-1940 however, the most pressing issue was not the administrative structure of the country, but whether Yugoslavia would join the Axis Powers and sign the Tripartite Pact. As pressure from Nazi Germany on the Yugoslav government mounted, public opposition to this idea grew. The Serbian anti-Pact opposition assembled around young Petar Karadjordjević, the heir to the throne. The Serbian Orthodox Church figured prominently among the military, political and public figures who opposed the agreement with Germany. The Patriarch repeatedly urged the Prince Regent not to sign the Pact. Amongst several prominent clerics Irinej Djordjevic and Nikolaj Velimirović were the most articulate critics of the agreement. Despite attempts by Prince Paul and Cvetković to convince the public of the need to join the Axis Powers to ensure the sovereignty and territorial integrity of Yugoslavia, they did not find the necessary support. On 27 March 1941, two days after Yugoslavia joined Germany, Italy and Japan, a coup d'état led by the General Dušan Simović and supported by the British brought down the regency and brought to power seventeen-year-old Petar II Karadjordjević, the last king of Yugoslavia.

That morning, Patriarch Gavrilo, in an address to the nation that was broadcast to radios all over the country (excluding Zagreb), supported the coup and praised the brave and courageous Yugoslav people who once again made the difficult choice in favour of 'the Kingdom of Heaven, that is, the kingdom of God's truth and justice, national unity and freedom'.[36] He appealed to the old tradition of martyrdom and past sufferings that had enriched and strengthened the nation spiritually. The reactions to the coup, the ensuing German attack and the occupation are discussed in the Epilogue.

Theorizing the nation

Nationalism as an ideology and as a political and cultural phenomenon has been on the radar of the Serbian Orthodox Church and other European Christian churches since the nineteenth century. In the nineteenth century, the attitude of East Orthodox churches to nationalism was generally hostile, they criticized it harshly due to its strong association with liberal secularism and materialism. There was no uniform East Orthodox theory of nationalism, and the individual churches and clerics made up their own minds guided by the specific circumstances in which they found themselves. The Ecumenical Patriarchate in Constantinople did officially condemn nationalism in the form of 'filetism' in 1872. From the mid-nineteenth century onwards, when many East Orthodox churches in Europe found themselves in independent or semi-independent nation-states, the issue of nationalism became tied to national sovereignty and thus to the issue of church–state relationship.

As the previous chapters have demonstrated, the Serbian Orthodox Church engaged with the question of national identity in a variety of ways, but it was only in the late 1930s that Serbian Orthodox intellectuals came to see the nation and nationalism as objects of theoretical or conceptual inquiry from a specifically Orthodox point of view. Some of the impulses for these theoretical considerations came from the Russian émigré community who settled in Belgrade in the early 1920s. Another source of inspiration was the theological thought of neighbouring Orthodox countries, namely Bulgaria and Romania.

Stefan Tsankov, a prominent Bulgarian theologian, and the head of the Theology department at Sofia University, was among those few Orthodox religious thinkers outside Russia who reflected on the matter. Tsankov reinterpreted the Byzantine tradition of *symphonia* to include nationalism as a category. In his words, 'in the Orthodox Church *the* nation is accepted and cherished as a historical given'.[37] Once the category of 'nation' exists, it ought to be included in the thinking on the relationship with the state and secular authorities. Tsankov differentiated between 'good' and 'bad' nationalisms – it was the bad version that got condemned in the nineteenth century. Meanwhile, 'good' nationalism did not contradict or undermine Christian beliefs and values and was very much acceptable and even desirable in modern society. The Church, of course, continued to be supra-national and universal in its nature. Tsankov embraced the fact that in modernity people were organized into nations. And since the church could not exist in isolation from society, it had to embrace the nation and nationalism, but it also had to make sure that it supported the 'good' kind. Tsankov presented the nation as a community, which served as a crucial link between family and humankind. This nation could and should be supported by an East Orthodox Church as it formed the 'body' of the Church, which the clergy and the institution of the church formed the 'spirit'. Should there be a conflict between the two, it is the task of the Church to persist and to bring the 'body' (i.e. the nation) into harmony with the 'spirit'.[38] Tsankov's reflection and rather eloquent theory was well known in Serbian Orthodox circles, and his reconsideration of the place of the nation vis-à-vis Christianity served as a model and an inspiration. It formed a coherent theoretic, but not yet theological, justification for the active national and political position of the Serbian Orthodox Church alongside that of Dimitrije Najdanović and the quest to nurture an Orthodox public.

Most scholarly overviews of the East Orthodox theological discussions of the period do not focus on nationalism. There was indeed very little international exchange amongst the representatives of East Orthodox Churches outside the ecumenical movement on the relationship between the Christian teaching and modern nationalism. The key theological discussion of the time had to do with the relationship with the Western theological traditions and the rise of the Neo-Patristic Movement. It was the Russian émigré theologian Georges Florovsky, who suggested at the First Congress of Orthodox Schools of Theology, held in Athens in 1936, that East Orthodox Christianity should renew itself and break free from the 'Babylonian captivity' to Western theology by liberating itself from the influences of Western scholasticism and returning to the Fathers of the Church.[39] This attitude was shared by many Russian émigré theologians and gained ardent supporters in Greece, Serbia and Romania. The Neo-Patristic movement 'became the hallmark of Orthodox theology in the 20th century', and the effort to de-Westernize East Orthodox theology 'overshadowed all other theological questions, as well as all the challenges the modern world had posed – and continues to pose – to Orthodox theology'.[40]

With this caveat in mind, it is possible and indeed important to discern the key ideas of the Serbian Orthodox intellectuals about nation and nationalism as modern phenomena. This aspect is often overlooked by historians of politics and society, as well as by the students of religious history. Radmila Radić, the leading authority on the twentieth-century history of the Serbian Orthodox Church, underlines the importance of the experience of living in a multinational and religiously diverse state, but does not delve into the nuances of the abstract arguments or the relationship with political modernity in general. In the second half of the 1930s for the Serbian Orthodox Church, the questions that structured the discussion were: the position of the Serbian Church vis-à-vis secular authorities and, increasingly, the emerging 'Serbian national question'. With rare exceptions, the more abstract conceptual claims are spread over several texts that dealt primarily with these very concrete socio-political issues.

Since the inception of Yugoslavia, the Serbian Orthodox Church thought of church–state relations differently from the secular authorities. From the clerics' point of view, church–state relations should be organized according to the nature of both the church and the state. While they did not spend too much time thinking about the theory of the state, they did spend considerable energy thinking about the church. In Christian thought the Church was not so much the sum of the clergy and its institutions as it was a community of believers. For the Serbian Orthodox Church it was also a national community. The Serbian clergy translated the Evangelical idea of Church as a community of believers into national terms and kept it as an axiom for much of its further thinking and reasoning.[41] The secular authorities, in their turn, saw the Church first and foremost as an institution and a legal entity. Such was the logic of a modern secular state, which at least nominally embraced the principle of equality of religions and was keen to regulate religious life. This explains the eagerness to sign the Concordat with the Vatican, or the rush to pass the Law on the

Serbian Orthodox Church in the 1920s. This fundamental difference between thinking about the Church as an institution versus community was at the core of the growing rift between the Yugoslav government and the Serbian Orthodox Church.

For all intents and purposes, the Serbian Church equated the community of East Orthodox Christians with the Serbian national community – that is, the nation – in order to create a 'national–ecclesiastical body' (*narodno-crkveno telo*).[42] This position was the most irksome to its opponents and the most cherished by its supporters because it gave the Church almost infinite possibilities for mass mobilization, including for political ends.

In Yugoslav context the consequences and implications of equating the community of believers to the national community were many. In the years from the death of Aleksandar Karadjordjević to the occupation of the country by the Axis Powers, some of the consequences became more apparent. The difference in rhetoric between the Patriarchs' enthronement speeches in 1924 and 1937 is a good example. As discussed in Chapter 2, in 1924 Patriarch Dimitrije lent his full support to Yugoslavia and, while making many references to the Serbian people, was careful to talk about other constitutive nations as well. In 1937, Gavrilo Dožić seemed oblivious to the existing religious and national differences in the country; and did not even hint at the heterogeneity and diversity of the state. His prime concern was his community – the community of the Serbian East Orthodox Christians. Dožić underlined the continuity between the medieval Serbian Church and the patriarchate, which he now headed. Thus, the more historically sensitive rhetoric from 1924 about *re*-establishing the patriarchate after centuries-long break was replaced by the rhetoric of an uninterrupted line between St Sava and the Serbian Orthodox Church of the 1930s.

This constitutes a major change in the official church discourse in just over a decade. The change becomes even more striking when compared to Yugoslav state rhetoric. Milan Simonović, Yugoslav minister of justice (religious affairs fell under his jurisdiction) present at the ceremony, underlined that the Serbs constitute a part of the Yugoslav nation, specifically mentioning the long tradition of the Serbian Church's tolerance towards other religions. In a rather stark contrast to the Patriarch, the minister emphasized the primacy of the state over church and of national unity over religious difference.

Another factor that contributed to the turning of the Serbian Orthodox Church away from the Yugoslav state and towards the Serbian national community was its anti-communism. 'It is a mistake [for the Church] to rely exclusively on the state. The state means nothing outside the nation and the church. It exists, really, as their function,' wrote the editor of *Hrišćanska misao*.⁴³ This radical statement was made in the context of the discussion of the 'Communist wave' in relation to the politics of the Soviet Union and the Spanish Civil War. It was not the first time that communism was condemned by the Christian hierarchs and intellectuals for its materialism, atheism and brutal anti-clericalism. Even if the danger of communism was exaggerated for the domestic Yugoslav context, it did loom large in the minds of more conservative public intellectuals, especially since the Russian émigrés arrived fleeing the horrors of the revolution, the civil war and Stalin's terror.

To sum up, a new conceptual understanding of nation underpinned the changing relationship between the Serbian Orthodox Church and the Yugoslav state and the change in attitude towards the Yugoslav state and the Serbian nation. In its most radical form, the new scheme suggested that neither the nation nor the state could survive without the support of the Church as the main guardian of East Orthodox Christianity. The next section will demonstrate how key Serbian Orthodox intellectuals came to support the Serbian nation, even if it had to happen at the expense of the Yugoslav state. What they had not envisaged was the disappearance of the state, as it happened in 1941. The Church, as it became clear soon afterwards, was bound if not to disappear with it, then to bear severe losses.

The national-religious synthesis

The end of the royal dictatorship and the willingness of the government to let go – at least to a degree – of the ideology of integral Yugoslavism coincided with the grand-scale nation-wide celebrations of St Sava held in 1935. The Serbian Orthodox Church led the people of Yugoslavia in celebrations commemorating the 700th anniversary of the death of Saint Sava, the founder of the Serbian Orthodox Church and patron saint of the Serbian nation. It announced 1935 to be the 'Year of Saint Sava', the so-called *Svetosavska godina*.⁴⁴ A sharp increase in the number of publications aimed at the general public accompanied the festivities. Combined, all of this led to an increased visibility of East Orthodox Christianity in the public sphere and to the Serbian Orthodox Church gaining new supporters as well as enemies.

Festivities were not limited to the East Orthodox religious community or ethnic Serbs. While many of the events and accompanying publishing campaign did indeed originate from the Serbian Orthodox Church, the state authorities lent their support to the many societies and clubs that organized celebrations locally. More importantly, festivities and celebrations were to be held in all schools across the country and in the army. The press was flooded with the texts of greater or lesser quality that reflected on the life and deeds of St Sava and his intellectual and spiritual heritage.

Vjekoslav Perica argued that 'historically the most relevant church-led myth-making in Yugoslavia began with a sequence of grand religious festivals and commemorations held between 1939 and 1941. These events expressed the ethnic churches' disillusionment with the Yugoslav idea and state, and called for a better future to be achieved, the clergy believed, by returning to ethnic roots and identities'.[45] In fact, the first significant public expression of the Yugoslav religious communities turning away from the Yugoslav project can be traced back earlier, to 1935 and the *Svetosavska godina*. The prominence of religion in national celebrations was typical for the interwar period in East Central Europe. As Cynthia J. Paces has argued at the example of Czechoslovakia, 'perhaps the appeal was the spirituality, passion, and magic that the era's liberal rationality otherwise stifled'.[46] Even in more secularized Czechoslovakia 'religious symbolism dominated nationalist commemorations in this era'.[47] Two of the three largest state celebrations in the 1920s commemorated medieval religious leaders – Jan Hus and Saint Wenceslas. The choice to celebrate Jan Hus, the famous heretic, left the Roman Catholic Church uneasy, but the significance of Hus as the national hero outweighed the potential undermining of Catholic authority. This tension between the emphasis on the national versus religious aspect of the medieval hero's heritage was central to the debates around St Sava.

Despite St Sava being one of the central characters of the Serbian oral culture, religious tradition and national epic, his cult in its present form can be traced back only to the early nineteenth century. Bojan Aleksov has noted that in Serbian nationalism, the cult of St Sava represented and reproduced 'powerful images of a national Golden Age, of national reconciliation and unification, and of martyrdom for the Church and the nation'.[48] It is fitting that his name was borrowed to define an ideology and a trend in religious-philosophical thought – *Svetosavlje* – which represents one of the most curious responses to the challenges of modernity as presented by the Yugoslav state, ideology of Yugoslavism and secularization.

The defining manifesto of the Svetosavlje ideology, 'The Nationalism of St Sava', was delivered by Nikolaj Velimirović in 1935 as a lecture at Kolarčev University during a week dedicated to East Orthodox Christianity. In this lecture, which was published later that year as a separate brochure, Velimirović discussed how St Sava had created the Serbian Church *and* defined the Serbian nation and thus essentially laid the foundations for the entirety of the Serbian national culture.⁴⁹

Velimirović regarded the establishment of what he called the 'national church' in the Middle Ages as the basis on which Serbian nationalism has been built ever since. Hence, the credit for everything created in the Serbian national sphere should be given to St Sava who founded the Church and gave the direction of the national development.⁵⁰ Velimirović interpreted nationalism very broadly, it encompasses the national Church as its basis and focal point, the national dynasty, the nation-state, national education, national culture and the feeling of national assertion. The Church acts as a spirit that resuscitates the entire national organism by illuminating it, inspiring it, and uniting it with one faith, one hope and one love.⁵¹ Because the Serbian Orthodox Church faithfully followed the direction indicated by St Sava, it is his rightful 'heir' or rather the embodiment of his spirit and ideas, and should be given credit for the establishment, endurance and survival of the Serbian nation.

The exact understanding of what church can be truly qualified as 'national Church' becomes of utmost importance in this argument. The national church, according to Velimirović, was

> an independent church organisation with the central authority coming from the nation and directed to the nation, with the national clergy, national language and national traditional expression of its faith. In opposition to such a national church stands a non-national or international church, with its centre outside the nation, with the clergy coming from everywhere, with a foreign language and with the unified, uniform expression of its faith. ⁵²

The national church was not only superior to a non-national one, but also more 'natural'. Clearly, Velimirović contrasts here the Serbian Orthodox Church (or any East Orthodox Church) to the Roman Catholic Church, which is more centralized with the Holy See in the Vatican and its clergy being more international, although the latter claim was far from the truth in interwar Europe. As this chapter demonstrated at the example of the Concordat crisis of 1935–7, such an animosity towards the Catholic Church, which in the Yugoslav context primarily meant the Catholic Church in Croatia, was not unique to Velimirović's thinking and was shared by a vast majority of clergy and common people in Serbia.

The genuinely new aspect of Velimirović's thought was not that the Serbian Orthodox Church made a significant contribution to the development of the

Serbian nation – this has been a widely accepted claim in Serbian historiography in the nineteenth and twentieth centuries. It was the claim that the Serbian Orthodox Church of the 1930s is the true and only possible foundation for the Serbian national culture and the Serbian nation. Velimirović's opponents, who advocated a secular, more modern path of development, did not contend his claims about the past, but did not agree with his vision for the future, especially when it came to the level of influence exercised by the Church.

Velimirović persistently argued for the closest possible ties between the Serbian nation and East Orthodox Christianity, which also implied the existence of the intimate connection between the nation-state and the Church. In the same 1935 lecture the archbishop cited the separation of church and state in many European nations as evidence of the ongoing crisis of morality in Europe. He called this decision of European intellectual and political leaders an 'act of desperation'.[53] Those representatives of the Serbian elite who saw these European developments as positive were, according to Velimirović, severely mistaken, as that was not progress, but nothing other than despair.[54]

This line of reasoning led Velimirović to make his most criticized statement, usually taken out of context:

> Hence, we see in these Western states an unbridgeable gap between the intelligentsia that is in pain because it does not believe in anything and the people that want to uphold their faith. Thus, respect should be paid to today's German leader who, being a simple craftsman and man of the people, saw that nationalism without faith is an anomaly, a cold and unsecured mechanism.[55]

It is not entirely clear what prompted Velimirović to praise German National-Socialists and their handling of the national question, especially given the importance of the pagan mythology and racial symbolism in Nazi public rituals and propaganda and less-than-perfect relationship with the Christian churches. It is likely, that Velimirović admired the anti-modernist attitude, the opposition to modern liberal secularism and the fact that the most important aspects of Nazi policy on religion were protecting the 'Germanic race'.[56]

Despite its common and frequent usage, Svetosavlje remained loosely defined throughout the interwar period, although the core ideas were always recognizable. In 1937, Danilo R. Medan in an article with the promising title 'The contours of St Sava's ideology and its meaning in the past and present' attempted to sketch the main points of this ideology. He followed Velimirović in stating that Svetosavlje emerged as the sum of deeds and teaching of St Sava, and that since then it has had the most profound impact upon Serbian nation, 'all our cultural and educational currents are inspired by St Sava's ideas'.[57] Projecting back into the thirteenth century the modern divisions between Eastern and Western Christianity, Medan claimed that Svetosavlje, and by extension the Serbian nation, was specifically Eastern Orthodox in its character, it was 'the beginning and the base of the national culture, which has been developing on the foundations of Orthodoxy'.[58] In short, Serbian culture and national character are essentially Orthodox.

Despite its seeming simplicity, Svetosavlje included a complex set of ideas that were not easily reconcilable. Sometimes it included a pan-Slavic idea (in its Orthodox form). Most often its proponents commented on the particular East Orthodox character of Svetosavlje and at the same time it was said to have a 'mission and character for all of humanity', that it was supposed to transcend national boundaries.[59] Klaus Buchenau remarks that Svetosavlje resembles the integral Yugoslavism of King Aleksandar, which also had claims of supra-national character, while keeping traditional Serbian iconography,[60] but this seems to be a superficial comparison as no Yugoslavism of any kind had ever had universal aspirations. For Velimirović, Medan and others, the importance of the spiritual legacy of St Sava was precisely because it opened a way for the Serbian culture to occupy its rightful place in world civilizations and an alternative to secular Yugoslavism, which, in their eyes, threatened the existence of the Serbian nation and culture. They saw St Sava as the first Serbian nationalist, but not a chauvinistic or intolerant one (quite in line with Stefan Cankov's idea of 'good nationalism'). 'Through Svetosavlje the Serbian racial element was absorbed into the Slavic element, which was absorbed into an evangelical or all-human one. In this way a unique and harmonious entity was created whose component parts maintain their racial characteristics'.[61] The tension between the universal religious component and the particular national one was the focal point of the debates about the legacy of St Sava that preoccupied the Serbian intellectual elite in the 1930s.

The year of St Sava with its abundance of publications led to the crystallization of distinct narratives and interpretations of St Sava's life and legacy, the role and place of the Serbian Orthodox Church, and the public role of religion more generally. The key difference in interpretation of Sava's historical and cultural significance was between those who saw him as primarily a national figure and a statesman and those who emphasized his activities as a religious figure. Both opinions had firm historical ground to be based upon. The debate revolved around the question of the 'true virtues' and Sava's historical legacy. Some Serbian clergy were unhappy that Sava was increasingly seen as a political figure, a secular national hero at the expense of downplaying his Christianity.

This meant a disagreement over what was more important: the foundation of the Serbian Orthodox Church as a *national institution* and Sava's efforts to emancipate it from the Greek hierarchs, or the Christian virtues he represented and promoted by his life and deeds?

Many secular intellectuals, artists and writers contributed to the glorification of Sava as a national hero. Miloš Crnjanski, one of the leading Serbian writers and poets of the interwar period published a book in 1934 under the simple title 'Saint Sava', in which he told the story of Sava's life and praised his diplomatic success in strengthening the medieval Serbian state.[62] The critical reaction by the Serbian Church followed almost immediately. In early 1935, Djoko Slijepčević published a detailed review of Crnjanski's work in *Hrišćanska misao*. Among other things Slijepčević was critical of the author's emphasis on Sava's nationalism rather than his piety. Slijepčević underlined Sava's ability to combine work towards building a national state with being the 'spiritual reviver' of the nation and, above all, Christ's missionary.[63]

Another contributor to *Hrišćanska misao* argued along similar lines, this time in a response to a polemical article by Sava M. Stedimlija published in the Zagreb-based journal *Nova Evropa*. There is no doubt that Milutin Devrnja's harsh response to Stedimlija had many supporters among Serbian clergy and the public. Devrnja strongly opposed claims by *Nova Evropa*'s journalist that St Sava was a powerful statesman, genius diplomat and politician, but had no connection to true Christianity.[64] Views similar to Crnjanski's disturbed the clergy so much that, a few months later, Devrnja published an article 'On the true understanding of the personality of St Sava' in which he continued to argue against overemphasizing Sava's political success at the expense of forgetting his spiritual experiences as a monk in Hilandar and his being 'a great Man of God, and of great religious and moral character'.[65]

The lesson drawn from the experience of having their main national saint 'highjacked' was that there was no more time left to waste. The Church had to act fast if it were to resist the corrupting, de-Christianizing secularization tendencies that had now been so clearly revealed. Proposed solutions included better organization of the Church and establishing and supporting local societies. It was at this time, that the Serbian Church became interested in and supportive of the grassroots movement of the God Worshippers, who had a broad network across the country and seemed open to exactly these issues, as discussed in the previous chapter.

These ideas reinforced and worked well together with the views expressed by the contributors to the journal *Svetosavlje* since the late 1920s. Najdanović and

Velimirović, who worked closely with the journal, steered it towards becoming more nationally exclusive and politically involved. The concept of Svetosavlje, as it has been described above, offered a new and powerful framing for the old problem of an a-religious national elite. One of the journal authors remarked that in Serbia, the intelligentsia learns about Orthodoxy from national songs and poems and through reading Dostoyevsky, which 'is enough to inspire, but not enough to incorporate' intellectuals into the religious community.[66] In the late 1930s the editorial position shifted from the earlier focus on social work and piety to calls for an active engagement by the Serbian Orthodox intellectuals in political debates in Yugoslavia and in Europe, primarily with the task to oppose anti-clericalism of liberal, fascist and communist modern ideologies. Svetosavlje was presented as an ideological alternative, which promoted Serbian national interests without sacrificing Christian values.

The establishment, popularity and long life of the Svetosavlje ideology supports the argument that modern nationalism as an ideology and practice is not necessarily confined to secular politics and culture. It is an interesting example of both religious nationalism and the sacralization of nation. It demonstrates how a nation can acquire characteristics of a sacred entity not by imitation of a religious ritual or by replacing an established religion, but by effacing the boundaries between national and religious communities. In this sense, the Serbian case fits a broader European pattern of establishing one's nation as 'the chosen nation' and incorporating religion in modern nation-building practices.

On 28 June 1939, the St Vitus (Serb. *Vidovdan*) was celebrated on a magnificent scale throughout the Kingdom of Yugoslavia to mark the 550th anniversary of the medieval Kosovo Battle. 'Massive outbursts of ethnic nationalist euphoria' accompanied the festivities.[67] All key national institutions, that is, the army, Orthodox Church, schools and Sokol societies were involved in the festivities. The festivals thus had religious, national and military character all at once, a powerful blend of mobilization techniques. Celebrations in Kosovo were by far the largest in the country, with Patriarch Gavrilo, Prime Minister Cvetković, Military Minister Milutin Nedić and representatives of the Parliament and the Senate present at Ravanica monastery which was central to the festivities. The *Naša Krila* aero club from Pristina took part with an impressive performance in the sky above Kosovo field. Military parades and performances by Sokol groups accompanied religious services, official speeches and wreath-laying ceremonies. Ravanica monastery in Fruska Gora, Vojvodina, where the relics of the Kosovo hero Prince Lazar were kept and displayed to the public in an icon case, also held grand-scale celebrations. Pilgrims from all over the country and as far away as

Sandžak attended the festivities. General Plecničar acted as a representative of the royal family at the ceremonies in Vojvodina.

Festivities were held very widely and were reported by the Church and national press. The official Church publication, *Glasnik Srpske Patrijaršije*, transformed seemingly overnight from a journal with strict rubrics and rather boring ecclesiastical content into an illustrated magazine with many pictures and relatively little text. In 1937 the journal started to publish numerous images to accompany the articles, mostly photographs capturing celebrations that featured high clergy and/or state officials. The editorial board of *Glasnik* found a way to make a contribution to nurturing an 'Orthodox public'.

The May 1939 issue of *Glasnik* was filled by a report on laying the foundations of the Cathedral of St Sava in Belgrade. The photographs in the report (in order of appearance) depicted the view of the imagined 'Future church of St Sava on the Vračar Hill in Belgrade'; 'Clergy and monks in a solemn procession' – an impressive scene of hundreds of people walking in a Belgrade street; 'Clergy in vestments in a magnificent liturgy' – also on the streets of Belgrade; 'Clergy and monks in an impressive manifestation of Orthodoxy' – rows of Orthodox priests going through a square in an orderly, almost military fashion; 'His Holiness Patriarch of Serbia Dr Gavrilo with Hierarchs in a procession', and six more including masses of people attending the ceremony and the Patriarch signing papers and sanctifying the foundations.[68] The ceremony and the procession were indeed unprecedented in their scale and organization. It must have been an overwhelming scene and experience for participants and observers capable to overshadow the memories of the preceding long and painful debates about the Cathedral.

Although the idea to build a church on Vračar Hill in Belgrade had appeared in the nineteenth century, it was only in 1935 that the construction works began. It took the Serbian Church many decades to come even to this point; projects, discussions and committees concerning the construction of the Church on Vračar Hill took a long time and displayed a range of opinions and visions.[69]

> The idea behind Belgrade's most ambitiously conceived architectural project was clearly to replicate the most exceptional magnificence and grandeur of the church [Cathedral of St Sofia] in Constantinople. The size and design were combined to anticipate the Serbian Church's success in overcoming the deep polarization of the Serbian society and to show that Serbs could unite and grow with their Orthodox Church.[70]

The debates in the committee who oversaw the future construction works would most likely have lingered on indefinitely (opposition to the neo-Byzantine style pushed by the Serbian Church was strong, and supporters of a more modern stylistic approach were many), if King Aleksandar had not used his powers of veto and granted permission to start the works in 1935. Another serious obstacle was the lack of active public interest and consequent lack of funds. A 1938 report explained this inertia by 'poverty, poor performance of the fund-raising committees [...and] disputes among political parties which prevented any common actions. The [Serbian Orthodox] Church itself was not spared from these disputes.'[71] The greatness of the 1939 celebrations marking the start of construction was meant to counterbalance the weakness displayed at the preceding phase.

Public displays of East Orthodox symbols reached its climax in 1939 demonstrating not only the apparent success of the Serbian Orthodox Church but also that the alternative, previously articulated options, however weak and marginal they may had been, had now completely disappeared and were beyond the horizon of the imaginable. A question remains whether there was an alternative path at least hypothetically available to the Serbian Orthodox Church leading to similar levels of public prominence without resorting to nationalist mobilization.

One alternative was presented by the God Worshipper movement, which by the mid-1930s had a well-developed network of local organizations, led by priests or lay activists. Although it is best known for its association with the fascist movement *Zbor* of Dimitrije Lotić, the members and leaders of the God Worshippers articulated a variety of opinions alternative to the 'national' path offered by Svetosavlje. Živan Marinković, an insider to the movement – he served as editor of *Hrišćanska Zajednica* in the early 1930s – believed that the movement offered a perfect solution to the problem of the people abandoning their Christian faith and 'religious-ethical ideals' in favour of materialism. People must have a 'healthy spirit' and 'strong faith' to be able to withstand the challenges of the 'difficult times'.[72] He suggested that the scale of the problem required a 'planned action', an 'Orthodox action' [Serb. *Pravoslavna akcija*] to be mounted by the Serbian Orthodox Church. Such an action would 'require manpower, and that [would require] effort and sacrifice'.[73] The Serbian Church, however, did not possess the manpower and was unlikely to succeed in this. The reason, according to Marinković, was simple – the Church had been weakened by its focus on national politics and lack of interest in social issues, which broke down the intimate connection between clergy and the community of believers. To restore this link and ultimately to successfully implement this Orthodox action, the Serbian Orthodox Church should use the God Worshipper movement as its base, for it had the required elements.

According to Marinković, the aims of this Orthodox action should be strengthening the people's religious-moral consciousness and the protection of the people and their souls from foreign influences and lies.[74] In this, he comes close to Najdanović's vision of political Orthodoxism, but in contrast to Najdanović, Marinković sought to revive parish life and reorient clergy from politics towards social and charitable work, and the help for the poor and disadvantaged.

His attempts were unsuccessful, as he calls, frustrated, for the Church to catch up with the world:

> New conditions and circumstances have been guiding the Church to move its activities from the national level to its own, [the level of] pastoral work. Meanwhile, our clergy especially older members, primarily in Serbia and Southern Serbia, who are used, in accordance with the acquired tradition, to work on the national level and with a cross in one hand and a gun in another, to leading people in the struggle 'for the holy cross and golden freedom' [*za krst časni i slobodu zlatnu*], today cannot deal with new conditions, nor can they see the need for reorientation in pastoral work, the need for return into their own sphere of work.[75]

There were other marginalized voices, mostly coming from the parish priests that supported Marinkivć's vision. One of the attendees of the conference held in Niš in 1939 argued that the times when work on the national level was needed were over, and in the current conditions the clergy should focus on their social and parish work. To this end, the movement of the God Worshippers seemed to offer a meaningful model.[76]

Marinković had several sources of inspiration, including the examples of revivalist religious movement in Bulgaria and West European lay activism. The Bulgarian experience was relevant for him insofar as it concerned the reorganization of the Church and the establishment of a special administrative unit for 'internal missionary work', an innovation that took place in Bulgaria in 1933. The Bulgarian Church was challenged by the revivalist Good Samaritan Movement, which combined two elements: royalist nationalism and religious mysticism. The political position of Good Samaritans was rather conservative. Their narrative of Bulgaria as the 'New Israel' was a type of post–First World War nationalist revisionism.[77] The movement worked closely with some of the most famous seers of the time, and in this capacity, as Valtchinova argued, rejected the official Church as the only institution with the authority to establish communication with God and established itself as an alternative religious authority. It was this claim that provoked the Bulgarian Church into harsh criticism and eventual subjugation of the movement. Valtchinova claims that 'in a sense, the Good Samaritan movement acted as a missionary church, in the face of an Orthodox Church that has never developed missionary policies aimed at what the Post-Reformation Roman Catholic Church called "inner conversion".'[78] The establishment of the special unit for missionary work was to fill this gap. Interest in spiritualism was not limited to the Serbian and Bulgarian contexts. In Romania, members of the group around the *Gindirea* journal 'were attracted to the speculative thought, mystical and religious experiences, and the primitive spirituality of folklore, and they were anxious to communicate their ideas in a modern idiom'.[79] West European influences include a multitude of phenomena ranging from pastoral work in Protestant sects to lay youth organizations of the Roman Catholic Church. Marinković's goal was not the isolation of the Serbian Orthodox Church from public life. But he disagreed with the use of national rhetoric and symbols to achieve a position of prominence. He aimed to reverse the opinion that faith and Church were not necessary for a modern person. His contribution was to the struggle against secularization and de-Christianization of the world. It went largely unnoticed.

The *Vidovdan* and other commemorations of 1939 are often cited as representative examples of the nationalist leaning of the Serbian Orthodox Church and as an indication of the failure of the Yugoslav political project based on the existence of a single Yugoslav nation.[80] They are however rarely interpreted as an element in a long line of developments, or even a culmination of these developments, which encompass the realization that the Serbian Orthodox Church needs to pursue a public campaign in the face of the crisis of modernity, a new theological take on modern nationalism, the response to secular Yugoslav nationalism in the form of the ideology of Svetosavlje, and finally the completion of the shift from the focus on piety and social work to the national issue, as exemplified by the evolution of the God Worshippers' movement.

The public embrace of nationalism by the Serbian Orthodox Church in 1939 is often discussed together with the parallel developments in the Roman Catholic Church, where the 1937 pilgrimage by the Archbishop Stepinac to Jerusalem kicked off a series of public events and celebrations intended to celebrate the 'thirteen centuries of Christianity in the Croat people'. This competition between the two churches is often interpreted as a competition between the two nations and a proof of the rising tensions between the Croats and Serbs in the kingdom. It should *also* be interpreted as an illustration of the lengthy transformation process that took place within the religious communities and led to their disillusionment with the Yugoslav political project. The turn to ethnic nationalism was neither natural nor easy for the Serbian Orthodox Church.

The themes discussed and questions faced by the Serbian Orthodox Church remained more or less constant throughout the interwar period. However, in the late 1930s the emphasis was on the national question. The years on the eve of the Second World War were characterized by an open conflict between the Serbian Orthodox Church and the Yugoslav government, which developed against the background of the continuous effort by the Serbian Orthodox Church to fight its main enemies: modernity and secularization. The idea of a synthesis between East Orthodox Christianity and Serbian nation prevailed and other options that were more cautious about such mixture were marginalized. This development by no means strengthened the Yugoslav political project, and only added fuel to the disagreement with the government, which was trying to save the common state by accommodating Croatian demands. The weakened Yugoslav state succumbed to the German attack in 1941. The impact of the state collapse and the Second World War on the Serbian Orthodox Church's relationship with the modern world is discussed in the next chapter.

Epilogue: The war

The story of the Serbian Orthodox Church grappling with modern politics told in this book is chronologically framed by the events of the two world wars. The First World War and its memory were paramount to the processes described and analysed in the four chapters. The role and place of the Serbian Orthodox Church in the Second World War probably deserve a book, or several, of their own. These undoubtedly will be written in the future. For this book, it is important that the political life of the Serbian Orthodox Church did not end in April 1941, when the Yugoslav government signed the armistice agreement, the army surrendered unconditionally and the country was divided into occupation zones by the Axis Powers. The Serbian Orthodox Church was instrumental during the March 1941 coup d'état and continued to play a role during the war years. After two decades of warnings about the crisis and a looming disaster, Serbian Orthodox thinkers continued to reflect on modernity, modern politics, state and nation, and the role and place of their religious institution – now in the circumstances of war and occupation, which presented new challenges.

This short epilogue to the story of the 1920s and 1930s sketches some of the intellectual and political choices made by the high-ranking representatives of the Serbian Orthodox Church in wartime. This is not a comprehensive account of the Church's actions in 1941–5. It focuses on Archbishop Nikolaj Velimirović, his associate Dimitrije Najdanović and a few others. They shared a political vision of the future of Yugoslavia and the Serbian Church in the prewar years. Still, they followed radically different paths after the occupation – of active resistance and collaboration. Henry Rousso emphasized the interconnectedness of the prewar status of an individual or a group and the war experience itself:

> Wars concern individuals with faces. These individuals belong to social groups that existed prior to, or developed in the course of the conflict. … Whatever the specific situation may have been, social groups and individuals were shaped by specific experiences during the war, which were frequently characterised by the

suddenness of events, by fear and uncertainty, sometimes even by fatalism, but at times also by a certain excitement in the face of the extraordinary nature of the events.¹

In line with Rousso's argument, to understand the political and moral choices of the Serbian Orthodox hierarchs and thinkers, we must look at their intellectual trajectories that have their roots in the prewar period. These stories also provide perfect proof that even minute differences in intellectual position can have significant political consequences, especially in extreme circumstances of war.

The memory of the Second World War

The Second World War occupied an important place in the ideological base of Socialist Yugoslavia and remains essential in the post-socialist period.² Under socialism, 'the People's Liberation War', the idea of 'brotherhood and unity' and antifascism were the centrepieces of historical narratives and official memory of the war. The legitimacy of Tito's Yugoslavia rested in part on the popular wartime support for the communist Partisans. Conflicts between various Yugoslav forces, the Holocaust, including Porajmos (the Romani genocide), were irrelevant to this discourse.³

As the socialist regime in Yugoslavia weakened in the 1980s and nationalist ideologies became stronger, the Second World War provided a fertile ground for disputes, disagreements and mutual accusations between the 'brotherly Yugoslav nations' instead of serving as a source of cohesion. From this new nationalist vantage point, victimhood and heroism became the key components of historical narratives and memorialization practices. In Serbia, the victimization narrative, which became a subject of controversy, 'focused on the genocide against Serbs in the Independent State of Croatia'.⁴ The urgent nature of the re-evaluation of the legacy of the Second World War was reinforced by the violence that accompanied the dissolution of Yugoslavia in the 1990s, and the widespread use of historical symbols and memories for political mobilization during the conflict.

While important for the relationship between the Yugoslav successor states, debates also took place *within* Serbian, Croatian and Bosnian national communities as academics, politicians and the public re-discovered the events of the Second World War. They were used to justify new political regimes, claims of autonomy and independence, to establish moral superiority, or reinforce a sense of national identity.⁵ The war continues to inform fierce public debates that divide the public in Serbia and other Yugoslav successor states. As part of the process, the role of the Serbian Orthodox Church as a national institution was also re-assessed. However, it appears to be secondary to the conversation about the key military players: the Chetniks of Draža Mihajlović, Partisans of Josip Broz Tito, the Zbor movement of Dimitrije Lotić and the collaborationist government of Milan Nedić. The primacy of political ideologies and coming to terms with the communist past directed the conversation about the role and place of the Serbian Orthodox Church during the war.

Even though socialist Yugoslavia was more tolerant of religious communities than the Soviet Union or GDR and religious institutions enjoyed some freedom and autonomy, they were constantly suspected of subversive action. In the immediate postwar years, the victorious communist regime engaged in a short-lived crackdown on religious institutions using allegations of wartime collaboration to undermine their leaders. The trial of Alojzije Stepinac is the most well-known illustration of this process. Assessment of the role and place of the Serbian Orthodox Church followed the general trajectory of the memory work in Serbia closely, at the centre of which since the 1980s was the rehabilitation of anti-communist forces. As Jelena Djurejnović demonstrated, the process was primarily limited to 'the rehabilitation of Chetniks and fascist collaborators as full-fledged patriots who fought the good fight against the onslaught of communist totalitarianism and for the preservation of the Serbian "golden era", the Kingdom of Yugoslavia'.[6] Attitudes to the Serbian Orthodox Church ranged from 'the saviour of the nation' to the accusations of betrayal and collaboration with the Nazi regime and its allies. The Serbian Orthodox Church had a role to play in memorialization practices as 'religious memorial services ... became a vital part of commemorations of victims of communism ... often involving the highest clergy of the Serbian Orthodox Church'.[7] In line with the well-established tradition, the Serbian Orthodox Church used these opportunities to underline its victimhood during the war and under communism by tying itself ever closer to the suffering of the Serbian nation.

The end of the Kingdom of Yugoslavia

The Second World War began for the Kingdom of Yugoslavia on 6 April 1941, with the bombardment of its capital, Belgrade. The German attack was caused by the coup d'état that took place some days earlier on 27 March, when the then seventeen-year-old prince Petar Karadjordjević became the king, and his uncle, the prince-Regent Paul, was overthrown. The main reason for the coup, organized by the military and widely supported by a coalition of the Serbian elite, was the signing of the Tri-Party Pact with the Axis Powers. The famous patriotic speech in favour of the putsch, which Serbian Patriarch Gavrilo Dožić read out on national radio shortly after the fall of Prince Paul, is widely believed to have been written or at least inspired by Velimirović.[8]

Shortly before the coup, Dimitrije Ljotić wrote a letter addressed to the Patriarch and two influential archbishops, Nikolaj Velimirović and Irinej Djordjević. He warned them not to take any abrupt actions regarding the already signed Tri-Party Pact. He suggested they demand from Prince Paul that a new strong government be formed to convince the people that their freedom, independence and well-being are not endangered. Ljotić pleaded and threatened at the same time: 'And if you are deaf to my plea and continue your anti-Pact activities, then you will put all responsibility for the collapse of the state and the nation on your shoulders and will stand in front of God as men who search the fame with people, not with God.'[9] Two aspects of Ljotić's letter stand out. Firstly, he must have been close to desperation to choose open confrontation with Velimirović, whom he held in high regard and whose idea of *Svetosavlje* he admired. Secondly, it is curious that in 1944 Najdanović employed a similar argument about the responsibility of Draža Mihailović's Chetniks for state collapse and the nation's suffering due to their support of the March coup and the monarchy. By 1944 Najdanović was closer to Ljotić than to Velimirović when it came to collaboration and support for Yugoslavia.

German occupation authorities targeted those members of the Serbian clergy who supported or participated in the coup d'état, opposed the occupation and supported the Serbian national cause. In the eye of the occupation regime, they were a potential source of disturbance and opposition within the country. The leaders of the Serbian Orthodox Church, Patriarch Gavrilo Dožić, and bishops Nikolaj Velimirović and Irinej Djordjević were placed under surveillance as important participants of the coup.

Not unlike the Yugoslav state-builders in the late 1910s, the German authorities did not trust the Serbian Orthodox Church and wanted to have its support at the same time. They viewed the Serbian Orthodox clergy with suspicion because of its national leanings and historical allegiance to the Serbian national cause and presumed sympathies towards the Anglican Church, and consequently, England. The latter view was based on the record of cooperation between the Serbian and Anglican Churches during the First World War and in the 1920s. They were equally aware of the prominent place of the Church in Serbian society and wanted to harness its moral authority. An SS officer reported: 'The Orthodox Church has always been the backbone of the Serbian nation. It has always had a great influence on the population of this country. For this reason, the Church must be involved in the work for the renewal of the state. But it is unclear, to the German side yet, how the Church could be most useful.'[10] This was especially true for Velimirović, whom the German intelligence service considered a potential ally before the invasion based on his support and even admiration of Adolf Hitler in the mid-1930s. Back then, Velimirović praised Hitler for recognizing the importance of spirituality for the national cause – Velimirović interpreted it as Hitler's embrace of Christianity. Their mistrust, however, was stronger due to Velimirović staunch opposition to the occupation.

Lower Orthodox clergy suffered as much as other civilians, and even more, in the intra-Yugoslav struggle between the Croatian Ustaša, communist Partisans and Serbian Chetniks. The tragic fate of the Orthodox population and clergy in the Independent State of Croatia (Nezavisna Držva Hrvatska, NDH), which resembled that of the Jewish people in Germany, has been discussed elsewhere on many occasions.[11] Vjekoslav Perica quotes the following numbers of victims and material damage: 217 priests and 3 bishops killed, 334 priests expelled to Serbia, 350–400 Orthodox Churches destroyed.[12] This was, in a nutshell, the narrative promoted by the Serbian Orthodox Church and its political supporters. Because the Serbian Orthodox population was targeted in NDH, the 'suffering church' narrative is powerful and convincing. It also builds upon an older tradition of emphasis on the sacrifice and martyrdom of the Serbian Orthodox Church in defence and support of the Serbian nation.

Some nuances are omitted from this narrative, as they contradict the image of the suffering and heroic Orthodox Church. While under house arrest, Patriarch Gavrilo, reportedly, performed the critical function of intermediary between the forces of Draža Mihailović, Dimitrije Ljotić and the quisling government of Milan Nedić. The lower clergy supported and joined all possible military and paramilitary groups in a given region, ranging from extreme nationalists to communists.

With the collapse of the common Yugoslav state in April 1941, the Serbian Orthodox Church found itself in instability and danger. As the country was divided into occupation zones and the Independent State of Croatia was established, the Serbian Patriarchate lost control over a considerable part of its structures that now fell under the jurisdiction of other authorities. Out of twenty-one eparchies that the Serbian Church had at the beginning of 1941, only six remained under its direct control.[13] The united Serbian Patriarchate was divided into eight entities located in different occupation zones and the NDH. The Serbian Orthodox Church had enjoyed its unity, which it had longed for so badly, only for twenty years. One could argue that once it had lost the support and protection of the sovereign Yugoslav state, the Serbian Church also lost the battle for the prominence and influence it seemed to be winning in the two interwar decades.

In 1942 the so-called Orthodox Church in Croatia was established on the territory of the NDH. It has been argued that the German and Ustaša authorities expected the Serbian Orthodox Church to acknowledge and accept the new Church as legitimate. However, that did not happen. The official Serbian Orthodox Church never accepted the new institution and urged other Orthodox Churches, including the Russian Orthodox Church Abroad, to follow suit. After several unsuccessful attempts to find a Serbian hierarch to lead the new Church, a Russian archbishop in exile Germogen (Maksimov), who at the time resided in a monastery on the Croatian territories, became the head of the Orthodox Church in Croatia.[14] Germogen failed to secure any significant support for his Church from other East Orthodox institutions. He was arrested, tried and executed in May 1945 by Yugoslav partisans for his collaboration with the Ustaša and Nazi regimes.

Meanwhile, the Serbian Patriarchate continued to exist, although with substantially curtailed territory, autonomy and authority. After the first bombing of Belgrade in April 1941, the Serbian Patriarch left the capital first for the Rakovica Monastery, then for Zića and finally went to Montenegrin Ostrog. While in Montenegro, Gavrilo refused the offer of the king and the government to leave the country with them. A few days later, the Patriarch was arrested and moved first to Sarajevo, then to Belgrade. Fairly soon, the occupying authorities realized that harsh treatment of the Patriarch would only contribute to his image as the leader and an undisputed moral authority for the oppressed nation. Given these considerations and the intervention of the collaborating Serbian politicians, Gavrilo was moved back to the Rakovica Monastery near Belgrade, where he stayed until 1943. Nikolaj Velimirović, the second most influential person in the Church, was interned in the Vojlovica monastery. In 1943 he was joined there by the Patriarch, who was moved to that monastery after the information of his planned liberation by the forces of Draža Mihajlović reached the Germans.

In the absence of the Patriarch and other high-profile Serbian hierarchs, metropolitan Josif Cvijović, who stayed in Belgrade, effectively led the Serbian Church. The Metropolitan Josif and the members of the Synod who remained free, with the unofficial approval and encouragement of the Patriarch, tried to maintain the basic structure and function of the Church. To survive, the Synod had to cooperate with the government of Milan Nedić, who generally supported Church appeals against the persecution of the Orthodox population and clergy in NDH and the demolishing of Church properties.

The attempts of the Germans to receive a written statement of support and loyalty from the interned Patriarch and Velimirović continuously failed, which did not improve the overall attitude of the occupants towards the Orthodox clergy. Milan Nedić advocated for more careful handling of the problem. He argued that it would be tough to convince the Serbian people to join the anti-Communist struggle on the side of the Germans if their two main national symbols, the king and the church, were under German attack. As a result of this, from October 1941, the position of the Serbian Church was somewhat eased.

In 1944 Patriarch Gavrilo and Archbishop Velimirović were moved from Serbia to Austria and then to the infamous Dachau concentration camp in Germany, where they spent several months as 'honorary guests'. Velimirović later on, upon his arrival to the United States, would claim that he spent two full years in the camp.[15] After the intervention of Dimitrije Ljotić, they were released from the camp and relocated to Vienna and afterwards to Slovenian Gorica. In April 1945, Ljotić, who stayed in Slovenia from late 1944 to prepare for a massive military operation, died in a car accident. Velimirović and Dožić, after attending Ljotić's funeral, went to Austrian Kitzbühel, although they thought they were going to Switzerland. There they met the American troops who liberated the region. Both hierarchs left the place in July 1945. After months of staying in different European cities, a disappointing visit to London and a refusal of the Greek government to issue a visa, the Patriarch, who had grown frail, decided to return to Yugoslavia. He entered the country in November 1946. Gavrilo Dožić died on 7 May 1950 and was buried in Belgrade *Saborna Crkva*. Velimirović never went back to Yugoslavia after he left Slovenia in the spring of 1945. He spent the last years of his life in the United States, where he died on 18 March 1956, at the age of seventy-six.

Resistance or collaboration? The continuation of the interwar Serbian Orthodox political thought in the war

The wartime history of the Yugoslav religious communities remains sadly under-researched. Yugoslav socialist historiography made sweeping accusations of fascism and collaboration for all churches and religious institutions. In the post-socialist period, heroism and victimhood came to the fore. Elements of socialist ideological judgement were retained by new national historiographies when it suited. For instance, many Serbian historians continued to emphasize that the Vatican and the Croatian Catholic clergy actively supported the persecution of Orthodox Serbs and Jews in NDH and the occupied territories. Archbishop Alojzije Stepinac was singled out as an avid supporter of the Pavelić regime. However, more recently, Mark Biondich presented a more nuanced judgement and argued that the archbishop's position was far from straightforward. While Stepinac supported the cause of independent Croatian statehood, he loathed the racism of the new regime, and the deportation of Jews and Serbs seriously worried him. Biondich claims that the support of the Catholic clergy and intellectuals of the Ustaša state was a logical result of the preceding development of the Catholic movement in Croatia and the problems of interwar Yugoslavia.[16]

Framing the analysis of the wartime experience as a simple choice between resistance and collaboration is riddled with potential pitfalls. Firstly, The narratives of resistance and collaboration in the Second World War have been ideologically driven since the end of the war. The circumstances of the divided state determined early German discussion. Both German states used the memory of resistance as a legitimation for their existence, essentially creating two parallel histories. As Hans Mommsen argued, it was only in the 1970s that historical research began 'to view the resistance in all its forms as the expression of an anti-fascist consensus', at the same time developing 'a critically distanced perspective on the history of resistance … that has been able to focus more clearly on its political ambivalence'.[17] In the case of the countries controlled by the Axis Powers, foreign occupation, loss of sovereignty and nationalism form an additional layer that makes it difficult to disentangle historical narratives of resistance and collaboration from the processes of power struggle and identity-building, especially in cases where the dominant ideological and historiographical framework has collapsed with the end of the Cold War.

Secondly, our understanding of what constitutes resistance and collaboration has evolved not least due to political changes in Europe since the fall of Communism. As Jill Stephenson has put it, instead of being seen in black and white, the history of one's involvement with the Second World War is nowadays predominantly seen as being coloured in various shades of grey.[18] Resistance and collaboration were fragmentary, situational and reactive, meaning that they were reactions to immediate circumstances and past histories. This recognition of their complex nature often makes it impossible to pass a moral judgement on either of them. The growing awareness that wartime actions are intimately linked with prewar histories has been summarized perfectly by Tony Judt:

> The conflicts of World War II, which we too easily package as 'collaboration' and 'resistance', were themselves echoes and transpositions of political, ideological, religious, local, and ethnic disagreements and disputes whose roots lay variously in interwar politics, post-World War I state making, pre-World War I small wars, and even ... the imperfect and incomplete forms of state making of the earlier nineteenth century.[19]

Political involvement of the Serbian Orthodox Church in the war years was multilayered and can hardly be brought to a common denominator. This variety is usually explained by historians from a secular point of view and in political terms, as though they are oblivious to the fact that most clerics were religious Christians. Jozo Tomasevich, in his classic study on collaboration and resistance in Yugoslavia, noted that

> the problems facing the Serbian Orthodox Church and clergy in Serbia proper during the Second World War were relatively simple. Differences of opinion among priests and the population did surface, dividing those who supported Mihailovic, Nedic, Ljotic, or the Partisans, and bloody struggles did ensue, but these were the result of political and ideological differences, without the admixture of any religious or national factors.[20]

This appears to be a widely accepted position that fails to explain where and how these differences may have originated while recognizing the diversity of opinion within the Serbian Church. In some instances, the answer is more straightforward, as in the Macedonian case, where orthodox clergy worked closely with the Partisans united by the idea of the Macedonian national cause and inspired by the communists' promise of national recognition and autonomy, not least from the institution of the Serbian Orthodox Church. The Partisans, in their turn, were aware of the importance of the church institutions locally for boosting morale and the day-to-day success of military operations and recruited Orthodox priests to join their ranks. In 1943, to cement this cooperation, the Bureau of Religious Affairs was created as part of the Partisan Chief Staff for Macedonia.[21] The Macedonian case demonstrates with all clarity that hopes for a better political future were essential when making alliances. In a sense, Tomashevich is correct that the choice was ideological. But for religious thinkers, one's imagination of politics and an understanding of a good political outcome has everything to do with the nuances of religious thinking, specifically with one's sense of modernity, interpretation of the church–state relationship and nationalism.

Such overwhelming support was not typical for the Serbian clergy, many of whom sympathized with the Royalist Chetniks. They shared their values of Serbian nationalism and loyalty to the king. In 1943, Patriarch Gavrilo Dožić declared that he would, until the very end, in good and evil, stand by Draža Mihailović.[22] At the same time, the clergy were wary of provoking the aggression or hostility of the already anti-Orthodox occupation forces and tried to maintain the balance between the support of Mihailović and the cooperation with the government of Milan Nedić. The Synod of the Serbian Church provided financial help to Mihailović. In 1943 and 1944, two liturgies were held in Belgrade to commemorate the fallen Chetniks. Two Serbian clerics took part in the Ravna Gora congress in 1944. Still, the Chetnik commanders were unable to recruit many for their units. At the same time, Čedomir Marjanović served as the minister of justice in the Nedić government. According to some testimonies, he was shot in Belgrade in 1944.[23] It is not clear whether Marjanović's motivation was similar to Germogen's or if he had held a grudge against the official Serbian hierarchy for not implementing his suggestions in the 1920s. Did he know that collaboration would ruin his career in the Church at the very least but did not care?

The Chetniks' political programme met some fierce criticism despite all the support. In June 1941, Stevan Moljević published 'Homogeneous Serbia', a short programmatic statement in which he presented the Chetniks' political and social vision for postwar Serbia and Yugoslavia. This royalist and nationalist program called for the Serbian hegemony in postwar Yugoslavia and the Balkan region. It stipulated that freedom of religion, freedom of the press and freedom of thought were guaranteed, as long as they were not 'abused'. The programme used the familiar anti-Catholic argument and stipulated that only internationally independent religious institutions, whose head resides in the country, will be legally recognized.[24] It was thus more restrictive than the Kingdom of Yugoslavia at any moment of its existence. More importantly, the programme restricted political activities of religious institutions and, similarly to the legislation under the dictatorship, banned any political party based on religious principles. This rule was directed against the political mobilization of the Bosnian Muslims, who in Moljević's plan did not deserve political autonomy. The programme was generically anti-Catholic, anti-Muslim and pro-Serbian Orthodox.

Moljević and other Chetnik leaders made declarations of support and respect for East Orthodox Christianity and the Serbian Orthodox Church. They expected the embrace of the Church. But the limitation of political engagement was contrary to what the Serbian Orthodox leaders believed was an essential part of their work and mission. Moljević, like many nationalist ideologues before and after him, did not think that the Serbian Orthodox Church has an independent political agenda, which goes beyond supporting a secular political force. Therefore, any claims of 'Orthodox character' should be interpreted as an attempt to harness the symbolic capital of the Church to their political ends. What seems as ideological proximity can, in fact, be superficial. This can possibly explain why, in 1944, Dimitrije Najdanović wrote a fierce critique of the Chetnik actions and their political agenda. Among other things, he accused Draža Mihajlović and his fellows of betraying the Serbian interests and of following the Judeo-Masonic conspiracy plan. He also held them responsible for the sufferings of the Serbian nation after the coup d'état in March 1941, repeating Ljotić's argument from before the coup.[25] This is not surprising, as Najdanović, a close associate of Velimirović, was an active supporter of Ljotić. He was arrested in 1940 while partaking in the activities of the outlawed Zbor movement and was released only after the intervention of Velimirović, who wrote a letter of protest to the Prime Minister Dragiša Cvetković, in which he referred to Ljotić as a man of 'great character' and a true Christian.[26]

The Zbor movement of Dimitrije Ljotić, with its incorporation and use of the Orthodox rhetoric and symbols, is a widely cited example of the affirmed Christian character of a political movement and its ideology. A close intellectual affinity between Ljotić and Nikolaj Velimirović has been well documented. Most famously, Velimirović, while giving the eulogy at Ljotić's funeral, referred to him as 'a politician with the cross', who always adhered to the interests and values of Orthodoxy. Their relationship could be described as spiritual guidance; Ljotić publicly referred to the archbishop as his mentor, and Velimirović never denied the connection.

Ljotić's movement failed miserably in the Yugoslav elections of 1935. It most probably would have remained marginal if it were not for the support of the German authorities and the government of Milan Nedić. Ljotić's ideology combined Italian, Mussolini-type corporatism, organic thought, Serbian nationalism, anti-Semitism and diffused Orthodox spirituality.[27] Zbor's motto was 'With faith in God and the victory of Zbor'. On multiple occasions, Ljotić wrote that there is no other life outside 'the life and the truth of Christ', that there was no other way to reach salvation for an individual – or a nation – outside Christ and the Orthodox Church.[28] Ljotić wrote that he spent every minute of each day working to find what would please God and to then pass this knowledge on to his followers.²⁹ At the same time, Ljotić claimed to be no better than any other member of the movement and humbly referred to himself as a 'sinful and unworthy man' whose only merit was that he could communicate the will of God.³⁰

In the winter of 1944, Ljotić spoke about the importance of spiritual values and keeping the national morale high and referenced the 'nationalism of St Sava', closely following Velimirović's lecture from 1935. He talked about St Sava as the 'original nationalist' and underlined that nationalism was born not in the French Revolution but in medieval Serbia. Ljotić argued that the greatest achievement of St Sava was the unification of nationalism and Christianity: 'If we study his life, then we see that he was a nationalist in the deepest sense of the word, and on the other hand, [he was] a Christian in the most sublime sense.'³¹

Velimirović, an exceptional theologian and thinker in many ways, was one of the few Serbian hierarchs whose political contribution also came from the wartime period. In 1944, while being interned as 'an honorary guest' in the concentration camp Dachau, Velimirović wrote his most controversial book, 'Speeches to the Serbian people through the dungeon window'.³² The book was published for the first time in 1985 in Great Britain, but according to the testimonies of Velimirović's close circle, it was written during his imprisonment.

In contrast to the Patriarch, who was a firm anti-fascist, Velimirović's attitude to National-Socialism was not straightforwardly negative. His flirting with the Nazi ideology was most visible in his anti-Semitic views. 'Through the Dungeon Window', written at the same time the Holocaust was taking place, is full of references to the Jews who have tried and murdered Christ, 'inspired by the stinking breath of Satan'. This continues Velimirović's earlier anti-Semitic statements of Jews as Christ-killers and enemies of Christianity that can be found in other writings: 'New Sermons under the Mountain', 'Ohrid Prologue' and 'Indian Letters'. As early as the late-1920s, Velimirović's allegorical sermon 'The Story of the Wolf and the Lamb' 'provoked a bitter reaction from the Belgrade Rabbi Dr Isaac Alkalai' when it was first published in 1928.³³

His wartime and postwar texts continue other themes he picked up in the late-1930s. Velimirović wrote about the reasons for the collapse of the Yugoslav state. He explained the failure of the state by the 'sin of the people' and that sin was the rejection of God in the name of the false, godless culture and civilization, which Velimirović compared to the biblical dry wells that cannot keep the water.³⁴

And yet, despite all this, Velimirović strongly opposed the occupation of Yugoslavia. Najdanović, however, was happy to work with Ljotić, who collaborated. One way to explain this difference is to look at the critical distinction in their vision for the role of the East Orthodox Christianity, the Serbian Orthodox Church and the nation in the face of the crisis of modernity, which spans wider than the war itself.

Najdanović believed that Ljotić could help ensure that his religious-political idea of political Orthodoxism has a chance to be implemented and was disappointed with Chetniks who denied the possibility of an active political position to religious institutions and communities. For Velimirović and Dožić, loyalty to the nation (not to the Yugoslav state, which they were happy enough to see dismantled) trumped all other considerations. There was no salvation outside the nation, and the occupation threatened it.

After the war

The end of the Second World War and Josip Broz Tito's coming to power signified the end of an era for the Serbian Orthodox Church and other religious institutions in Yugoslavia. Many prominent members of the Serbian Orthodox clergy left the country and spent the rest of their lives in voluntary exile in Europe and North America. Patriarch Gavrilo Dožić, however, chose to return home. Velimirović spent the last years of his life in the United States. After initial participation in émigré anti-communist activities, he became 'disenchanted with the divisions within the Serbian diaspora in North America and aware of his diminishing influence in the homeland ... withdrew from public life and retreated to the Russian St Tikhon Monastery in South Canaan, Pennsylvania.'[35] In 1991 Velimirović's remains were transported and reburied in a chapel in his native village of Lelić in Central Serbia. In 2003, he was canonized as a Serbian Orthodox saint, causing a scandal and a public debate about his intellectual and political legacy.

Najdanović spent more than a decade between 1948 and 1960 in England, moved to Canada in 1960, and eventually to the United States in 1967, where he stayed until his death in 1986. He continued to write and publish both in North America and Germany.[36] Other members of Zbor, including the church historian Slijepčević, ended up in Germany. Slijepčević left Yugoslavia during the war, spent a few years interned in Italy and Germany and finally settled down in Switzerland, researching at the Old Catholic Department of the University of Bern. In 1954, he moved to Munich, where he worked at the Institute for Southeastern Europe. He reportedly kept in touch with Munich-based publishing house 'Iskra', which specialized in memoirs of the former Zbor members and anti-Communist publications. He died in 1992 in Cologne.

The visions of the interwar Serbian Orthodox intellectuals did not disappear after 1945. Most notably, the idea of Svetosavlje was sustained and developed further by Velimirović writing in emigration and by Justin Popović at home. Velimirović focused on the concept of the exceptionality of the Serbian people and formulated a theory of 'the Serbian nation as a Theodulus' or God's servant, which is also the name of his most famous book to date. Velimirović's writings were banned in socialist Yugoslavia, and he was a persona non grata, an accused traitor and collaborator. Nevertheless, his texts circulated underground, were published anonymously or under a false name and were smuggled from abroad.[37]

Velimirović's ideas were further developed by his disciple and a younger colleague Justin Popović, who is considered the second greatest Serbian theologian of the twentieth century. Popović remained in Yugoslavia after the end of the Second World War, but because of his anti-Communist record he was placed under police surveillance and was essentially confined to living in the monastery of Ćelije, where he could write, contribute to church affairs, but was not allowed to teach and his public appearances were minimal. He died in Ćelije on 7 April 1979. He was canonized as a saint of the Serbian Orthodox Church on 2 May 2010.[38]

Popović received an excellent international education, including in Russia, England and Greece. Unlike Velimirović, who was both critical of and open to international developments in religious thought, theology and ecumenism, Popović provided 'a scathing critique of the contemporary ecumenical process and of Western Christianity and "Western culture" in general. The crux of his critique is his belief that the "West" abandoned Christ (i.e., the God-man) in favour of Adam (i.e., a man).'[39] He was greatly influenced by Russian conservative religious thought and especially by the philosophy of Dostoevsky, who was the subject of his doctoral thesis.[40] In this sense, Popović resembles the Romanian philosopher Nichifor Crainic, who was also fascinated by Dostoevsky's spirituality. Popović turned *svetosavlje* into a holistic philosophy, which provided an alternative to the 'lost ways' of the West and allowed for the continuation of Christian belief in cultural, social and political life.[41]

Svetosavlje as a religious philosophy open to nationalist (ab)use resurfaced in the late 1980s with the weakening of Socialist Yugoslavia and the rise of nationalist political forces and ideologies in the region. A group of Popović's students, including such high-profile members of the Serbian Orthodox Church as Atanasije Jevtić, Amfilohije Radović, and Irinej Bulović, have been working on popularizing it. Through his well-established connections in the Greek Orthodox Church, Popović was able to send his best students to Greece, where many of them fell under the influence of radical Greek neo-Orthodox current and Christos Yannaras, who shared Popović's strong anti-Westernism.[42] The popularity of *svetosavlje* in Serbia has been growing since, but often at the expense of intellectual complexity. Much of the original sophistication of the religious-political thought of the 1930s got lost, as the emphasis has been shifted to anti-Communism, anti-Westernism and Serbian ethnonationalism.

As the Serbian Orthodox Church once again became a powerful political actor in the national arena, it retained those aspects of the original teaching created by Velimirović, Najdanović and others that suited the current political needs of the Church. The key characteristics of the Serbian Church's political programme since the 2000s were 'nationalism, conservatism, homophobia, and religious intolerance'.[43] In this sense, the story repeated itself, and *svetosavlje* of the twenty-first century is as much a product of its political context as it had been in the 1930s.

Notes

Introduction

1 J. G. A. Pocock, 'The Concept of a Language and the Métier d'Historien: Some Considerations on Practice', in *The Languages of Political Theory in Early-Modern Europe*, ed. Anthony Pagden (Cambridge: Cambridge University Press, 1987), 19–38.
2 Roger Woods, 'The Radical Right: The "Conservative Revolutionaries" in Germany', in *The Nature of the Right: European and American Politics and Political Thought since 1789*, ed. Roger Eatwell and Noël O'Sullivan (London: Pinter Publishers, 1989), 128.
3 Reinhart Koselleck, 'Social History and Begriffsgeschichte', in *History of Concepts: Comparative Perspectives*, ed. Iain Hampsher-Monk, Karin Tilmans and Frank van Vree (Amsterdam: Amsterdam University Press, 1998), 23–35.
4 Brian Porter-Szűcs, 'Introduction', in *Christianity and Modernity in Eastern Europe*, ed. Bruce R. Berglund and Brian Porter-Szűcs (Budapest: Central European University Press, 2010), 9.
5 Hartmut Lehman, 'History of Twentieth-Century Christianity as a Challenge for Historians', in *Transformationen der Religion in der Neuzeit: Beispiele aus der Geschichte des Protestantismus*, ed. Hartmut Lehmann (Göttingen: Vandenhoeck and Ruprecht, 2007), 219.
6 Ronald Grigor Suny and Michael D. Kennedy, eds, *Intellectuals and the Articulation of the Nation* (Ann Arbor: University of Michigan Press, 2002), 2.
7 David Martin, *On Secularization: Towards a Revised General Theory* (Aldershot: Ashgate, 2005); Owen Chadwick, *The Secularization of the European Mind in the Nineteenth Century* (Cambridge: Cambridge University Press, 1991).
8 Jeffrey Cox, 'Master Narratives of Long-term Religious Change', in *The Decline of Christendom in Western Europe, 1750–2000*, ed. Hugh McLeod and Werner Ustorf (Cambridge: Cambridge University Press, 2003), 201.
9 Talal Asad, *Formations of the Secular: Christianity, Islam, Modernity* (Stanford, CA: Stanford University Press, 2003).
10 Charles Taylor, *A Secular Age* (Cambridge, MA: Belknap Press of Harvard University Press, 2007).
11 José Casanova, *Public Religions in the Modern World* (Chicago: University of Chicago Press, 1994).

12 Mark Edward Ruff, 'The Postmodern Challenge to the Secularization Thesis: A Critical Assessment', *Schweizerische Zeitschrift für Religions-und Kulturgeschichte* 99 (2005): 385–401.

13 Renato Moro, 'Religion and Politics in the Time of Secularization: The Sacralization of Politics and Politicization of Religion', *Totalitarian Movements and Political Religions* 6, no. 1 (June 2005): 75, https://doi.org/10.1080/146907 60500099796.

14 Homi K. Bhabha, 'Introduction', in *Nation and Narration*, ed. Homi K. Bhabha (London: Routledge, 1990), 3.

15 Graham Day and Andrew Thompson, eds, *Theorizing Nationalism* (Basingstoke, Hampshire: Palgrave Macmillan, 2004), 102.

16 Rogers Brubaker, 'Religion and Nationalism: Four Approaches', *Nations and Nationalism* 18, no. 1 (2011): 1–19, https://doi.org/10.1111/j.1469-8129.201 1.00486.x.

17 George Th. Mavrogordatos, 'Orthodoxy and Nationalism in the Greek Case', in *Church and State in Contemporary Europe: The Chimera of Neutrality*, ed. John T. S. Madeley and Zsolt Enyedi (London: Frank Cass, 2003), 117.

18 George L. Mosse, *The Nationalization of the Masses: Political Symbolism and Mass Movements in Germany from the Napoleonic Wars through the Third Reich* (New York: Howard Fertig, 1975).

19 Ibid., 14.

20 Talal Asad, 'Religion, Nation-State, Secularism', in *Nation and Religion: Perspectives on Europe and Asia*, ed. Peter van der Veer and Hartmut Lehmann (Princeton, NJ: Princeton University Press, 1999), 187.

21 Anthony D. Smith, *Chosen Peoples: Sacred Sources of National Identity* (Oxford: Oxford University Press, [2003] 2008), 25.

22 Ibid., 28–31.

23 Adrian Hastings, *The Construction of Nationhood: Ethnicity, Religion, and Nationalism* (Cambridge: Cambridge University Press, 1997).

24 Pål Kolstø, 'Introduction', in *Myths and Boundaries in South-Eastern Europe*, ed. Pål Kolstø (London: Hurst, 2005), 21.

25 Mary Anne Perkins, *Nation and Word, 1770–1850: Religious and Metaphysical Language in European National Consciousness* (Aldershot: Ashgate, 1999), 155. Emphasis is mine.

26 Friedrich Wilhelm Graf, *Die Wiederkehr der Götter. Religion in der modernen Kultur* (München: C. H. Beck Verlag, 2004), 119.

27 Ibid., 119.

28 Perkins, *Nation and Word*, 14–15.

29 Stefan Samerski, ed., *Die Renaissance der Nationalpatrone: Erinnerungskulturen in Ostmitteleuropa im 20./21. Jahrhundert* (Köln: Böhlau Verlag, 2007).

30 Miroslav Hroch, 'National Movements with and without Religion: The Nation and Religion in a Historical Perspective', *Studies in Religion / Sciences Religieuses* 50, no. 4 (December 2021): 493–512, https://doi.org/10.1177/0008429820978970.

31 Doris L. Bergen, 'Christianity and Germanness: Mutually Reinforcing, Reciprocally Undermining?', in *Religion und Nation, Nation und Religion: Beiträge zu einer unbewältigten Geschichte*, ed. Michael Geyer and Hartmut Lehmann (Göttingen: Wallstein, 2004), 89.

32 John Kent, 'Religion and Nationalism', in *Religion in Europe: Contemporary Perspectives*, ed. Sean Gill, Gavin D'Costa and Ursula King (Kampen: Kok Pharos, 1995), 180.

33 For an account of the changes in the discipline, see Cox, 'Master Narratives of Long-Term Religious Change', 201–17. For the discussion of the secularization theory, see Steve Bruce, ed., *Religion and Modernization: Sociologists and Historians Debate the Secularization Thesis* (Oxford: Clarendon Press, 1992).

34 Franziska Metzger, *Religion, Geschichte, Nation: Katholische Geschichtsschreibung in der Schweiz im 19. und 20. Jahrhundert – kommunikationstheoretische Perspektiven* (Stuttgart: Kohlhammer, 2010); Hans-Christian Maner, *Multikonfessionalität und neue Staatlichkeit. Orthodoxe, griechisch-katholische und römisch-katholische Kirche in Siebenbürgen und Altrumänien zwischen den Weltkriegen: 1918–1940* (Stuttgart: Steiner, 2007); Ricarda Vulpius, *Nationalisierung der Religion. Russifizierungspolitik und ukrainische Nationsbildung: 1860–1920* (Wiesbaden: Harrassowitz, 2005).

35 Martin Schulze Wessel, ed., *Nationalisierung der Religion und Sakralisierung der Nation im östlichen Europa* (Stuttgart: Steiner, 2006), 7.

36 Moro, 'Religion and Politics', 73.

37 Ibid., 77.

38 Emilio Gentile, 'Political Religion: A Concept and Its Critics – A Critical Survey', *Totalitarian Movements and Political Religions* 6, no. 1 (June 2005): 29, https://doi.org/10.1080/14690760500099770.

39 The concept 'political religion' was first introduced by Eric Vögelin in 1938 and later picked up by scholars analysing totalitarian regimes and ideologies. Its usage and applicability have been debated for many years, and no agreement has been reached. In the narrow sense, 'political religion' refers to an ideology (normally totalitarian, e.g. Fascism, National Socialism or Stalinism) that has a pseudo-religious nature and whose cults, rites and a salvation theory have a religious character. Emilio Gentile remarked that

> although the expression 'political religion' was born before totalitarianism, only after it was associated with Bolshevism, fascism and Nazism in early comparative analyses of those regimes, did the concept of political religion become more prominent. It was employed to define the absolute exaltation

of the party and of the state, the cult of the leader, mass fanaticism, rites and symbols of collective liturgies, which were fundamental aspects of the new totalitarian regimes. (Gentile, 'Political Religion', 25)

In a broader meaning (which is a source of dispute), 'political religion' stands for a type of 'true' religion that became a political ideology. Whichever the position, scholars agree that the phenomenon is closely related to secularization, modernity and 'the rebellion against God'.

40 Heinz Schilling quoted in Thomas A. Brady Jr., 'Confessionalization – The Career of a Concept', in *Confessionalization in Europe: 1555 – 1700. Essays in Honor and Memory of Bodo Nischan*, ed. John M. Headley (Aldershot: Ashgate, 2004), 4.

41 Wolfgang Reinhard, 'Reformation, Counter-Reformation, and the Early Modern State: A Reassessment', *Catholic Historical Review* 75, no. 3 (July 1989): 399.

42 Olaf Blaschke, 'Das 19. Jahrhundert: Ein Zweites Konfessionelles Zeitalter?', *Geschichte und Gesellschaft: Zeitschrift für historische Sozialwissenschaft* 26 (2000): 38–75; Helmut Walser Smith, *German Nationalism and Religious Conflict: Culture, Ideology, Politics, 1870-1914* (Princeton, NJ: Princeton University Press, 1995).

43 Smith, *German Nationalism and Religious Conflict*, 54.

44 Ibid., 236–7.

45 Michael B. Petrovic, *A History of Modern Serbia: 1804–1918* (New York: Harcourt Brace Jovanovich, 1976), 10.

46 Paul Mojzes, *Yugoslavian Inferno: Ethnoreligious Warfare in the Balkans* (New York: Continuum, 1994); Nathalie Clayer and Xavier Bougarel, eds, *Europe's Balkan Muslims: A New History* (London: Hurst, 2017).

47 Detlef Pollack, 'Modifications in the Religious Field of Central and Eastern Europe', *European Societies* 3, no. 2 (2001): 135–65, https://doi.org/10.1080/14616690120054 302; Detlef Pollack and Gert Pickel, *The Vitality of Religion-Church Integration and Politics in Eastern and Western Europe in Comparison* (Frankfurt(Oder): Frankfurter Institut für Transformationsstudien, 2000); Mattei Dogan, 'Accelerated Decline of Religious Beliefs in Europe', *Comparative Sociology* 1, no. 2 (2002): 127–49, https://doi.org/10.1163/156913302100418466.

48 Lucian N. Leustean, 'Orthodox Christianity and Nationalism: An Introduction', in *Orthodox Christianity and Nationalism in Nineteenth-Century Southeastern Europe*, ed. Lucian N. Leustean (New York: Fordham University Press, 2014), 12.

49 Barbara Jelavich, *History of the Balkans. Vol. 1 Eighteenth and Nineteenth Centuries* (Cambridge: Cambridge University Press, 1983), 50.

50 Paschalis M. Kitromilides, *Enlightenment, Nationalism and Orthodoxy: Studies in the Culture and Political Thought of Southeastern Europe* (Aldershot, Hampshire: Variorum, 1994). For a critical interpretation of Kitromilides's argument and its applicability to other Balkan cases, see Carsten Riis, *Religion,*

Politics, and Historiography in Bulgaria (Boulder, CO: East European Monographs, 2002), 129–34.

51 Vangelis Kechriotis, 'Greek Historiography and the Role of the Orthodox Church', in *Battling over the Balkans: Historiographical Questions and Controversies*, ed. John R. Lampe and Constantin Iordachi (Budapest: Central European University Press, 2020), 56–64.

52 Peter F. Sugar, 'Religion, Nationalism and Politics', in *Nationalism and Religion in the Balkans since the Nineteenth Century*, ed. Peter F. Sugar (Seattle: University of Washington Press, 1996), 7.

53 Pedro Ramet, ed., *Eastern Christianity and Politics in the Twentieth Century* (Durham, NC: Duke University Press, 1988).

54 Sabrina P. Ramet, ed., *Orthodox Churches and Politics in Southeastern Europe: Nationalism, Conservativism, and Intolerance* (Cham, Switzerland: Palgrave Macmillan, 2020).

55 Makridies and Uffelmann observed that 'the comparative analysis and examination of two or more Orthodox cultures not only in terms of anti-Western discourses and practices, but also in terms of their interrelations, the transfer of ideas from one Orthodox culture to the other and their differences' was missing in the early 2000s. Vasilios N. Makridies and Dirk Uffelmann, 'Studying Eastern Orthodox Anti-Westernsim: The Need for a Comparative Research Agenda', in *Orthodox Christianity and Contemporary Europe: Selected Papers of the International Conference Held at the University of Leeds, England in June 2000*, ed. Jonathan Sutton and Wil van den Bercken (Leuven: Peeters, 2003), 87–120. The Hidden Galleries ERC project, led by James Kapalo at the University College Cork, is an excellent recent example of a transnational approach to religious history http://hiddengalleries.eu/.

56 Lucian N. Leustean, 'Orthodoxy and Political Myths in Balkan National Identities', *National Identities* 10, no. 4 (December 2008): 421–32, https://doi.org/10.1080/14608940802519045; Pål Kolstø, ed., *Myths and Boundaries in South-Eastern Europe* (London: Hurst, 2005); Martin Schulze Wessel, ed., *Nationalisierung der Religion und Sakralisierung der Nation im östlichen Europa* (Stuttgart: Steiner, 2006); Hans-Christian Maner and Martin Schulze-Wessel, eds, *Religion im Nationalstaat zwischen den Weltkriegen 1918–1939: Polen, Tschechoslowakei, Ungarn, Rumänien* (Stuttgart: Steiner, 2002).

57 John T. S. Madeley and Zsolt Enyedi, eds, *Church and State in Contemporary Europe: The Chimera of Neutrality* (London: Frank Cass, 2003); Lucian N. Leustean, 'Religion and Politics in the European Union', in *The Oxford Handbook of Religion and Europe*, eds. Grace Davie and Lucian N. Leustean (Oxford: Oxford University Press, 2021), 287–306.

58 Bruce R. Berglund and Brian Porter-Szűcs, eds, *Christianity and Modernity in Eastern Europe* (Budapest: Central European University Press, 2010).
59 Brian Porter-Szűcs, 'Introduction' to *Christianity and Modernity in Eastern Europe*, eds. Bruce R. Berglund and Brian Porter-Szűcs, 5–6.
60 Vasa Čubrilović, 'Srpska Pravoslavna Crkva pod Turcima od XV do XIX veka', *Zbornik Filozofskog fakulteta* 5, no. 1 (1960): 163–88. The same narrative can be found in I. V. Tchurkina, ed., *Rol' religii v formirovanii yuzhnoslavyanskikh naciy*. (Moscow: URSS, 1999).
61 The first to voice a substantial critique of this point was the American historian of Serbia Gale Stokes in Gale Stokes, 'Church and Class in Early Balkan Nationalism', *East European Quarterly* 13 (1979): 259–70.
62 Yuriy Kostyashov, *Serby v Avstriiskoi monarkhii v XVIII veke* (Kaliningrad: Kaliningrad University, 1997); Bojan Aleksov, *Religious Dissent between the Modern and the National: Nazarenes in Hungary and Serbia, 1850–1914* (Wiesbaden: Harrassowitz Verlag, 2006).
63 Djoko Slijepčević, *Istorija Sprske Pravoslavne Crkve*, Vols 1–3 (Belgrade: JRJ 1991).
64 Wayne Vucinich commented: 'Since the author is deeply engaged in church politics, the book cannot claim to be a model of dispassionate historical analysis. Yet, it is the only work on the subject, and, thus, will be of considerable interest to contemporary historians and to church scholars.' Wayne Vucinich, 'Review article of "Istorija Srpske Pravoslavne Crkve" by Djoko Slijepčević', *Slavic Review* 48, no. 3 (Autumn 1989): 526.
65 Mark Biondich observed:

> In Serbian nationalist historiography, virtually all Serb actions of the interwar era are seen as defensive and an attempt to save the Yugoslav state from Croat secessionist intrigues, which were ultimately to blame for the country's dysfunctional parliamentary system. According to this interpretation, the Kingdom of Serbs, Croats and Slovenes stood a good chance of evolving into a liberal democratic society had it not been for Croat recalcitrance. The nascent state found itself under constant attack by disaffected Croat intellectuals and politicians who, working in conjunction with the Catholic Church, Vatican, and revisionist powers like Italy and Hungary, worked to sabotage the state.

Mark Biondich, 'The Historical Legacy: The Evolution of Interwar Yugoslav Politics, 1918–1941', in *State Collapse in South-Eastern Europe: New Perspectives on Yugoslavia's Disintegration*, ed. Lenard J. Cohen and Jasna Dragović-Soso (West Lafayette, IN: Purdue University Press, 2008), 45. The examples of this approach include Nikola Žutić, *Kraljevina Jugoslavija i Vatikan: Odnos jugoslovenske države i Rimske Crkve, 1918–1935* (Belgrade: Arhiv Jugoslavije, 1994), Nikola Žutić, *Rimokatolička crkva i hrvatstvo od ilirske ideje do velikohrvatske realizacije,*

1453–1941 (Belgrade: Institut za savremenu istoriju, 1997) and Dragoljub R. Živojinović, *Varvarstvo u ime Hristovo: prilozi za Magnum Crimen* (Belgrade: Nova knjiga, 1988).

66 Miloš Mišović, *Srpska Crkva i konkordatska kriza* (Belgrade: Sloboda, 1983), 23.

67 Radmila Radić, *Država i verske zajednice: 1945–1970* (Belgrade: Institut za noviju istoriju Srbije, 2002); Radmila Radić, *Život u vremenima: Gavrilo Dožić, 1881–1950* (Belgrade: Institut za noviju istoriju Srbije, 2006); Radmila Radić, *Narodna verovanja, religija i spiritizam u srpskom društvu 19. i u prvoj polovini 20. veka* (Belgrade: Institut za noviju istoriju Srbije, 2009).

68 Klaus Buchenau, *Kämpfende Kirchen: Jugoslawiens religiöse Hypothek* (Frankfurt am Main: Peter Lang, 2006).

69 Thomas Bremer, *Ekklesiale Struktur und Ekklesiologie in der Serbischen Orthodoxen Kirche im 19. und 20. Jahrhundert* (Würzburg: Augustinus-Verlag, 1992) was the first work of its kind. Serbian translation: Tomas Bremer, *Vera, kultura i politika: eklezijalna struktura i ekleziologija u Srpskoj pravoslavnoj crkvi u XIX i XX veku* (Niš: Gradina: Jugoslovensko udruženje za naučno istraživanje religije, 1997); Klaus Buchenau, 'Svetosavlje und Pravoslavlje: Nationales und Universales in der serbischen Orthodoxie', in *Nationalisierung der Religion und Sakralisierung der Nation in Ostmittel-, Südost- und Osteuropa im 19. und 20. Jahrhundert*, ed. Martin Schulze Wessel (Stuttgart: Steiner, 2006); Klaus Buchenau, *Auf russischen Spuren. Orthodoxe Antiwestler in Serbien, 1850–1945* (Wiesbaden: Harrassowitz, 2011).

70 Predrag J. Markovic, Milos Kovic and Natasa Milicevic, 'Developments in Serbian Historiography since 1989', in *(Re)Writing History: Historiography in Southeast Europe after Socialism*, ed. Ulf Brunnbauer (Münster: Lit, 2004), 277–316; Vladan Jovanović, 'Recent Serbian Historiography on the Interwar Period', in *Battling over the Balkans: Historiographical Questions and Controversies*, ed. John R. Lampe and Constantin Iordachi (Budapest: Central European University Press, 2020), 121–9.

71 Anti-Westernism of the Serbian clergy is also tackled in Bojan Aleksov, 'History Taught Us Not to Fear Anything from the East and Everything from the West. A Historical Perspective on Serbian Occidentalism', in *Prowestliche und antiwestliche Diskurse in den Balkanländern/ Südosteuropa*, ed. Gabriella Schubert and Holm Sundhaussen (Munich: Südosteuropa-Gesellschaft, 2008), 31–46.

72 Neven Vukic, 'The Church in a Communist State: Justin Popovic (1894–1979) and the Struggle for Orthodoxy in Serbia/Yugoslavia', *Journal of Church and State* 63, no. 2 (Spring 2021): 278–99, https://doi.org/10.1093/jcs/csaa033; Bogdan Lubardic, ' "Revolt against the Modern World": Theology and the Political in the Thought of Justin Popović', in *Political Theologies in Orthodox Christianity: Common Challenges – Divergent Positions*, ed. Kristina Stoeckl, Ingeborg Gabriel and Aristotle Papanikolaou (London: Bloomsbury, 2017), 207–26.

73 Radovan Bigović, *Od svečoveka do bogočoveka: Hrišćanska filosofija vladike Nikolaja Velimirovića* (Belgrade: Društvo Raška škola, 1998).
74 Jovan Byford, *Denial and Repression of Anti-Semitism: Post-Communist Remembrance of the Serbian Bishop Nikolaj Velimirović* (Budapest: Central European University Press, 2008); Predrag Ilić, *Srpska pravoslavna crkva i tajna Dahaua: mit i istina o zatočeništvu patrijarha Gavrila i episkopa Nikolaja u koncentracionom logoru Dahauu* (Belgrade: P. Ilić, 2006).
75 Milan Vukomanović, 'Religious Freedoms in Yugoslavia and the Relations between Religious Communities and the State', *Religion in Eastern Europe* 22, no. 1 (February 2002): 38–44; Milan Vukomanović, 'Srpska pravoslavna crkva izmedju tradicionalizma, konzervatizma i fundamentalizma', in *Istorija i sećanje*, ed. Olga Manojlović Pintar (Belgrade: Institut za noviju istoriju Srbije, 2006), 175–90; idem, *Homo viator: religija i novo doba* (Belgrade: Čigoja štampa, 2008).
76 Milorad Ekmečić, *Stavaranje Jugoslavije*, Vols 1–2 (Belgrade: Prosveta, 1989); Milorad Ekmečić, *Srbija izmedju srednje Evrope i Evrope* (Belgrade: Politika, 1992).
77 Ivo Banac, *The National Question in Yugoslavia: Origins, History, Politics* (Ithaca: Cornell University Press [1984] 1993).
78 Dejan Djokić, *Elusive Compromise: A History of Interwar Yugoslavia* (New York: Columbia University Press, 2007).
79 Jovo Bakić, *Ideologije jugoslovenstva između srpskog i hrvatskog nacionalizma 1918–1941: sociološko-istorijska studija* (Zrenjanin: Gradska narodna biblioteka 'Žarko Zrenjanin', 2004).
80 John Paul Newman, *Yugoslavia in the Shadow of War: Veterans and the Limits of State Building, 1903–1945* (Cambridge, Cambridge University Press, 2015); Pieter Troch, *Nationalism and Yugoslavia: Education, Yugoslavism and the Balkans before World War II* (London: I.B. Tauris, 2015).
81 Emily Greble, *Muslims and the Making of Modern Europe* (Oxford: Oxford University Press, 2021).

1 Religion and Serbian state- and nation-building before 1918

1 Mary E. Durham, *Through the Lands of the Serb* (London: E. Arnold, 1904), 155.
2 Ivo Banac, *The National Question in Yugoslavia: Origins, History, Politics* (Ithaca, NY: Cornell University Press, [1984] 1993, 107). Italics are mine.
3 'Program of the Liberal Party' [1889], in *Programi i statuti Srpskih političkih stranaka do 1918. godine*, ed. Vasilije Krestić and Radoš Ljušić (Belgrade: Književne novine, 1991), 171.

4 Maroš Melichárek offers an informative overview in 'Great Migration of the Serbs (1690) and Its Reflections in Modern Historiography', *Serbian Studies Research* 8, no. 1 (2017): 87–102.
5 Nicholas Doumanis, *Before the Nation: Muslim-Christian Coexistence and Its Destruction in Late Ottoman Anatolia* (Oxford: Oxford University Press, 2013), 2.
6 Ronald Grigor Suny, *'They Can Live in the Desert but Nowhere Else': A History of the Armenian Genocide* (Princeton, NJ: Princeton University Press, 2015), 11.
7 Peter F. Sugar, *East European Nationalism, Politics and Religion* (Aldershot: Ashgate, 1999); Peter F. Sugar, *Nationality and Society in Habsburg and Ottoman Europe* (Aldershot: Variorum, 1997).
8 Pieter M. Judson, *The Habsburg Empire: A New History* (Cambridge, MA: Harvard University Press, 2016), 41–2.
9 Robert A. Kann and Zdenek V. David, *The Peoples of the Eastern Habsburg Lands, 1526-1918* (Seattle: University of Washington Press, 1984), 181; Johan Hajinrih Šviker (Johann Heinrich Schwicker), *Politička istorija srba u Ugarskoj*, trans. Tomislav Bekić (Novi Sad: Matica srpska, 1998), 25.
10 Jelavich, *History of the Balkans*, vol. 1, 149.
11 Ibid.
12 Stevan K. Pavlowitch, *Serbia: The History behind the Name* (London: Hurst, 2002), 20.
13 Kostyashov, *Serby v Avstriiskoy monarkhii*, 38.
14 Judson, *The Habsburg Empire*, 40.
15 Banac. *The National Question in Yugoslavia*, 65.
16 For instance, Jovan Rajić's four-volume *Istoriia slavenskikh narodov, naipache Bolgar, Khorvatov i Serbov*, the first significant history of the Serbs, appeared in Vienna in 1794–5.
17 Balázs Trencsényi, Maciej Janowski, Mónika Baár, Maria Falina and Michal Kopeček, *A History of Modern Political Thought in East Central Europe. Volume I: Negotiating Modernity in the 'Long Nineteenth Century'* (Oxford: Oxford University Press, 2016), 36.
18 Ljubinka Trgovčević, 'The Enlightenment and the Beginnings of Modern Serbian Culture', *Balcanica: Godišnjak instituta za balkanologiju* 37 (2006): 110.
19 Robin Okey, *Taming Balkan Nationalism: The Habsburg 'Civilizing Mission' in Bosnia 1878-1914* (Oxford: Oxford University Press, 2007), 30.
20 Edin Hajdarpasic, *Whose Bosnia? Nationalism and Political Imagination in the Balkans, 1840-1914* (Ithaca, NY: Cornell University Press, 2015), 32
21 Ibid.
22 For detailed accounts of the Serbian Church's involvement in the national liberation struggle, see I. V. Tchurkina, ed., *Rol' religii v formirovanii yuzhnoslavyanskikh naciy* (Moscow: URSS, 1999); VasaČubrilović, 'Srpska Pravoslavna Crkva pod

Turcima od XV do XIX veka'. *Zbornik Filozofskog fakulteta* 5, no. 1 (1960): 163–88; DjokoSlijepčević, *Istorija Sprske Pravoslavne Crkve*, Vol. 2 *Od početka XIX veka do kraja drugog svetskog rata* (Belgrade: JRJ, 1991).

23 Ramet, *Eastern Christianity*, 7.
24 Ibid., 18.
25 Kitromilides, *Enlightenment, Nationalism and Orthodoxy*, Carsten Riis, *Religion, Politics, and Historiography in Bulgaria*.
26 Aleksa Ilić, 'Naša prva reč pravoslavnom Srpskom sveštenstvu u svima pokrajinama Srpskim', *Hrišćanski vesnik*, 1 January 1901.
27 Mojsej, episkop, *Crkveno pitanje u Srbiji* (Belgrade: Štamparija Pere Todorovića, 1895), 83.
28 Sabrina Petra Ramet, *Balkan Babel: Politics, Culture, and Religion in Yugoslavia* (Boulder, CO: Westview Press, 1992), 51.
29 Radić, 'Verska elita i modernizacija: Teškoće pronalaženja odgovora', in *Srbija u modernizacijskim procesima 19. i 20. veka*, ed. Latinka Perović (Belgrade: Authors, 2003), 169.
30 Ramet, *Eastern Christianity*, 233.
31 Milica Bakic-Hayden, 'National Memory and Narrative Memory: The Case of Kosovo', in *Balkan Identities: Nation and Memory*, ed. Maria Todorova (New York: New York University Press, 2004), 34.
32 Ibid.
33 The significance of 'life after death' of historical figures is discussed in Katherine Verdery, *The Political Lives of Dead Bodies: Reburial and Postsocialist Change* (New York: Columbia University Press, 1999), Thomas W. Laqueur, *The Work of the Dead: A Cultural History of Mortal Remains* (Princeton, NJ: Princeton University Press, 2015).
34 Lj. Kalušević, 'Čuvajmo naše moralno blago', *Vesnik Srpske Crkve* (1904): 125.
35 Nikola D. Božić, 'Sveštencima narodnim poslanicima', *Vesnik Srpske Crkve* (1903): 980.
36 Dubravka Stojanovic, *Srbija i Demokratija, 1903–1914: Istorijska Studija o 'Zlatnom dobu srpske demokratije'* (Belgrade: Udruženje za društvenu istoriju, Čigoja, 2003).
37 Nikola Pašić, *Sloga Srbo-Hrvata* (Belgrade: Vreme knjige, 1995). Contextual analysis and the English translation of a representative excerpt is available in Diana Mishkova, Marius Turda and Balázs Trencsényi, eds. *Discourses of Collective Identity in Central and Southeast Europe, 1770–1945. Volume IV Anti-modernism. Radical revisions of collective identity* (Budapest: Central European University Press, 2014), 47–55.
38 Božić, 'Sveštencima narodnim poslanicima', 982–4.
39 D. D., 'Pred izbore narodnih poslanika',*Vesnik Srpske Crkve* (1912): 98.
40 Petar S. Protić, 'O moralnom vaspitavanju u školama', *Vesnik Srpske Crkve* (1895): 2.

41 Miloš Andjelković, 'Bez vere nema morala', *Vesnik Srpske Crkve* (1895): 916–17.
42 Protić, 'O moralnom vaspitavanju u školama', 5.
43 D. Mihajlović, 'Savremena pitanja u Srpskoj Crkvi', *Vesnik Srpske Crkve* (1905): 678.
44 Mihajlović, 'Savremena pitanja u Srpskoj Crkvi', 359.
45 'Iz narodne Skupštine' [A speech of archpriest Milan Djurić], *Vesnik Srpske Crkve* (1909): 309. The same argument is present in many other articles, e.g. 'Narodnoj Skupštini' (1904): 979–82.
46 'Iz narodne Skupštine', 938.
47 Ibid., 940.
48 Ibid., 941–3.
49 A. L. Shemiakin, 'Serbskoye obtshestvo na rubezhe XIX-XX vv.: tradicionalizm i modernizatsiya. Vzgliad iznutri', in *Chelovek na Balkanah v epohu krizisov i etnopoliticheskih stolknoveniy XX v.*, ed. G. Litavrin and R. Grishina (St Petersburg: Aleteyia, 2002), 48; Milan Stojadinović, *Ni Rat Ni Pakt: Jugoslavija izmedju dva rata* (Belgrade: Glas, 2002), 11.
50 Nikola Božić, 'Sveštenici i učitelji u službi narodne prosvete', *Vesnik Srpske Crkve* (1903): 215.
51 Božić, 'Sveštencima narodnim poslanicima', 981.
52 Milentije, episkop Timočki, 'Istorijske zasluge srpskog sveštenstva u službi Sv. Pravoslavlja i naroda svog', *Vesnik Srpske Crkve* (1899): 215.
53 Lazar R. Petrović, 'Beseda na proglas kraljevine', *Vesnik Srpske Crkve* (1899): 622.
54 Jevrem Bojović, 'Istorijski zakon', *Vesnik Srpske Crkve* (1897): 105.
55 Ibid., 109–10.
56 Čeda Marjanović, *Socjializam: Kritički pregled najosnovnijih tačaka socijalističkog učenja* (Belgrade: Državna štamparija Kraljevine Srbije, 1907).
57 Čedomir Marjanović, 'Veronauka u našim srednjim školama', *Vesnik Srpske Crkve* (1905): 1068.
58 Ibid., 1069.
59 Ibid., 1068.
60 Ibid., 1072.
61 Miloš Anđelković, 'Bez vere nema morala', *Vesnik Srpske Crkve* (1895): 917–18.
62 Ibid., 923.
63 This conflict is described in greater detail in Aleksa Ilić, *Moji doživljai* (Belgrade: Štamparija Sv. Sava, 1931), 287–91. According to Ilić, the Metropolitan was infuriated by Marjanović's complaints that a person without proper theological training was occupying such a high position.
64 Klaus Buchenau, 'Just as Real-Life Brothers: Serb-Russian Contacts in the Ecclesiastical Academy of Kiev (1850–1914) and in Orthodox Schools of Interwar Yugoslavia (1920–1941)', *Tokovi Istorije* 3/4 (2005): 57.

65 *Vesnik Srpske Crkve* published a translation of excerpts from his work *Christianisme et démocratie, christianisme et socialisme* (Paris: Bloud, 1905) under the title 'Hrišćanstvo i Demokratija', *Vesnik Srpske Crkve* (1906): 856–63. Leroy-Beaulieu wrote extensively on the Liberal Catholics of France in the nineteenth century, and his book *La papauté, le socialisme, et la démocratie* was the first to welcome Leo XIII's Encyclical 'Rerum Novarum'.
66 'Hrišćanstvo i Demokratija', 856.
67 'Zakletva socialističkih odbornika u Belgradu i Kragujevcu', *Vesnik Srpske Crkve* (1906): 116–22.
68 Ibid., 70.
69 V. Vitorović, 'Vera i moral u narodu našem nekad i sad', *Vesnik Srpske Crkve* (1903): 352.
70 Milos S. Pantelic, 'Nasa inteligencija i religija', *Vesnik Srpske Crkve* (1899): 230.
71 Mihajlović, 'Savremena pitanja u Srpskoj Crkvi', 239.
72 P. R., Milojević, 'Naše sveštenstvo i savremeni pogled našega obrazovanog društva na isto', *Vesnik Srpske Crkve* (1902): 208–11.
73 'Pjesnik o sveštenstvu', *Vesnik Srpske Crkve* (1900): 90.

2 New Church for the new state: 'Liberation and unification' of lands, people and institutions

1 Andrew B. Wachtel, *Making a Nation, Breaking a Nation: Literature and Cultural Politics in Yugoslavia* (Stanford, CA: Stanford University Press, 1998), 114.
2 Ibid., 71.
3 On the Christian character of interwar Yugoslavia, see: Maria Falina, 'Religious Diversity and Equality in Interwar Yugoslavia', *Studies in Religion / Sciences Religieuses* 50, no. 4 (December 2021): 539–59, https://doi.org/10.1177/0008429820978967.
4 Milorad Ekmečić, *Stavaranje Jugoslavije*; Milorad Ekmečić, *Srbija između srednje Evrope i Evrope*.
5 Ivo Banac, *The National Question in Yugoslavia*.
6 Dr Joseph Smodlaka, the founder of the Croat Democratic Party in Dalmatia, and a member of the Parliament for Spalato, in R. W. Seton-Watson's words, was 'one of the ablest and most attractive Southern Slav politicians, and what is still better, "a modern of the moderns" in the midst of medieval conditions'. (R. W. Seton-Watson, *The South Slav Question and the Habsburg Monarchy* (London: Constable, 1911), 406.
7 Josip Smodlaka, 'Ime Države', in *Srpski književni glasnik* 7, no. 4 (16 October 1922): 293.

8 Jovo Bakić, *Ideologije jugoslovenstva*, 73.
9 Ibid.
10 Viktor Novak, ed., *Antologija jugoslovenske misli i narodnog jedinstva: 1390-1930* (Belgrade: Štampa državne štamparije, 1930), 569.
11 Josip Jelačić, 'Narodnu hrvatskome i srpskome u trojedinoj kraljevini Dalmacije, Hrvatske i Slavonije ljubezni pozdrav', in *Antologija jugoslovenske misli*, ed. Novak, 128.
12 'Poziv Srpske Skupšine u Karlovcima od 10/22 maja 1848 "Slavenima Rimske cerkve u Bačkoj, Banatu, Sremu i Baranji, koji jednim sa Serbljima jezikom govore"', in *Antologija jugoslovenske misli*, ed. Novak, 140.
13 Vladika Strossmayer, 'Poslanica' (1877), in *Antologija jugoslovenske misli*, ed. Novak, 403.
14 Falina, 'Religious Diversity and Equality in Interwar Yugoslavia'.
15 Vladimir Ćorović, *Srpski Književni glasnik* (1919), 57.
16 Banac, *The National Question in Yugoslavia*, 49-58.
17 Radić, *Država i verske zajednice*, 21.
18 For a detailed discussion of the challenges of practical implementation of religious equality, see Falina, 'Religious Diversity and Equality in Interwar Yugoslavia'.
19 AJ 69/182/286, Note from the Ministry of the Interior to the Minister of Religions, 21 January 1928.
20 Blagota Gardašević, 'Organizaciono ustrojstvo i zakonodavstvo pravoslavne crkve izmedju dva svetska rata', in *Sprska Pravoslavna Crkva 1920-1970: Spomenica o 50 -godíšnjici vaspostavljanja Srpske Patriašije*, ed. Vladislav (Metropolitan). (Belgrade: Sveti arhijerejski sinod Srpske pravoslavne crkve, 1971), 40.
21 Mark Biondich, 'Religion and Nation in Wartime Croatia: Reflections on the Ustaša Policy of Forced Religious Conversions, 1941-42', *Slavonic and East European Review* 83, no. 1 (January 2005): 71-116, http://www.jstor.org/stable/4214049.
22 Pedro Ramet, 'From Strossmayer to Stepinac: Croatian National Ideology and Catholicism', *Canadian Review of Studies in Nationalism* 12, no. 1 (1985): 131.
23 Zlatko Matijević, 'Pokušaj ustavopravnog definiranja položaja Katoličke crkve u Kraljevini Srba, Hrvata i Slovenaca: 1918-1921', in *Liberalizam i Katolicizam u Hrvatskoj*. II Dio, ed. Hans-Georg Fleck (Zagreb: Zaklada Friedrich Naumann, 1999), 11-25.
24 M. Jaksić, 'Uloga crkve u ujedinjenoj državi', *Nova Evropa* 7, no. 1 (1923): 1-6.
25 Radmila Radić, 'Religion in a Multinational State: The Case of Yugoslavia', in *Yugoslavism: History of a Failed Idea*, ed., Dejan Djokić, 199.
26 Ibid., 198.
27 Francine Friedman, *The Bosnian Muslims: Denial of a Nation* (Boulder, CO: Westview Press, 1996), 96-7.

28 Mitja Velikonja, *Religious Separation and Political Intolerance in Bosnia-Herzegovina* (College Station: Texas A&M University Press, 2003), 147.
29 Okey, *Taming Balkan Nationalism*, 30.
30 Fikret Karčić, 'The Reform of Shari'a Courts and Islamic Law in Bosnia and Herzegovina 1918–1941', in *Islam in Interwar Europe*, ed. Nathalie N. Clayer and Eric Germain (London: Hurst, 2008), 253–70.
31 *Krfska konferencija. Beleške sa sednica vlade Kraljevine Srbije i predstavnika jugoslovenskog odbora, držanih na Krfu 1917 godine, na kojima je donesena Krfska Deklaracija* (Belgrade: Štamparija Skerlić, 1924), 34.
32 Mitja Velikonja, *Religious Separation*, 147.
33 Zlatko Matijević, 'Pokušaj ustavopravnog definiranja', 20.
34 The issue of political participation by the clergy and lay members of religious communities had a regional, if not pan-European, scope as well. In 1922 Pope Pius XI in his formative encyclical *Ubi Arcano Dei* stated that the aim of Catholic Action was to bring the laity into the apostolate of the Church, in order to work towards the establishment of 'Christ's rule across the World'. The Pope surely was not unique in his wish to ensure the prevalence of religious values in social and political spheres, nor was this the first occasion where this wish was articulated. However, the encyclical served as a powerful stimulus for the development of political life in Catholic communities across Europe. The question of direct political participation by the clergy was hotly debated throughout the period in several national and denominational contexts. The Yugoslav debate demonstrated that all religious communities had a vested interest in having their clergy in politics. At the same time in Poland the debate of the early 1920s revealed that a segment of Catholic political circles was not in favour of the creation of a 'Catholic' political party, on the grounds that 'the ablest Catholic people involved in politics' were already members of one or another structure, thus a new party would be doomed to be intellectually weak and politically meaningless. Brian Porter-Szűcs, *Faith and Fatherland: Catholicism, Modernity, and Poland* (Oxford: Oxford University Press, 2011).
35 Radić, *Država i verske zajednice*, 35.
36 Prior to 1918 there were three independent church bodies: the Serbian Orthodox Church in the Kingdom of Serbia, the Serbian Orthodox Church in Montenegro and the Serbian Orthodox Metropoly in Sremski Karlovci in Vojvodina in Southern Hungary. Three others enjoyed different degrees of autonomy from the Constantinople Patriarchate: the Orthodox Church in Bosnia and Herzegovina, the Serbian Orthodox Church in Southern Serbia and Macedonia, and the Bukovina-Dalmatian Metropoly. Between December 1918 and May 1919, two conferences of clergy were held where all necessary steps for the unification of the Serbian Church in accordance with the canonical law of the Orthodox Church were made. Dioceses

that previously belonged to the Metropolies whose heads resided outside Yugoslavia (Dalmatia was part of the Metropoly of Dalmatia-Bukovina, whose head resided in Romania; Old Serbia fell under the jurisdiction of the Patriarch of Constantinople) were negotiated to fall under the jurisdiction of the Serbian Church. Djoko Slijepčević, *Istorija Sprske Pravoslavne Crkve*, vol. 2, 558.

37 The Orthodox community of the Habsburg Empire historically enjoyed a considerable degree of autonomy. The Metropoly of Sremski Karlovci had also been acting for decades as the national institution of the Serbian community in the empire. Once the state took over, the hierarchy of Sremski Karlovci inevitably had to give up its position as the national leader. It also had to bid farewell to its aspirations of being the spiritual leader of the community now that Belgrade was taking over.

38 Radmila Radić, *Država i verske zajednice*, vol. 1, 20.

39 Radmila Radić, *Život u vremenima*, 129.

40 Gardašević, 'Organizaciono ustrojstvo', 47.

41 Radmila Radić, *Život u vremenima*, 113.

42 Djoko Slijepčević, *Istorija Sprske Pravoslavne Crkve*, vol. 2. Od početka XIX veka do kraja Drugog svetskog rata, 562; see also: *Crkveno zakonodavstvo Srpske pravoslavne crkve*. Knj. 3 (Belgrade: Geca Kon, 1933).

43 Dimitrije Pavlović was born in 1846 in Požarevac where he spent his first years of study, before moving to Belgrade. In the capital, after finishing high school, the future Patriarch enrolled in the seminary from which he successfully graduated in 1868. After graduating from the Department of Philosophy of Belgrade University, Dimitrije Pavlović in 1882 became a Professor of theology there, one of the first in Serbia. During the conflict of Metropolitan Mihailo with King Milan, he became the Bishop of Niš. After Mihajlo's return from exile, D. Pavlović, together with some other clerics, left for France, where he spent several years studying literature, philosophy and economics. After Mihailo's death, he returned to Serbia to become first the bishop of Šabac, and in 1905, the Metropolitan of Serbia.

44 Djoko Slijepčević, *Istorija Sprske Pravoslavne Crkve*, vol. 2, 559–60.

45 Gavrilo Dožić writes in his memoirs that General Petar Živković, the head of the government after 1929, openly expressed his opinion that the real intention of the Serbian Church in the debate about the church–state relationship was to mobilize political opponents of the general and his government and force it to step down. Gavrilo Dožić, *Memoari Patrijarha Srpskog Gavrila* (Belgrade: Sfairos, 1990), 34–8.

46 Slijepčević, *Istorija Sprske Pravoslavne Crkve*, vol. 2, 565.

47 'Sednica Ministarskog Saveta Kraljevine SHS, 11. jan 1930'. in *Zapisnici sa sednica ministarskog saveta kraljevine Jugoslavije, 1929–1931*, ed. Ljubodrag Dimić, Nikola Žutić and Blagoje Isailović (Belgrade: Službeni list, Arhiv Jugoslavije, 2002), 134.

48 Meyendorf cited in Zoe Katrina Knox, *Russian Society and the Orthodox Church: Religion in Russia after Communism* (London: Routledge Curzon, 2005), 106.
49 Leustean, 'Orthodoxy and Political Myths', 423.
50 Dimitrije, Archbishop of Belgrade and Metropolitan of Serbia, 'Speech Held in the Serbian Church on the Island of Corfu on the St. Peter's Day in 1917', *Glasnik Ujedinjene Srpske Pravoslavne Crkve*, no. 1 (1920): 15. Note the symptomatic *ujedinjena* (united) in the name of the journal. The prewar title did not contain it, nor was it kept for a longer period of time in the interwar period.
51 Rajko Veselinović, 'Ujedinjenje pokrainskih crkva i vaspostavljenje Srspke Patrijaršije', in *Sprska Pravoslavna Crkva 1920–1970: Spomenica o 50-godíšnjici vaspostavljanja Srpske Patriašije*, 17.
52 Cited in Rajko Veselinović, 'Ujedinjenje pokrainskih crkva i vaspostavljenje Srspke Patrijaršije', 25.
53 John Paul Newman, 'Forging a United Kingdom of Serbs, Croats and Slovenes: The Legacy of the First World War and the "Invalid Question"', in *New Perspectives on Yugoslavia*, ed. Dejan Djokić and James Ker-Lindsay, 46–61.
54 'Naša Reč', *Glasnik Ujedinjene Srpske Pravoslavne Crkve*, no. 1 (1920): 16.
55 The original uses the Serbian word 'narod', which can be translated as both 'people' or 'nation'. King Petar I's order on the re-establishment of the Patriarchate (30 August/12 September 1920), in *Sprska Pravoslavna Crkva 1920–1970*, 29.
56 King Petar I's order on the re-establishment of the Patriarchate, 29.
57 Slijepčević, *Istorija Sprske Pravoslavne Crkve*, vol. 2, 556.
58 Momir Lečić, 'Izgradnja i obnova crkava i manastra od 1920–1941', in *Sprska Pravoslavna Crkva: 1920–1970*, 65.
59 King Petar I's order from 1920 on the re-establishment of the Serbian Patriarchate, in *Sprska Pravoslavna Crkva: 1920–1970*, 29.
60 'Aleksandar's charter on the enthronement of Dimitrije in Peć', in *Sprska Pravoslavna Crkva: 1920–1970*, 35.
61 Tens of thousands of Serbian soldiers found refuge on Corfu in the period from 1916 to 1918, but many died on their way through the mountains and during the winter spent on the Adriatic coast due to exhaustion, harsh conditions, snipers' bullets, diseases and food shortages. An estimated number of the military and civilian deaths amounts to 210,000 people (70,000 soldiers and *c.*140,000 refugees). Dušan Bataković, 'Srpska vlada i Esad-Paša Toptani', in *Srbi i Albanci u XX veku: Ciklus predavanja*, ed. Andrej Mitrović (Belgrade: SANU, 1991), 48. Mitrović cites somewhat different numbers: 70,000 soldiers and civilians missing during the actual withdrawal, with more dying on the coast before the evacuation to Corfu and other safe locations. Andrej Mitrović, *Serbia's Great War, 1914–1918* (West Lafayette, IN: Purdue University Press, 2007), 152. The Island of Vido near Corfu,

where a hospital was located, came to be known as the 'island of death', while the waters around it are even today known as 'the Blue Graveyard' (*Plava Grobnica*), after a poem written by Milutin Bojić. In 1923, King Aleksandar erected a memorial cross, and in 1938, a mausoleum was built on Vido to commemorate fallen Serbian soldiers and to express gratitude to the Greek and French governments who organized the rescue operation. In 1930 a *Monument of Gratitude to France*, designed by Ivan Meštrovic, was unveiled in the presence of King Aleksandar in Belgrade's city park and Kalemegdan fortress. For an account of the retreat and its broader significance, see: 'Golgotha: The Retreat of the Serbian Army and Civilians in 1915–16', in *Europe on the Move. Refugees in the Era of the Great War*, ed. Peter Gatrell and Lyubov Zhvanko (Manchester: Manchester University Press, 2017), 236.

62 'Naša Reč', 15.
63 Andjelković, 'Apologija crkve', *Glasnik Srpske Pravolsavne Patrijaršije*, no. 4 (1921): 55.
64 Miloš Andjelković, 'Apologija crkve', *Glasnik Srpske Pravolsavne Patrijaršije*, no. 4 (1921): 54–6 and no. 5 (1921): 75.
65 Jaroslav Pelikan, *Christian Doctrine and Modern Culture: Since 1700* (Chicago: University of Chicago Press, 1991, c.1989), 282.
66 Mary B. Cunningham and Elizabeth Theokritoff, eds, *The Cambridge Companion to Orthodox Christian Theology* (Cambridge: Cambridge University Press, 2008), 122.
67 Ibid., 125.
68 Initially a religious notion, it was introduced to the Serbian political language and thought by Nikola Pašić. He borrowed this religious concept from the Russian Slavophile philosopher Khomiakov but transformed it into a secular one. Khomiakov himself connected the idea of the spiritual Church community to the Russian peasant commune, but never left completely the theological grounds. He used the concept in order to analyse and criticize church–state relationship in the Romanov Empire after the reforms of Peter I. Martin Schulze Wessel, 'Rechtgläubigkeit und Gemeinschaft: Ekklesiologische und politische Bedeutungen des "sobornost" Begriffs in Russland', in *Baupläne der sichtbaren Kirche: Sprachliche Konzepte religiöser Vergemeinschaftung in Europa*, ed. Lucian Hölscher (Göttingen: Wallstein, 2007), 196–211. For Pašić the notion signified the importance of the traditional peasant commune – *zadruga* – and even more importantly its democratic spirit to Serbian political and social life. But unlike Khomiakov, Pašić left the theological connotations aside and focused exclusively on the application of the term to the secular context of politics.
69 Pelikan, *Christian Doctrine and Modern Culture*, 287.
70 Miloš Andjelković, 'Savrmena crkva', *Glasnik Ujedinjene Srpske Pravoslavne Crkve*, no. 12 (1920): 182.

71 Pelikan, *Christian Doctrine and Modern Culture*, 289–90.
72 Miloš Andjelković, 'Prava religija i autoritativna crkva', *Glasnik Ujedinjene Srpske Pravoslavne Crkve*, no. 6 (1920): 93.
73 András Bozóki and Miklós Sükösd, *Anarchism in Hungary: Theory, History, Legacies* (Boulder, CO: Social Science Monographs; New York: Columbia University Press, 2006), 88.
74 Bojan Aleksov, *Religious Dissent between the Modern and the National*, 143–5.
75 Katić, *Narodna crkva sa gledišta narodnih potreba* (Jagodina: Knijžara Ž. D. Kostića, 1921), 8–9.
76 Ljudevit Gaj, 'O "Zahtevanju naroda trojedne kraljevine", 1848 na pitanja jednog Beograđanina', in *Antologija jugoslovenske misli*, ed. Novak, 126.
77 Pelikan, *Christian Doctrine and Modern Culture*, 283–4.
78 https://www.oikoumene.org/resources/documents/unto-the-churches-of-christ-everywhere-encyclical-of-the-ecumenical-patriarchate-1920.
79 The new calendar was proposed for adoption by the Orthodox Churches at a synod in Constantinople in May 1923. The synod, chaired by controversial Patriarch Melentije IV of Constantinople, and called Pan-Orthodox by its defenders, did not have representatives from many Orthodox Churches, including the largest one, the Russian Orthodox Church. This synod synchronized the new calendar with the Gregorian calendar by specifying that the next 1 October of the Julian calendar would be 14 October in the new calendar, thus dropping thirteen days. It then adopted a leap year rule that differs from that of the Gregorian calendar. Years evenly divisible by four are leap years, except that years evenly divisible by 100 are not leap years, unless they leave a remainder of 200 or 600 when divided by 900, then they are leap years. This means that the two calendars will first differ in 2800, which will be a leap year in the Gregorian calendar, but a common year in the new calendar. This leap year rule was proposed by the Serbian scientist Milutin Milanković, an astronomical delegate to the synod representing the Kingdom of Serbs, Croats and Slovenes.
80 Jovan Byford, *Denial and Repression of Anti-Semitism: Post-communist Remembrance of the Serbian Bishop Nikolaj Velimirović* (Budapest: Central European University Press, 2008), 23.
81 His standing as a modernist and progressive, with sympathy towards Protestant Churches, together with his obvious erudition and knowledge of languages made the Serbian government send Velimirović on a fundraising mission to the United States and England during the war. He spent four years from 1915 to 1919 mostly in England. His activities abroad were part of the actions taken by the more nationally oriented Serbian Relief Fund and the more inclusive Yugoslav Committee.

82 Byford states that this friendliness was only the political, superficial layer of Velimirović's view, and that his true beliefs were quite the opposite: hostile to Catholicism and Islam, etc. Byford, *Repression and Denial*, 30.
83 AJ 69/182/285, Report by the Bishop of Timisoara to the minister of religions, 12 January 1920.
84 AJ 69/182/286, Note from the Ministry of the Interior to the minister of religions, 21 January 1928.
85 Falina, 'Religious Diversity and Equality', 549–50.
86 George L. Mosse, *The Nationalization of the Masses: Political Symbolism and Mass Movements in Germany from the Napoleonic Wars Through the Third Reich* (New York: Howard Fertig, 1975), 8.
87 Melissa Bokovoy, 'Scattered Graves, Ordered Cemeteries: Commemorating Serbia's Wars of National Liberation, 1912–1918', in *Staging the Past: The Politics of Commemoration in Habsburg Central Europe, 1848 to the Present*, ed. Maria Bucur and Nancy M. Wingfield (West Lafayette, IN: Purdue University Press, 2001), 239.
88 Ibid., 251.
89 For a detailed account of these attempts at reinterpretation, see Wachtel, 'How to Use a Classic', 131–53 and Wachtel, *Making a Nation, Breaking a Nation*.
90 Before his death, Njegoš had asked to be buried in a chapel on top of Mount Lovćen in Montenegro. His will was fulfilled several years after his death, only to be revoked during the war years, when his body was moved back to Cetinje. Once the war was over, Church authorities in Montenegro, now a part of the Kingdom of Serbs, Croats and Slovenes, decided to move Njegoš's remains back to Mount Lovćen. The chapel was in very poor condition and was to be either renovated or built anew.
91 Dožić, *Memoari*, 18.
92 Ibid., 23.
93 S. Budim, 'Hrvatski problem i vera', *Glasnik Srpske Pravolsavne Patrijaršije*, no. 9 (1922): 134.
94 Ibid.

3 The Serbian Orthodox Church faces the challenge of modernity

1 D. J. Vasić, 'Pravoslavlje i naša narodna budućnost', *Pravoslavlje*, no. 1 (1934): 8.
2 Dožić, *Memoari*, 36.
3 Ibid., 34.
4 Miloš Parenta, 'Opasnosti za pravoslavlje', *Glasnik Srpske Pravoslavne Patrijaršije*, no. 12 (1927): 180.

5 Malbone W. Graham Jr., 'The Dictatorship in Yugoslavia', *American Political Science Review* 23, no. 2 (May 1929): 454.
6 Aleksandar Karadjordjević, *Mome dragom narodu svima Srbima, Hrvatima i Slovencima* (Belgrade, 6 January 1929).
7 Ljubodrag Dimić, *Istorija Srpske državnosti. Vol. 3 Srbija u Jugoslaviji* (Novi Sad: Srpska akademija nauka i umetnosti. Ogranak, 2001), 137.
8 Ljubomir Petrović, 'U Potrazi za izmišljenom stvarnošću: Jugoslovenski identitet u časopisu "Jugosloven" 1931–1932', *Istorija 20. veka* 25, no. 1 (2007): 37.
9 Dimić, *Istorija Srpske državnosti*, 142.
10 Cited in Ivana Dobrivojević, *Državna represija u doba diktature kralja Aleksandra, 1929–1935* (Belgrade: Institut za savremenu istoriju, 2006), 63.
11 Dožić, *Memoari*, 48–9.
12 Ibid., 31.
13 Radić, *Život u vremenima*, 144.
14 Minister of religions at the cabinet meeting on 14 March 1929. 'Sednica Ministarskog Saveta Kraljevine SHS, 14. mart 1929', in *Zapisnici sa sednica ministarskog saveta kraljevine Jugoslavije, 1929–1931*, 50.
15 Ibid., 52.
16 'Referat Pretsedinka Ministarskog saveta gen. Petra R. Živkovića Hj. V. Kralju o radu Kraljevske vlade u godini 1929. Podnesen 31. Decembra god. 1929', in *Zapisnici sa sednica ministarskog saveta kraljevine Jugoslavije, 1929–1931*, 123–7.
17 Slijepčević, *Istorija Srpske pravoslavne crkve*, vol. 2, 564.
18 'Poslanica Nj. Sv. Patrijarha i Sv. Arh. Sinoda (Povodom obnarodovanog ustava Srpske pravoslavne crkve i božićnih praznika', *Bratstvo*, no. 1 (1931): 184–7.
19 Radić, *Život u vremenima*, 145.
20 Karčić, 'The reform of Shari'a courts', 261.
21 Christian Axboe Nielsen, *Making Yugoslavs: Identity in King Aleksandar's Yugoslavia* (Toronto, ON: University of Toronto Press, 2014), 157–64.
22 Milan Mratinković, 'Ljubav prema kralju i otadžbini', *Bratstvo*, no. 1 (1932): 29–33.
23 Svetozar Pribićević, *Diktatura Kralja Aleksandra*, trans. Andra Milosavljević (Belgrade: Prosveta, 1952).
24 This motto can be loosely translated as 'For faith and freedom'. Literal translation reads, 'For the Holy cross and golden freedom'.
25 Dožić, *Memoari*, 36–7.
26 Ibid., 37.
27 Miloš Parenta, 'Srpsko-Bugarsko bratstvo', *Glasnik Srpske Pravoslavne Patrijaršije*, no. 6 (1927): 27.
28 Vladimir Ćorović, *Istorija Srba*, 4th edition (Niš: Zograf, 2001), 745.
29 Miloš Parenta, 'Proslava dana ujedinenja', *Glasnik Srpske Pravoslavne Patrijaršije*, no. 23 (1925): 359.

30 'Sednica Ministarskog Saveta Kraljevine SHS, 07 feb 1930', in *Zapisnici sa sednica ministarskog saveta kraljevine Jugoslavije, 1929-1931*, 142-5.
31 Ljubodrag Dimić, *Kulturna politika u kraljevini Jugoslaviji*, vol. 2 (Belgrade: Stubovi kulture), 487.
32 Sandra Prlenda, 'Young, Religious and Radical: The Croat Catholic Youth Organizations, 1922-1945', in *Ideologies and National Identities: The Case of Twentieth-Century Southeastern Europe*, ed. John Lampe and Mark Mazower (Budapest: Central European University Press, 2004), 86.
33 Falina, 'Religious Diversity and Equality'.
34 Pieter Troch, *Nationalism and Yugoslavia: Education, Yugoslavism and the Balkans before World War II* (London: Bloomsbury Academic, [2015] 2020), 43-50.
35 Dr Dimitrje Kirilović (1884-1956) was an archivist and educational historian working in Novi Sad. He started his education in a seminary in Sresmki Karlovci, but became disappointed in his studies and continued education in other secular institutions: he studied philosophy in Budapest, Prague and Zagreb. In 1924, he received doctorate from the University of Zagreb for his thesis 'Serbian primary schools in Vojvodina in the 18th c.'.
36 Aleksandar Živanović, 'Da li se predavanje nauke o veri ostaje sveštenicima?' *Glasnik Srpske Pravoslavne Patrijaršije*, no. 22 (1926): 344.
37 Dr Jure Turić, ,Versko vaspitanje i konfesijska nastava u našim školama', *Glasnik Srpske Pravoslavne Patrijaršije*, no. 5 (1924): 74.
38 'Zakon o Srpskoj Pravoslavnoj Crkvi', § 17 *Glasnik Srpske Pravoslavne Patrijaršije*, no. 22 (1929): 337-41.
39 Ibid.
40 *Glasnik Srpske Pravoslavne Patrijaršije*, no. 15 (1930): 225.
41 Vladan Jovanović, *Vardarska banovina, 1929-1941* (Belgrade: Institut za noviju istoriju Srbije, 2011), 304.
42 'Zakon o Srpskoj Pravoslavnoj Crkvi', § 68.
43 Kristina Stöckl, 'Modernity and Its Critique in Twentieth-century Russian Orthodox Thought', *Studies in East European Thought* 58, no. 4 (2006): 248, http://www.jstor.org/stable/23317542.
44 Ibid.
45 Editorial to Čedomir Marjanović, *Izbacivanje veronauke iz naših gimnazija* (Belgrade: Štamparija 'Sv. Sava', 1921), 192.
46 Branislav Gligorijević, 'Russkya pravoslavnaya tserkov' v period mezhdu dvumya mirovymi voinami', in *Russkaya Emigratsiya v Yugoslavii*, ed. A. Arsenyev (Moscow: Indrik, 1996), 109-17.
47 Slijepčević, *Istorjia Srpske Pravoslavne crkve*, vol. 2, 570.
48 *Glasnik Srpske Pravoslavne Patrijaršije*, nos 15-16 (1933): 250.

49 Dr A. J., 'Povodom dvoju zakonskih predloga u Narodnoj skupštini', *Katolički list*, no. 9 (1933): 90–1.
50 Miloš Parenta, 'Crkvena politika', *Glasnik Srpske Pravoslavne Patrijaršije*, no. 2 (1928): 21.
51 Pelikan, *Christian Doctrine and Modern Culture*, 317.
52 Miloš Parenta, 'Klerikalizam i liberalizam', *Glasnik Sprske Pravoslavne Patrijaršije*, no. 21 (1925): 327.
53 Buchenau, 'Just as Real-life Brothers', 65.
54 Ibid., 54–66.
55 Miloš Parenta, ‚Opasnosti za pravoslavlje', *Glasnik Srpske Pravoslavne Patrijaršije*, no. 12 (1927): 180.
56 'Da li imamo pravoslavno javno mišlenje?' *Glasnik Srpske Pravoslavne Patrijaršije*, nos 15–16 (1933): 251.
57 Ljub Stojanović, 'O našoj inteligenciji: Pamet i srce', *Nova Evropa* 22, no. 1 (1930): 2.
58 C. D. Booth, 'Politički utisci iz Jugoslavije', *Nova Evropa* 19, no. 1 (1929): 22.
59 Slijepčević, *Istorija Srpske Pravoslavne crkve*, vol. 2, 572.
60 For an overview of the debates surrounding the creation of the Theology Faculty, see: Bogoljub Šijaković and Akelksandar Raković, *Univerzitet i srpska teologija: Istroijski i prosvetni kontekst osnivanja Pravoslavnog bogoslovskog fakulteta u Beogradu* (Belgrade: Pravoslavni bogoslovski fakultet, 2010).
61 Irinej Djordjević, after having studied in Belgrade, went on to Saint Petersburg and Oxford where he received a doctoral degree in theology. Justin Popović spent a year in Saint Petersburg and more than ten years (1916–26) in England, in Oxford and London, where he studied theology and philosophy.
62 Slijepčević, *Istorija Srpske Crkve*, vol. 3, 17.
63 'Naša reč', *Svetosavlje*, no. 1 (1932): 2.
64 Dionisije, Jeromonah, ‚Velike stvari u sitnim vermenima', *Glasnik Srpske Pravoslavne Patrijaršije*, no. 24 (1932): 379.
65 See e.g. 'Crkvena aktuelna pitanja', *Glasnik Srpske Pravoslavne Patrijaršije*, no. 35 (1932): 550–2.
66 'Tri konjaka iz apokalipse', *Glasnik Srpske Pravoslavne Patrijaršije*, no. 8 (1933): 121–3.
67 Djokić, *Elusive Compromise*, 60.
68 AJ 69/182/288, The representative reports include the following: Report from the Ministry of the Interior to the Ministry of Religions detailing the support for Radić by a Catholic parson from Križ, 28 January 1925; Report from the Ministry of Army and Navy to the minister of religion detailing that Catholic of Petrijna have announced 'national mourning' due to the government's actions against the Croatian Peasant Party, 24 January 1925; Report from the Ministry of Army and

Navy to the minister of religion detailing how Catholic priests campaign for Radić in churches and schools in the regions of Baranja and Podravina, 27 February 1925.

69 AJ 69/182/288, Report from the Ministry of Army and Navy to the minister of religion detailing how Catholic priests campaign for Radić in churches and schools in the regions of Baranja and Podravina, 27 February 1925.

70 AJ 69/182/288, Report from the Ministry of Army and Navy to the minister of religion, 28 January 1925.

71 Pieter Troch, 'The Intertwining of Religion and Nationhood in Interwar Yugoslavia: The School Celebrations of St Sava's Day', *Slavonic and East European Review* 91, no. 2 (2013): 244–6, https://doi.org/10.5699/slaveasteurorev2.91.2.0235.

72 J. A. B., 'Katolička djeca i svetosavska zabava', *Katolički list*, no. 11 (1933): 129–30.

73 Troch, 'The Intertwining of Religion and Nationhood', 255.

74 Ibid., 251.

75 Iemima Ploscariu, *A Dappled People: Jewish, Roma, and Romanian Evangelicals Challenging Nationalism in Interwar Romania* (PhD diss., Dublin City University, 2021) discusses in great detail the Romanian case.

76 The name is normally translated into English either as the 'God Worshipper movement', which is a literal translation, or as the 'Devotionalist movement'.

77 For a new and to date the most detailed and evidence-based history of the movement, see Radmila Radić and Aleksandra Djurić Milovanović, 'The God Worshipper Movement in Serbian Society in the Twentieth Century: Emergence, Development, and Structures', in *Orthodox Christian Renewal Movements in Eastern Europe*, ed. Aleksandra Djurić Milovanović and Radmila Radić (Cham, Switzerland: Palgrave Macmillan, 2017), 137–72.

78 Metropolitan Dimitrjie cited in Slijepčević, *Istorija Srspke Pravoslavne crkve*, vol. 2, 575.

79 Radić and Djurić Milovanović, 'The God Worshipper Movement in Serbian Society', 139.

80 Milan Bozoljac, 'Bogomoljac – svešteničkoj skupštini', *Hrišćanski život* (1925): 397–400.

81 Monah, 'Pokret Bogomoljca', *Glasnik Srpske Pravoslvane Patrijaršije*, no. 16 (1922): 258.

82 Dragan Subotić, *Episkop Nikolaj i Pravoslavni bogomoljački pokret* (Belgrade: Nova Iskra, 1996). The God Worshippers themselves estimated their numbers to be 300–400,000. Bozoljac, 'Bogomoljac – svešteničkoj skupštini', 400.

83 Radić and Djurić Milovanović, 'The God Worshipper Movement in Serbian Society', 145.

84 Nikolaj Velimirović, 'Ne odbacujte ih. Jedna napomena sveštenicima', *Glasnik Srpske Pravoslvane Patrijaršije*, no. 17 (1921): 273.

85 Djoko Slijepčević, 'Inteligencija i narod', *Hrišćanska misao*, no. 1 (1936): 2.

86 N.E.O., 'Sta je prirodno za nas', *Bratstvo* (1929): 52.
87 Ibid.
88 Dr Savo Ljubibratić, 'Bratstvo Sv. Save', *Bratstvo* (1925): 1–6.
89 Miloš Parenta, 'Opasnosti za pravoslavlje', *Glasnik Srpske Pravoslavne Patrijaršije*, no. 12 (1927): 180.
90 Radić, *Život u vremenima*, 154.
91 Ionut Biliuta, 'The Ultranationalist Newsroom: Orthodox "Ecumenism" in the Legionary Ecclesiastical Newspapers', *Review of Ecumenical Studies* 10, no. 2 (2018): 186–211, https://doi.org/10.2478/ress-2018-0015.
92 *Rapport de la Conférence Régionale Balkanique Sociale et Internationale tenue à Bucarest du 14 au 19 mai 1933 sous les auspices de L'Alliance universelle pour l'amitié internationale par les Eglises et du Conseil Œcuménique du Christianisme pratique*, 20. (N.p., 1933) Collection of the Library of the Serbian Patriarchate.
93 Ibid., 20–1.
94 S., 'Mi odveć mnogo čuvamo, a malo osvajamo', *Glasnik Srpske Pravoslavne Patrijaršije*, no. 37 (1932): 582–3.
95 Dimitrije Najdanović, 'Jugoslovenstvo i crkve', *Hrišćanska misao*, no. 7 (1935): 3.
96 Dimitrije Najdanović, 'Udruženim snagama', *Hrišćanska misao*, no. 1 (1935): 5.
97 Najdanović, 'Jugoslovenstvo i crkve', 2.
98 Ibid.
99 Najdanović, 'Udruženim snagama', 4–5.
100 Ivan Meštrović, *Uspomene na politicke ljude i dogadjaje* (Zagreb: Matica Hrvatska, 1993), 218.

4 Climax: The Serbian Orthodox Church enters politics

1 Their Orthodoxism was primarily a literary and cultural phenomenon, but it had had significant political effects as well. Crainic was closely associated with the Romanian fascist movement, the Iron Guard. He propagated spiritualised traditionalism with East Orthodox Christianity as its foundation; Blaga was fascinated by Romania's mythologised folk culture. Both deemed necessary the spiritual revival of the Romanian nation, the intellectual and cultural elite of which, they argued, followed incorrect, mostly French models, and thus betrayed the essence of the national character. Keith Hitchins, 'Gindirea: Nationalism in a Spiritual Guise', in *Social Change in Romania: 1860–1940: A Debate on Development in a European Nation*, ed. Kenneth Jowitt (Berkeley: Institute of International Studies, University of California, 1978), 140–73.
2 Patrijarh Varnava, 'Gospodinu D-ru Milanu Stojadinoviću Pretsedniku Ministarskog Saveta', *Glasnik Srpske Pravoslavne Patrijaršije*, no. 15 (1937): 450.

3. Dimitrije Najdanović, 'Prolegomena religiozne politike', *Hrišćanska misao*, no. 5 (1936): 69.
4. Miloš Misović, *Zatamnjena istorija. Tajna testamenta kralja Aleksandra i smrt patrijarha Varnave* (Belgrade: Službeni list, 1994).
5. Djokić, *Elusive Compromise*, 115.
6. Stojadinovic, *Ni rat, ni pakt*, 533.
7. Djokić, *Elusive Compromise*, 117.
8. 'Deveti Oktobar', *Hrišćanska misao*, no. 9 (1939): 122.
9. 'Parastosi Blaženopičivšem Kralju Akeksandru I Ujedinitelju o petogodišnjici smrti', *Glasnik Srpske Pravoslavne Patrijaršije*, nos 23–4 (1939): 563.
10. Varnava, 'Gospodinu D-ru Milanu Stojadinoviću Pretsedniku Ministarskog Saveta', 449–52.
11. Radić, *Država i vjerske zajednice*, 36–8. Miloš Misović, *Zatamnjena istorija*. As the Church archive in Belgrade is barely available to scholars, this issue remains underresearched.
12. Djokić, *Elusive Compromise*, 155. The English public's interest in religious affairs in Yugoslavia partially comes from the fact, that in the second half of the 1930s, contacts between the Serbian Church and the Anglican Church intensified and mutual visits were paid to discuss ecumenical work and European security.
13. Djokić, *Elusive Compromise*, 157.
14. Djokić, *Elusive Compromise*; Dejan Djokić, 'National Mobilisation in the 1930s: The "Serb Question" in the Kingdom of Yugoslavia', in *New Perspectives on Yugoslavia: Key Issues and Controversies*, ed. Dejan Djokić and James Ker-Lindsay (New York: Routledge, 2010), 62–81.
15. 'Oko konkordata', *Glansik Srpske Pravoslavne Patrijaršije*, nos 1–2 (1937): 2–4.
16. Ivan Ribar, 'Konkordat', *Glasnik Srpske Pravoslavne Patrijaršije*, nos 1–2 (1937): 10–13. Dr Ivan Ribar (1881–1968) was a Belgrade-based lawyer of Croatian descent and future prominent member of the Communist party of Yugoslavia. Ribar served as president of the Parliamentary Assembly in 1920–2. He belonged to the secular political left (the left wing of the Democratic Party), thus his strong opposition to the Concordat, which, in his view, gave too much power to the Catholic Church at the expense of the state.
17. 'Nekoliko objašnenja o konkordatu', *Glasnik Srpske Pravoslavne Patrijaršije*, nos 5–6 (1937): 149–50.
18. Ibid.
19. Though exaggerated, this fear was not completely groundless. Just a few months earlier, Antun Bauer, the Archbishop of Zagreb, reported considerable growth in Catholic Action clubs and societies in Croatia.
20. AJ 63/105, Note from the Ministry of the Interior to the Ministry of Justice (Section of Religions) containing a transcript of the sermon given by Martin Bešenić, parson at the church of St Peter, Orehovac. 2 November 1932.

21 'Zar se zbog ovogo borio šumadijski narod?' *Glasnik Srpske Pravoslavne Patrijaršije* nos 1–2 (1937): 7–28.
22 'Oštar protest protiv konkordata: Glas sveštenstva i naroda crnogorsko-primirskog', *Glasnik Srpske Pravoslavne Patrijaršije*, nos 3–4 (1937): 107.
23 Ibid.
24 The original uses '*srspkopravoslavni*' which literally translates as 'Serbo-orthodox' and was not a term used commonly at that time. It is an instance of a full equation of categories of religious and national. A noteworthy fact, as the authors came from Montenegro and not Serbia. Macedonian national/ethnic identity does not feature in the entire discussion on any occasion.
25 Patriarch Varnava cited in Miloš Mišović, *Srpska crkva i konkordatska kriza*, 61.
26 Velimirović, quoted in Vjekoslav Perica, *Balkan Idols: Religion and Nationalism in Yugoslav States* (Oxford: Oxford University Press, 2002), 18.
27 Franklin D. Roosevelt, 'Annual Message to the Congress', 4 January 1939. Franklin D. Roosevelt, Annual Message to Congress Online by Gerhard Peters and John T. Woolley, The American Presidency Project https://www.presidency.ucsb.edu/node/209128; *Glasnik Srpske Pravoslavne Patrijršije*, no. 1 (1939): 3.
28 'Pravoslavna crkva pred problemima', *Glasnik Srpske Pravoslavne Patrijaršije*, nos 1–2 (1939): 22–3.
29 Ibid.
30 Quoted in Radić, *Država i verske zajednice*, vol. 1, 41.
31 Nebojša A. Popović, *Slobodan Jovanović i Jugoslovenska država* (Belgrade: Institut za savremenu istoriju, 2003), 212.
32 Dragoljub Jovanović, *Političke Uspomene*, cited it Nebojša A. Popović, *Slobodan Jovanović i Jugoslovenska država*, 213.
33 Ibid., 214.
34 Ibid.
35 Slobodan Jovanović, *Jugoslovenska misao u prošlosti i budućnosti. Predavanje održano u Srpskom kulturnom klubu na dan 4. decembra 1939. godine* (Belgrade: Sloboda, 1939).
36 Quoted in Radić, *Država i verske zajednice*, 44. The Patriarch included the text of his speech in his memoirs. Dožić, *Memoari*, 251–3.
37 Stefan Cankov, 'Crkva i nacija na pravoslavnom istoku', *Hrišćanska misao*, no. 3 (1936): 36. Emphasis in the original.
38 Cankov, 'Crkva i nacija', 36–8.
39 Viorel Coman, 'Revisiting the Agenda of the Orthodox Neo-Patristic Movement', *Downside Review* 136, no. 2 (2018): 99–117, https://doi.org/10.1177/0012580618770381.
40 Pantelis Kalaitzidis, 'From the "Return to the Fathers" to the Need for a Modern Orthodox Theology', *St Vladimir's Theological Quarterly* 54, no. 1 (2010): 7.

41 See e.g. the Speech by Patriarch Gavrilo on the occasion of his enthronement in Peć, *Glasnik Srpske Pravoslavne Patrijaršije*, nos 20–1 (1938): 522.
42 'Sumorne teze u obliku apela Crkvi', *Hrišćanska misao*, no. 10 (1939): 137.
43 Ibid. Emphasis is mine.
44 *Glasnik Srpske Pravoslavne Patrijaršije*, nos 40–1 (1934): 593–4.
45 Vjekoslav Perica, 'The Sanctification of Enmity', in *Myths and Boundaries in South-Eastern Europe*, ed. Pål Kolstø, 135.
46 Cynthia J. Paces, 'Religious Heroes for a Secular State: Commemorating Jan Hus and saint Wenceslas in 1920s Czechoslovakia', in *Staging the Past*, ed. Maria Bucur and Nancy M. Wingfield, 232.
47 Ibid., 209.
48 Bojan Aleksov, 'Nationalism in Construction: The Memorial Church of St Sava on Vračar Hill in Belgrade', *Balkanologie* 7, no. 2 (December 2003): 47.
49 Nikolaj Velimirović, 'Nacionalizam Svetoga Save', in *Srpska konzervativna misao*, ed. Mirko Djordjević (Belgrade: Helsinški odbor za ljudska prava u Srbiji, 2003), 57–63. The first publication of the text is Episkop Nikolaj, *Nacionalizam svetoga Save, predavanje održano na KNU 1935* (Belgrade: Izdanje Arhiepiskopije beogradsko-karlovačke, 1935). Hereafter citations are from the modern edition.
50 Velimirović, 'Nacionalizam Svetoga Save', 60.
51 Ibid., 58.
52 Ibid.
53 Ibid., 63.
54 Ibid.
55 Ibid.
56 Samuel Koehne, 'The Racial Yardstick: "Ethnotheism" and Official Nazi Views on Religion"' *German Studies Review* 37, no. 3 (October 2014): 575–96, http://www.jstor.org/stable/43556113; John S. Conway, 'Coming to Terms with the Past: Interpreting the German Church Struggles 1933–1990', *German History* 16, no. 3 (1998): 377–96.
57 Danilo R. Medan, 'Konture Svetosavske ideologije i njen značaj u prošlosti i sadašnjosti', *Svetosavlje*, no. 1 (1937): 88.
58 Ibid.
59 Ibid.
60 Buchenau, 'Pravoslavlje und Svetosavlje: Nationales und Universales in der serbischen Orthodoxie', 214.
61 Medan, 'Konture Svetosavske ideologije', 89.
62 Miloš Crnjanski, *Sveti Sava* (Belgrade: Zadruga Profesorskog društva, 1934).
63 Djoko Slijepčević, Review of Crnjainski's 'Sveti Sava', *Hrišćanska misao*, no. 1 (1935): 14.
64 Milutin P. Devrnja, 'Sava M. Stedimlija o Sv. Savi', *Hrišćanska misao*, no. 2 (1935): 12.

65 Milutin P. Devrnja, 'Za istinsko shvatanje ličnosti Sv. Save', *Hrišćanska misao*, nos 5–6 (1935): 20.
66 Priest Jovan (Rapajić), 'Untitled', *Svetosavlje*, no. 1 (1937): 41.
67 Perica, *Balkan Idols*, 20.
68 *Glasnik Srpske Pravoslavne Patrijaršije*, nos 10–11 (1939).
69 For a detailed history of the Cathedral, see Bojan Aleksov, 'Nationalism in Construction'.
70 Ibid., 13.
71 Ibid., 15.
72 Živan Marinković, 'Za aktivniju socijalnu delatnost naše Crkve', *Hrišćanska misao*, no. 1 (1939): 5.
73 Ibid., 5–6.
74 Ibid.
75 Živan Marinković, 'Za aktivniju socijalnu delatnost naše Crkve', *Hrišćanska Misao*, no. 2 (1939): 25.
76 Lj. A. (Ljubomir Antic), 'Reorganizacija rada pravoslavne narodne Hrišćanske zajednice u Niškoj eparhiji', *Glasnik Srpske Pravoslavne Patrijaršije*, no. 18 (1939): 416.
77 Galina Valtchinova, *Balkanski yasnovitki i prorotchitsi ot XX vek* (Sofia: Universitetsko izdatelstvo Sv. Kliment Ohridski, 2006), 254–5.
78 Valtchinova, *Balkanski yasnovitki*, 392.
79 Hitchins, 'Gindirea: Nationalism in Spiritual Guise', 147.
80 Perica, *Balkan Idols*, 18–20.

Epilogue: The war

1 Henry Rousso, 'A New Perspective on the War', in *Experience and Memory: The Second World War in Europe*, ed. Jörg Echternkamp and Stefan Martens (New York: Berghahn Books, 2010), 2.
2 Bette Denich, 'Dismembering Yugoslavia: Nationalist Ideologies and the Symbolic Revival of Genocide', *American Ethnologist* 21, no. 2 (May 1994): 367–90; Stef Jansen, 'The Violence of Memories: Local Narratives of the Past after Ethnic Cleansing in Croatia', *Rethinking History* 6, no. 1 (2002): 77–94, https://doi.org/10.1080/13642520110112128; Jelena Djureinović, *The Politics of Memory of the Second World War in Contemporary Serbia: Collaboration, Resistance and Retribution* (London: Routledge, 2020).
3 Ibid., 36–7.
4 Ibid., 45.
5 Sabrina P. Ramet and Ola Listhaug, eds., *Serbia and the Serbs in World War Two* (New York: Palgrave Macmillan, 2011).

6   Djureinović, *The Politics of Memory*, 68.
7   Ibid., 58.
8   Jovan Radosavljević, *Život i stradanja Žiče i Studenice pod okupatorom, 1938–1945* (Sveta Gora: Manastir Hilandar, 1993); Jevtić, 'The Kosovo Creed in Bishop Nikolaj's Writing', *Glas Crkve* 3 (1988): 19.
9   Dimitrije V. Ljotić, 'Pismo patrijarhu Gavrilu i episkopima Nikolaju i Irineju, Beograd, 25 March, 1941', in *Sabrana Dela, Vol. 10, 1941–1945*, ed. Dimitrije Ljotić (Novi Sad: Zadruga, 2001), 37.
10 Radic, *Život u vremenima*, 255.
11 Mark Biondich, 'Religion and Nation in Wartime Croatia'; Jozo Tomasevich, *War and Revolution in Yugoslavia, 1941–1945: Occupation and Collaboration* (Stanford, CA: Stanford University Press 2001); Aleksa Djilas, *The Contested Country: Yugoslav Unity and Communist Revolution, 1919–1953* (Cambridge, MA: Harvard University Press, 1991); Alexander Korb, *Im Schatten des Weltkriegs: Massengewalt der Ustaša gegen Serben, Juden und Roma in Kroatien 1941–1945* (Hamburg: Hamburger Edition, 2013).
12 Perica, *Balkan Idols*, 24.
13 Radić, *Držva i verske zajednice*, 47.
14 M. V. Shkarovskiy, 'Sozdaniye i deyatel'nost Khorvatskoy Pravoslavnoy Tserkvi v gody Vtoroy mirovoy voyny', *Vestnik Tserkovnoy Istorii* 3, no. 7 (2007): 238.
15 Radic, *Život u vremenima*, 286.
16 Mark Biondich, 'Radical Catholicism and Fascism in Croatia, 1918–1945', *Totalitarian Movements and Political Religions* 8, no. 2 (2007): 393. An apologetic view of the Catholic Church is presented by Jure Kristo, *Katolička crkva u Nezavisnoj Državi Hrvatskoj*, 2 vols (Zagreb: Hrvatski institut za povijest, 1998).
17 Hans Mommsen, 'The German Resistance against Hitler and the Restoration of Politics', *Journal of Modern History* 64 (December 1992): 113.
18 Jill Stephenson, 'Review Article: Resistance and the Third Reich', *Journal of Contemporary History* 36, no. 3 (July 2001): 507–16.
19 Tony Judt, 'Preface' to *The Politics of Retribution in Europe: World War II and Its Aftermath*, ed. István Deák, Jan Tomasz Gross, Tony Judt (Princeton, NJ: Princeton University Press, c.2000), ix.
20 Jozo Tomasevich, *War and Revolution in Yugoslavia*, 512.
21 Ibid., 515.
22 Radić, *Život u vremenima*, 275.
23 Urs von Arx, 'Episkop Nikolaj Velimirović (1880–1956) i njegoce studije u Bernu u okviru starokatoličkih i srpsko-pravoslavnih odnosa', in *Srspka teologija u dvadesetom veku: Istrazivacki problemi i rezultati*, ed. Bogoljub Šijaković (Belgrade: Pravoslavni bogoslovski fakultet, 2007), 20.
24 Stevan Moljević, 'Homogena Srbija' (June 1941), in *Srbija i Ravna Gora*, ed. Dragan Sotirović and Branko Jovanović (Belgrade: Institut za savremenu istoriju, 2004), 194.

25 Dimitrije Najdanović, *Ravna Gora: Zablude i samounistenje*, ed. Zeljko Z. Jelić (Belgrade: Slobodna knjiga, 2002). The text was initially published in Belgrade in 1944.
26 Milan D. Janković, *Sveti Episkop Nikolaj: život, misao i delo, Vol. III* (Valjevo: Eparhija Šabačko-Valjevska, 2003), 217.
27 Maria Falina, 'Between "Clerical Fascism" and Political Orthodoxy: Orthodox Christianity and Nationalism in Interwar Serbia', *Totalitarian Movements and Political Religions* 8, no. 2 (2007): 247–58, https://doi.org/10.1080/14690760701321155.
28 Dimitrije V. Ljotić, 'Pismo drugovima', in Dimitrije V. Ljotić, *Sabrana dela, Vol. 10, 1941–1945*, 194–201.
29 Ibid.
30 Ibid.
31 Dimitrije V. Ljotić, 'Srpski narod mora živeti po zakonu svoga bića (26 Feb 1944)', in Dimitrije V. Ljotić, *Sabrana dela, Vol. 10, 1941–1945*, 168.
32 Nikolaj Velimirović, *Govori Srpskom narodu kroz tamnički prozor* (Belgrade: Svetosavska književna zajednica, 1995).
33 Byford, *Denial and Repression of Antisemitism*, 43.
34 Velimirović, *Govori Srpskom narodu*, 5.
35 Byford, *Denial and Repression of Antisemitism*, 56.
36 Dimitrije Najdanović, *Blaženi i blaženstva: misao oboženja* (München: Štamparija Iskra, 1965); Dimitrije Najdanović, *Tri srpska velikana* (München: Svečanik-Verlag, 1975).
37 Klaus Buchenau, *Svetosavlje und Pravoslavlje*, 216.
38 Neven Vukic, 'The Church in a Communist State', 278–99.
39 Neven Vukic, 'Saintsavaism(s) and Nationalism: An Overview of the Development of the Serbian Orthodox Phenomenon of Saintsavaism, with a Special Focus on the Contribution of Justin Popovic (1894–1979)', *Exchange* 50 (2021): 78, https://doi.org/10.1163/1572543X-12341586.
40 Justin Popović, *Filosofija i religija F.M. Dostojevskoga* (Sremski Karlovci: Srpska manastirska stamparija, 1923).
41 Justin Popović, *Pravoslavna Crkva i ekumenizam* (1974); *Svetosavlje kao filosofija zivota* (1953).
Modern edition: Atanasije Jevtić, ed. *Sabrana dela oca Justina Popovića*, vol. 4 (Beograd: Manastir Celije; Naslednici Oca Justina, 2001).
42 Klaus Buchenau, 'Svetosavlje und Pravoslavlje', 222; Makrides and Uffelmann, 'Studying Eastern Orthodox Anti-Westernism', 116–17.
43 Jelena Subotić, 'The Church, the Nation, and the State: The Serbian Orthodox Church after Communism', in *Orthodox Churches and Politics in Southeastern Europe: Nationalism, Conservativism, and Intolerance*, ed. Sabrina P. Ramet (Cham, Switzerland: Palgrave Macmillan, 2019), 85–110.

Bibliography

Primary sources

Unpublished

Arhiv Jugoslavije (Archive of Yugoslavia, Belgrade)

Fond 69, Ministarstvo vera Kraljevine Srba, Hrvata i Slovenaca
Fond 63, Ministarstvo pravde Kraljevine Jugoslavije

Library of the Serbian Patriarchate

Rapport de la Conference Regionale Balkanique Sociale et Internationale tenue a Bucarest du 14 au 19 mai 1933 sous les auspices de L'Alliance universelle pour l'amitie internationale par les Eglise et du Conseil Oecumenigue du Christianisme pratique.

Published

Legislation, official transcripts

Crkveno zakonodavstvo Srpske pravoslavne crkve. Vol. 3. Belgrade: Geca Kon, 1933.
Dimić, Ljubodrag, Nikola Žutić and Blagoje Isailović, eds. *Zapisnici sa sednica ministarskog saveta kraljevine Jugoslavije,* 1929–1931. Belgrade: Službeni list, Arhiv Jugoslavije, 2002.
Karadjordjević, Aleksandar. *Mome dragom narodu svima Srbima, Hrvatima i Slovencima.* Belgrade, 6 January 1929.
Krestić, Vasilije, and Radoš Ljušić, eds. *Programi i statuti Srpskih političkih stranaka do 1918. g.* Belgrade: Književne novine, 1991.
Krfska konferencija. Beleške sa sednica vlade Kraljevine Srbije i predstavnika jugoslovenskog odbora, držanih na Krfu 1917 godine, na kojima je donesena Krfska Deklaracija. Belgrade: Štamparija Skerlić, 1924.
N. P. *Tekstovi projekta zakona o Konkordatu i odgovarajućih stavova iz zakonodavstva Srpske Pravolsavne Crkve. Uporedjeni i objašnjeni.* Belgrade: Izdanje 'Samouprave', 1937.

Journals and newspapers

Bogoslovlje: Organ Pravoslavnog bogoslovskog fakulteta u Beogradu (Belgrade), 1926–40.
Bratstvo: List za vjersko i narodno prosvjećivanje (Sarajevo), 1925–41.
Glasnik: Zvanični list Srpske Pravoslavne Patrijaršije (Belgrade), 1920–41. The subtitle changed several times, this version was used for most of the interwar period.
Hrišćanska misao: Časopis za hrišćanska i društvena pitanja (Belgrade), 1935–41.
Hrišćanski vesnik (Belgrade), 1896–1900, 1906–8, 1911–14.
Hrišćanski život: mesečni časopis za hrišćansku kulturu i crkveni život (Sremski Karlovci, Belgrade, Prizren), 1922–7.
Hrišćansko delo: Časopis za hrišćansku kulturu i crkveni život (Skopje), 1935–41.
Katolički list (Zagreb), 1933–7.
Nova Evropa (Zagreb), 1920–41.
Put: Časopis za hrišćansku kulturu (Belgrade), 1933–4.
Srpski književni glasnik (Belgrade), 1901–14, 1920–41.
Svetosavlje: Organ studenata Pravoslavnog bogoslovskog faulteta (Belgrade), 1932–41.
Vesnik: Crkveno-politički i društveni list (Belgrade), 1919–30.
Vesnik Srpske Crkve (Belgrade), 1898–1914, 1921–33.

Memoirs

Dožić, Gavrilo. *Memoari Patrijarha Srpskog Gavrila*. Belgrade: Sfairos, 1990.
Ilić, Aleksa. *Moji doživljai*. Belgrade: Štamparija Sv. Sava, 1931.
Meštrović, Ivan. *Uspomene na političke ljude i dogadjaje*. Zagreb: Matica Hrvatska, 1993 (first published in Buenos Aires in 1963).
Pribićević, Svetozar. *Diktatura kralja Aleksandra*. trans. Andra Milosavljević. Belgrade: Prosveta, 1952 (first published as *La dictature du roi Alexander*, Paris, 1933).
Stojadinović, Milan. *Ni Rat Ni Pakt: Jugoslavija izmedju dva rata*. Belgrade: Glas, 2002 (first published in 1963).

Anthologies

Djordjević, Mirko, ed. *Srpska konzervativna misao*. Belgrade: Helsinški odbor za ljudska prava u Srbiji, 2003.
Mishkova, Diana, Marius Turda and Balázs Trencsényi, eds. *Discourses of Collective Identity in Central and Southeast Europe, 1770–1945. Volume IV Anti-modernism. Radical revisions of collective identity*. Budapest: Central European University Press, 2014.

Novak, Viktor, ed., *Antologija jugoslovenske misli i narodnog jedinstva: 1390–1930*. Belgrade: Štampa državne štamparije, 1930.

Essay, pamphlets and other published primary sources

Bulgakov, S. N. *Sochineniya*. 2 Vols. Moscow: Nauka, 1993.
Crnjanski, Miloš. *Sveti Sava*. Belgrade: Prosveta, 1934.
Durham, Mary E. *Through the Lands of the Serb*. London: E. Arnold, 1904.
Jevtić, Atanasije, ed. *Sabrana dela oca Justina Popovića*. Vol. 4. Beograd: Manastir Celije; Naslednici Oca Justina, 2001.
Jovanović, *Slobodan. Jugoslovenska misao u prošlosti i budućnosti. Predavanje održano u Srpskom kulturnom klubu na dan 4. decembra 1939. godine*. Belgrade: Sloboda, 1939.
Katić, *Narodna crkva sa gledišta narodnih potreba*. Jagodina: Knijžara Ž.
   D. Kostića, 1921.
Leontev, Konstantin Nikolaevich. *Vostok, Rossiia i
   Slavianstvo: filosofskaia i politicheskaia publitsistika: dukhovnaia proza* (1872–1891). Moscow: Respublika, 1996.
Ljotić, Dimitrije V. *Sabrana Dela, Vol. 10 1941–1945*. Novi Sad: Zadruga, 2001.
Ljotić, Dimitrije V.. *Zatomljena misao: O političkim idejama Dimitrija Ljotića*, edited by Dragan Subotić. Belgarde: Klio, 1994.
Marjanović, Čedomir. *Izbacivanje veronauke iz naših gimnazija*. Belgrade: Štamparija Sv. Sava, 1921.
Marjanović, Čedomir. *Socjializam: Kritički pregled najosnovnijih tačaka socijalističkog učenja*. Belgrade: Državna štamparija Kraljevine Srbije, 1907.
Mojsej, episkop. *Crkveno pitanje u Srbiji*. Belgrade: Štamparija Pere Todorovića, 1895.
Najdanović, Dimitrije. *Blaženi i blaženstva: misao oboženja*. München: Štamparija Iskra, 1965.
Najdanović, Dimitrije. *Filosofija istorije Imanuela Hermana Fihtea i drugi spisi iz filosofije, bogoslovlja i kniževnosti*. Edited by Željko Z. Jelić. Belgrade: Jasen: Fond istine o Srbima, 2003.
Najdanović, Dimitrije. *Ravna Gora: Zablude i samounistenje*. Edited by Zeljko Z. Jelić. Belgrade: Slobodna knjiga, 2002. Originally published in Belgrade in 1944.
Najdanović, Dimitrije. *Tri srpska velikana*. München: Svečanik-Verlag, 1975.
Pašić, Nikola. *Sloga Srbo-Hrvata*. Belgrade: Vreme knjige, 1995.
Popović, Justin. *Filosofija i religija F.M. Dostojevskoga*. Sremski Karlovci: Srpska manastirska stamparija, 1923.
Velimirović, Nikolaj. *Govori Srpskom narodu kroz tamnički prozor*. Belgrade: Svetosavska književna zajednica, 1995.
Velimirović, Nikolaj. *Nacionalizam svetoga Save, predavanje održano na KNU 1935*. Belgrade: Izdanje Arhiepiskopije beogradsko-karlovačke, 1935.

Secondary literature

Aleksov, Bojan. 'History Taught Us Not to Fear Anything from the East and Everything from the West. A Historical Perspective on Serbian Occidentalism'. In *Prowestliche und antiwestliche Diskurse in den Balkanländern/ Südosteuropa*, edited by G. Schubert. and S. Sundhaussen, 31–46. München: Südosteuropa-Gesellschaft, 2008.

Aleksov, Bojan. 'Nationalism in Construction: The Memorial Church of St. Sava on Vracar Hill in Belgrade', *Balkanologie* 7, no. 2 (December 2003): 47–72.

Aleksov, Bojan. *Religious Dissent between the Modern and the National. Nazarenes in Hungary and Serbia 1850–1914*. Wiesbaden: Harrassowitz Verlag, 2006.

Allcock, John B. *Explaining Yugoslavia*. London: C. Hurst, 2000.

Anderson, Benedict. *Imagined Communities: Reflections on the Origin and Spread of Nationalism*. London: Verso, 2006.

Arjomand, Said Amir, ed. *The Political Dimensions of Religion*. Albany: State University of New York Press, 1993.

Arx, Urs von. 'Episkop Nikolaj Velimirović (1880–1956) i njegove studije u Bernu u okviru starokatoličkih i srpsko-pravoslavnih odnosa'. In *Srspka teologija u dvadesetom veku: Istrazivacki problemi i rezultati*, edited by Bogoljub Šijaković, 7–27. Belgrade: Pravoslavni bogoslovski fakultet, 2007.

Asad, Talal. *Formations of the Secular: Christianity, Islam, Modernity*. Stanford, CA: Stanford University Press, 2003.

Asad, Talal. 'Religion, Nation-State, Secularism'. In *Nation and Religion: Perspectives on Europe and Asia*, edited by Peter van der Veer and Hartmut Lehmann, 178–96. Princeton, NJ: Princeton University Press, 1999.

Augustinos, Gerasimos, ed. *Diverse Paths to Modernity in Southeastern Europe: Essays in National Development*. New York: Greenwood Press, 1991.

Bakić, Jovo. *Ideologije jugoslovenstva izmedu srpskog i hrvatskog nacionalizma 1918–1941: sociološko-istorijska studija*. Zrenjanin: Gradska narodna biblioteka 'Žarko Zrenjanin', 2004.

Bakic-Hayden, Milica. 'National Memory and Narrative Memory: The Case of Kosovo'. In *Balkan Identities: Nation and Memory*, edited by Maria Todorova, 25–41. New York: New York University Press, 2004.

Banac, Ivo. *The National Question in Yugoslavia: Origins, History, Politics*. Ithaca, NY: Cornell University Press, [1984] 1993.

Banac, Ivo, John G. Ackerman and Roman Szporluk, eds. *Nation and Ideology: Essays in Honor of Wayne S. Vucinich*. Boulder, CO: East European Monographs, 1981.

Banac, Ivo, and Katherine Verdery, ed. *National Character and National Ideology in Interwar Eastern Europe*. New Haven, CT: Yale Center for International and Area Studies, 1995.

Bauchman, Tom, and Martin Conway, eds. *Political Catholicism in Europe, 1918–1965*. Oxford: Clarendon Press, 1996.

Bellamy, Alex J. 'The Catholic Church and Croatia's Two Transitions'. *Religion, State and Society* 30, no. 1 (2002): 45–61.
Berend, Ivan T. *Decades of Crisis: Central and Eastern Europe before World War II*. Berkeley: University of California Press, 1998.
Bergen, Doris L. 'Christianity and Germanness: Mutually Reinforcing, Reciprocally Undermining?' In *Religion und Nation, Nation und Religion: Beiträge zu einer unbewältigten Geschichte*, edited by Michael Geyer and Hartmut Lehmann, 76–98. Göttingen: Wallstein, 2004.
Berglund, Bruce R., and Brian Porter-Szűcs, eds. *Christianity and Modernity in Eastern Europe*. Budapest: Central European University Press, 2010.
Bhabha, Homi K., ed. *Nation and Narration*. London: Routledge, 1990.
Bigović, Radovan. *Crkva i društvo*. Belgrade: Chilandar Fund at the Theological Faculty of the Serbian Orthodox Church, 2000.
Bigović, Radovan. *Od svečoveka do bogočoveka: Hrišćanska filosofija vladike Nikolaja Velimirovića*. Belgrade: Društvo Raška škola, 1998.
Biliuta, Ionut. 'The Ultranationalist Newsroom: Orthodox "Ecumenism" in the Legionary Ecclesiastical Newspapers'. *Review of Ecumenical Studies* 10, no. 2 (2018): 186–211. https://doi.org/10.2478/ress-2018-0015.
Biondich, Mark. 'The Historical Legacy: The Evolution of Interwar Yugoslav Politics, 1918–1941'. In *State Collapse in South-Eastern Europe: New Perspectives on Yugoslavia's Disintegration*, edited by Lenard J. Cohen and Jasna Dragović-Soso, 43–54. West Lafayette, IN: Purdue University Press, 2008.
Biondich, Mark. 'Radical Catholicism and Fascism in Croatia, 1918–1945'. *Totalitarian Movements and Political Religions* 8, no. 2 (2007): 383–99.
Biondich, Mark. 'Religion and Nation in Wartime Croatia: Reflections on the Ustaša Policy of Forced Religious Conversions, 1941–1942'. *Slavonic and East European Review* 83, no. 1 (January 2005): 71–116. http://www.jstor.org/stable/4214049.
Blaschke, Olaf. 'Das 19. Jahrhundert: Ein Zweites Konfessionelles Zeitalter?' *Geschichte und Gesellschaft: Zeitschrift für historische Sozialwissenschaft* 26 (2000): 38–75.
Blinkton, Martin. *Fascism and the Right in Europe, 1919–1945*. Harlow: Pearson Education, 2000.
Boia, Lucian. *Romania: Borderland of Europe*. London: Reaktion Books, 2001.
Bozóki, András, and Miklós Sükösd. *Anarchism in Hungary: Theory, History, Legacies*. Boulder, CO: Social Science Monographs, 2006.
Brady, Thomas A., Jr. 'Confessionalization – The Career of a Concept'. In *Confessionalization in Europe: 1555 – 1700. Essays in Honor and Memory of Bodo Nischan*, edited by John M. Headley, 1–20. Aldershot: Ashgate, 2004.
Bremer, Thomas. *Ekklesiale Struktur und Ekklesiologie in der Serbischen Orthodoxen Kirche im 19. und 20. Jahrhundert*. Würzburg: Augustinus-Verlag, 1992.
Broughton, David, and Hans-Martien ten Napel, eds. *Religion and Mass Electoral Behaviour in Europe*. London: Routledge, 2000.

Brubaker, Rogers. 'Religion and Nationalism: Four Approaches'. *Nations and Nationalism* 18, no. 1 (2011): 1-19. https://doi.org/10.1111/j.1469-8129.201 1.00486.x.

Bruce, Steve. *Politics and Religion*. Cambridge: Polity Press, 2003.

Bruce, Steve, ed. *Religion and Modernization: Sociologists and Historians Debate the Secularization Thesis*. Oxford: Clarendon Press, 1992.

Brunnbauer. Ulf, ed. *(Re)Writing History: Historiography in Southeast Europe after Socialism*. Münster: Lit, 2004.

Buchenau, Klaus. *Auf russischen Spuren. Orthodoxe Antiwestler in Serbien, 1850-1945*. Wiesbaden: Harrassowitz, 2011.

Buchenau, Klaus. 'Just as Real-Life Brothers: Serb-Russian Contacts in the Ecclesiastical Academy of Kiev (1850-1914) and in Orthodox Schools of Interwar Yugoslavia (1920-1941)'. *Tokovi Istorije* 3-4 (2005): 54-66.

Buchenau, Klaus. *Kämpfende Kirchen: Jugoslawiens religiöse Hypothek*. Frankfurt am Main: Peter Lang, 2006.

Buchenau, Klaus. *Orthodoxie und Katholizismus in Jugoslawien, 1945-1991: Ein serbisch-kroatischer Vergleich*. Wiesbaden: Harrassowitz, 2004.

Buchenau, Klaus. 'Svetosavlje und Pravoslavlje: Nationales und Universales in der serbischen Orthodoxie'. In *Nationalisierung der Religion und Sakralisierung der Nation in Ostmittel-, Südost- und Osteuropa im 19. und 20. Jahrhundert*, edited by Martin Schulze Wessel, 203-32. Stuttgart: Steiner, 2006.

Bucur, Maria, and Nancy M. Wingfield, eds. *Staging the Past: The Politics of Commemoration in Habsburg Central Europe, 1848 to the Present*. West Lafayette, IN: Purdue University Press, 2001.

Burrin, P. 'Political Religion: The Relevance of a Concept'. *History and Memory*, 9 (1997): 321-49.

Byford, Jovan. *Denial and Repression of Anti-Semitism: Post-Communist Remembrance of the Serbian Bishop Nikolaj Velimirović*. Budapest: Central European University Press, 2008.

Casanova, José. 'The Problem of Religion and the Anxieties of European Secular Democracy'. In *Religion and Democracy in Contemporary Europe*, edited by Gabriel Motzkin and Yochi Fischer, 63-74. London: Alliance Publishing, Van Leer Jerusalem Institute, 2008.

Casanova, José. *Public Religions in the Modern World*. Chicago: University of Chicago Press, 1994.

Chadwick, Owen. *The Secularization of the European Mind in the Nineteenth Century*. Cambridge: Cambridge University Press, 1991.

Cisarž, Branko A. *Jedan vek periodične štampe Srpske pravoslavne crkve: bibliografijski opis časopisa i listova sa pregledom-sadržajem svih radova objavljenih u njima od 1868-1970*. 2 Vols. Belgrade: Sveti arhijerejski sinod Srpske pravoslavne crkve, 1986.

Clayer, Nathalie, and Xavier Bougarel, eds. *Europe's Balkan Muslims: A New History*. London: Hurst, 2017.

Clayer, Nathalie N., and Eric Germain, eds. *Islam in Interwar Europe*. London: Hurst, 2008.
Čolović, Ivan. *The Politics of Symbol in Serbia: Essays in Political Anthropology*. London: Hurst, 2002.
Coman, Viorel. 'Revisiting the Agenda of the Orthodox Neo-Patristic Movement'. *Downside Review* 136, no. 2 (2018): 99–117. https://doi.org/10.1177/0012580618770381.
Conway, John S. 'Coming to Terms with the Past: Interpreting the German Church Struggles 1933–1990', *German History* 16, no. 3 (1998): 377–96.
Conway, Martin. *Catholic Politics in Europe: 1918–1945*. London: Routledge, 1997.
Ćorović, Vladimir. *Istorija Srba*. 4th edition. Niš: Zograf, 2001.
Ćorović, Vladimir. *Istorija Srpskog naroda*. 3 Vols. Cetinje: Svetigora, Podgorica: Oktoih: Jumedijamont, 2009.
Cox, Jeffrey. 'Master Narratives of Long-Term Religious Change'. In *The Decline of Christendom in Western Europe*, edited by David Hugh McLeod and Werner Ustorf, 201–18. Cambridge: Cambridge University Press, 2003.
Craciun, Maria, and Ovidiu Ghitta, eds. *Ethnicity and Religion in Central and Eastern Europe*. Cluj: Cluj University Press, 1995.
Crampton, R. J. *Eastern Europe in the Twentieth Century*. London: Routledge, 1994.
Crampton, R. J. *A Short History of Modern Bulgaria*. Cambridge: Cambridge University Press, 1993.
Cristi, Marcela. *From Civil to Political Religion: The Intersection of Culture, Religion and Politics*. Waterloo, ON: Wilfrid Laurier University Press, 2001.
Čubrilović, Vasa. *Istorija Političke misli u Srbiji XIX veka*. Belgrade: Prosveta, 1958.
Čubrilović, Vasa. 'Srpska Pravoslavna Crkva pod Turcima od XV do XIX veka'. *Zbornik Filozofskog fakulteta* 5, no. 1 (1960): 163–88.
Cunningham, Mary B., and Elizabeth Theokritoff, eds., *The Cambridge Companion to Orthodox Christian Theology*. Cambridge: Cambridge University Press, 2008.
Danopoulos, Constantine P. 'Religion, Civil Society, and Democracy in Orthodox Greece'. *Journal of Southern Europe and the Balkans* 6, no. 1 (April 2004): 43–55.
Daskalov, Roumen. *The Making of a Nation in the Balkans*. Budapest: Central European University Press, 2003.
Davie, Grace, and Lucian N. Leustean, eds. *The Oxford Handbook of Religion and Europe*. Oxford: Oxford University Press, 2021.
Day, Graham, and Andrew Thompson, eds. *Theorizing Nationalism*. Basingstoke: Palgrave Macmillan, 2004.
Deák, István, Jan Tomasz Gross and Tony Judt, eds. *The Politics of Retribution in Europe: World War II and Its Aftermath*. Princeton, NJ: Princeton University Press, 2000.
Denich, Bette. 'Dismembering Yugoslavia: Nationalist Ideologies and the Symbolic Revival of Genocide'. *American Ethnologist* 21, no. 2 (May 1994): 367–90.

Dimić, Ljubodrag. *Istorija Srpske državnosti. Vol. 3 Srbija u Jugoslaviji*. Novi Sad: Srpska akademija nauka i umetnosti. Ogranak, 2001.

Dimić, Ljubodrag. *Kulturna politika u Kraljevini Jugoslaviji, 1918–1941*. Belgrade: Stubovi kulture, 1996.

Dimitrova, Nina. *Religiya i natsionalizam: Idei za religiyata v mezhduvoenniya period v Bulgaria*. Sofia: Faber, 2006.

Djilas, Aleksa. *The Contested Country: Yugoslav Unity and Communist Revolution, 1919–1953*. Cambridge, MA: Harvard University Press, 1991.

Djokić, Dejan. *Elusive Compromise: A History of Interwar Yugoslavia*. New York: Columbia University Press, 2007.

Djokić, Dejan. 'National Mobilisation in the 1930s: The "Serb Question" in the Kingdom of Yugoslavia'. In *New Perspectives on Yugoslavia: Key Issues and Controversies*, edited by Dejan Djokić and James Ker-Lindsay, 62–81. New York: Routledge, 2010.

Djokić, Dejan. ed. *Yugoslavism: Histories of a Failed Idea, 1918–1992*. London: C. Hurst, 2003.

Djureinović, Jelena. *The Politics of Memory of the Second World War in Contemporary Serbia: Collaboration, Resistance and Retribution*. London: Routledge, 2020.

Djurović, Bogdan, ed. *Religija – crkva – nacija*. Niš: JUNIR; Subotica: Otvoreni univerzitet, 1996.

Dobrivojević, Ivana. *Državna represija u doba diktature kralja Aleksandra, 1929–1935*. Belgrade: Institut za savremenu istoriju, 2006.

Dobrivojević, Ivana. 'Izmedju kralja i naroda nema posrednika: dinastička propaganda u vreme šestojanuarskog režima'. *Tokovi istorije*, 4 (2006): 159 – 82.

Dogan, Mattei. 'Accelerated Decline of Religious Beliefs in Europe'. *Comparative Sociology* 1, no. 2 (2002): 127–49. https://doi.org/10.1163/156913302100418466.

Doumanis, Nicholas. *Before the Nation: Muslim-Christian Coexistence and Its Destruction in Late Ottoman Anatolia*. Oxford: Oxford University Press, 2013.

Eatwell, Roger. 'Reflections on Fascism and Religion'. *Totalitarian Movements and Political Religions* 4, no. 3 (2003): 145–66.

Eatwell, Roger, and Noël O'Sullivan, eds. *The Nature of the Right: European and American Politics and Political Thought since 1789*. London: Pinter, 1989.

Eatwell, Roger, and A. W. Wright. *Contemporary Political Ideologies*. London: Pinter, 1999.

Echternkamp, Jörg, and Stefan Martens, eds. *Experience and Memory: The Second World War in Europe*. New York: Berghahn Books, 2010.

Eisenstadt, S. N. 'Multiple Modernities'. *Daedalus* 129, no. 1 (Winter 2000): 1–29.

Ekmečić, Milorad. *Srbija izmedju srednje Evrope i Evrope*. Belgrade: Politika, 1992.

Ekmečić, Milorad. *Stavaranje Jugoslavije*, Vols 1–2. Belgrade: Prosveta, 1989.

Falina, Maria. 'Between "Clerical Fascism" and Political Orthodoxy: Orthodox Christianity and Nationalism in Interwar Serbia'. *Totalitarian Movements and*

Political Religions 8, no. 2 (2007): 247–58. https://doi.org/10.1080/1469076070 1321155.

Falina, Maria. 'Religious Diversity and Equality in Interwar Yugoslavia'. *Studies in Religion / Sciences Religieuses* 50, no. 4 (December 2021): 539–59. https://doi.org/10.1177/0008429820978967.

Fleck, Hans-Georg, ed. *Liberalizam i Katolicizam u Hrvatkskoj.* Vol. 2. Zagreb: Zaklada Friedrich Naumann, 1999.

Friedman, Francine. *The Bosnian Muslims: Denial of a Nation.* Boulder, CO: Westview Press, 1996.

Gašparić, Jure. *Diktatura kralja Aleksandra in politika Slovenske ljudske stranke v letih 1929-1935.* Ljubljana: Modrijan, 2007.

Gatrell, Peter, and Lyubov Zhvanko, eds. *Europe on the Move. Refugees in the Era of the Great War.* Manchester: Manchester University Press, 2017.

Gaut, Greg. 'Can a Christian Be a Nationalist? Vladimir Solov'ev's Critique of Nationalism'. *Slavic Review* 57, no. 1 (Spring 1998): 77–94.

Gentile, Emilio. 'Fascism as Political Religion'. *Journal of Contemporary History* 25, nos 2–3 (1990): 229–51.

Gentile, Emilio. 'Fascism, Totalitarianism and Political Religion: Definitions and Critical Reflections on Criticism of an Interpretation'. *Totalitarian Movements and Political Religions* 5, no. 3 (December 2004): 326–75.

Gentile, Emilio. 'Political Religion: A Concept and Its Critics – A Critical Survey'. *Totalitarian Movements and Political Religions* 6, no.1 (June 2005): 19–32. https://doi.org/10.1080/14690760500099770.

Gentile, Emilio. 'The Sacralization of Politics: Definitions, Interpretations and Reflections on the Question of Secular Religion and Totalitarianism'. *Totalitarian Movements and Political Religions* 1, no. 1 (2000): 18–55. https://doi.org/10.1080/14690760008406923.

Georgescu, Vlad. *The Romanians: A History.* Columbus: Ohio State University Press, 1991.

Georgiadou, Vassiliki. 'Greek Orthodoxy and the Politics of Nationalism'. *International Journal of Politics, Culture and Society* 9 no. 2 (1995): 295–316.

Geyer, Michael, and Hartmut Lehmann, eds. *Religion und Nation, Nation und Religion: Beiträge zu einer unbewältigten Geschichte.* Göttingen: Wallstein, 2004.

Gligorijević, Branislav. 'Russkya pravoslavnaya tserkov' v period mezhdu dvumya mirovymi voinami'. In *Russkaya Emigratsiya v Yugoslavii,* edited by A. Arsenyev, 109–17. Moscow: Indrik, 1996.

Graf, Friedrich Wilhelm. *Die Wiederkehr der Götter. Religion in der modernen Kultur.* München: C. H. Beck Verlag, 2004.

Graham, Malbone W., Jr. 'The Dictatorship in Yugoslavia'. *American Political Science Review* 23, no. 2 (May 1929): 449–59.

Greble, Emily. *Muslims and the Making of Modern Europe.* Oxford: Oxford University Press, 2021.

Griffin, Roger. *The Nature of Fascism*. London: Pinter, 1991.
Griffin, Roger. 'The Palingenetic Political Community: Rethinking Legitimation of Totalitarian Regimes in Interwar Europe'. *Totalitarian Movements and Political Religions* 2, no. 2 (2002): 24–43.
Hanson, Eric O. *The Catholic Church in World Politics*. Princeton, NJ: Princeton University Press, 1987.
Hastings, Adrian. *The Construction of Nationhood: Ethnicity, Religion, and Nationalism*. Cambridge: Cambridge University Press, 1997.
Hosking, Geoffrey A. *Church, Nation and State in Russia and Ukraine*. London: Macmillan, 1991.
Hroch, Miroslav. 'National Movements with and without Religion: The Nation and Religion in a Historical Perspective'. *Studies in Religion / Sciences Religieuses* 50, no. 4 (December 2021): 493–512/ https://doi.org/10.1177/0008429820978970.
Hughes, Stuart H. *Consciousness and Society: The Reorientation of European Social Thought, 1890–1930*. Brighton: Harvester Press, 1988.
Ilić, Predrag. *Srpska pravoslavna crkva i tajna Dahaua: mit i istina o zatočeništvu patrijarha Gavrila i episkopa Nikolaja u koncentracionom logoru Dahauu*. Belgrade: P. Ilić, 2006.
Jansen, Stef. 'The Violence of Memories: Local Narratives of the Past after Ethnic Cleansing in Croatia', *Rethinking History* 6, no. 1 (2002): 77–94. https://doi.org/10.1080/13642520110112128
Jelavich, Barbara. *History of the Balkans*. 2 Vols. Cambridge: Cambridge University Press, 1983.
Jelavich, Charles, and Barbara Jelavich. *The Establishment of the Balkan National States: 1804–1920*. Cambridge: Cambridge University Press, 1983.
Johnson, Matthew Raphael. 'Nation, State and the Incarnation in the Political Writings of Vladimir Solov'yev: The Transfiguration of Politics'. *Religion, State and Society* 30, no. 4 (2002): 347–55.
Jovanović, Vladan. *Vardarska banovina, 1929–1941*. Belgrade: Institut za noviju istoriju Srbije, 2011.
Jowitt, Kennet, ed. *Social Change in Romania, 1860–1940: A Debate on Development in a European Nation*. Berkley: Institute of International Studies, University of California, 1978.
Judah, Tim. *The Serbs: History, Myth, and the Destruction of Yugoslavia*. New Haven, CT: Yale University Press, 1997.
Judson, Pieter M. *The Habsburg Empire: A New History*. Cambridge, MA: Harvard University Press, 2016.
Hajdarpasic, Edin. *Whose Bosnia? Nationalism and Political Imagination in the Balkans, 1840–1914*. Ithaca, NY: Cornell University Press, 2015.
Hitchins, Keith. *Rumania: 1866–1947*. Oxford: Clarendon Press, 1994.
Kalaitzidis, Pantelis. 'From the "Return to the Fathers" to the "Need for a Modern Orthodox Theology"'. *St Vladimir's Theological Quarterly* 54, no. 1 (2010): 5–36.

Kann, Robert A., and Zdenek V. David. *The Peoples of the Eastern Habsburg Lands, 1526–1918*. Seattle: University of Washington Press, 1984.

Kent, John. 'Religion and Nationalism'. In *Religion in Europe: Contemporary Perspectives*, edited by Sean Gill, Gavin D'Costa and Ursula King, 170–96. Kampen: Kok Pharos, 1995.

Kitromilides, Paschalis M. *Enlightenment, Nationalism and Orthodoxy: Studies in the Culture and Political Thought of Southeastern Europe*. Aldershot, Hampshire: Variorum, 1994.

Kitromilides, Paschalis M. *An Orthodox Commonwealth: Symbolic Legacies and Cultural Encounters in Southeastern Europe*. Aldershot: Ashgate Variorum, 2007.

Knox, Zoe Katrina. *Russian Society and the Orthodox Church: Religion in Russia after Communism*. London: Routledge Curzon, 2005.

Koehne, Samuel. 'The Racial Yardstick: "Ethnotheism" and Official Nazi Views on Religion'. *German Studies Review* 37, no. 3 (October 2014): 575–96. http://www.jstor.org/stable/43556113.

Kolstø, Pål, ed. *Myths and Boundaries in South-Eastern Europe*. London: Hurst, 2005.

Korb, Alexander. *Im Schatten des Weltkriegs: Massengewalt der Ustaša gegen Serben, Juden und Roma in Kroatien 1941–1945*. Hamburg: Hamburger Edition, 2013.

Koselleck, Reinhart. 'Social History and Begriffsgeschichte'. In *History of Concepts: Comparative Perspectives*, edited by Iain Hampsher-Monk, Karin Tilmans and Frank van Vree, 23–35. Amsterdam: Amsterdam University Press, 1998.

Kosik, V. I. *Konstantin Leontev: Razmyshleniia na slavianskuiu temu*. Moskva: Zertsalo, 1997.

Kostyashov, Yuriy. *Serby v Avstriiskoi monarkhii v XVIII veke*. Kaliningrad: Kaliningrdaskii universitet, 1997.

Kristo, Jure. *Katolička crkva u Nezavisnoj Državi Hrvatskoj*. 2 Vols. Zagreb: Hrvatski institut za povijest, 1998.

Lampe, John R. *Yugoslavia as History: Twice There Was a Country*. 2nd edition. Cambridge: Cambridge University Press, 2000.

Lampe, John R., and Constantin Iordachi, eds. *Battling over the Balkans: Historiographical Questions and Controversies*. Budapest: Central European University Press, 2020.

Lampe, John, and Mark Mazower, eds. *Ideologies and National Identities: The Case of Twentieth-Century Southeastern Europe*. Budapest: Central European University Press, 2004.

Laqueur, Thomas W. *The Work of the Dead: A Cultural History of Mortal Remains*. Princeton, NJ: Princeton University Press, 2015.

Lehmann, Hartmut. 'Die Säkularisierung der Religion und die Sakralisierung der Nation im 20. Jahrhundert. Varianten einer komplementären Relation'. In *Religion im Nationalstaat zwischen den Weltkriegen 1918–1939*, edited by Hans-Christian Maner and Martin Schulze Wessel, 13–27. Stuttgart: Steiner, 2002.

Lehmann, Hartmut. 'History of Twentieth-Century Christianity as a Challenge for Historians'. In *Transformationen der Religion in der Neuzeit: Beispiele aus der Geschichte des Protestantismus*, edited by Hartmut Lehmann, 207–20. Göttingen: Vandenhoeck and Ruprecht, 2007.

Leustean, Lucian N., ed. *Orthodox Christianity and Nationalism in Nineteenth-Century Southeastern Europe*. New York: Fordham University Press, 2014.

Leustean, Lucian N. 'Orthodoxy and Political Myths in Balkan National Identities'. *National Identities* 10, no. 4 (December 2008): 421–32. https://doi.org/10.1080/14608940802519045.

Litavrin, G., and R. Grishina, eds. *Chelovek na Balkanah v epohu krizisov i etnopoliticheskih stolknoveniy XX v.* St Petersburg: Aleteyia, 2002.

Lubardic, Bogdan. ' "Revolt against the Modern World": Theology and the Political in the Thought of Justin Popović'. In *Political Theologies in Orthodox Christianity: Common Challenges – Divergent Positions*, edited by Kristina Stoeckl, Ingeborg Gabriel and Aristotle Papanikolaou, 207–26. London: Bloomsbury, 2017.

Makridies, Vasilios. 'Aspects of Greek-Orthodox Fundamentalism'. *Orthodoxes Forum* 5, no. 49 (1991): 49–72.

Makridies, Vasilios N., and Dirk Uffelmann. 'Studying Eastern Orthodox Anti-Westernsim: The Need for a Comparative Research Agenda'. In *Orthodox Christianity and Contemporary Europe: Selected Papers of the International Conference Held at the University of Leeds, England in June 2001*, edited by Jonathan Sutton and Wil van den Bercken, 87–120. Leuven: Peeters, 2003.

Maner, Hans-Christian. *Multikonfessionalität und neue Staatlichkeit. Orthodoxe, griechisch-katholische und römisch-katholische Kirche in Siebenbürgen und Altrumänien zwischen den Weltkriegen: 1918–1940*. Stuttgart: Steiner, 2007.

Maner, Hans-Christian and Martin Schulze-Wessel, eds. *Religion im Nationalstaat zwischen den Weltkriegen 1918–1939: Polen, Tschechoslowakei, Ungarn, Rumänien*. Stuttgart: Steiner, 2002.

Martin, David. *On Secularization: Towards a Revised General Theory*. Aldershot: Ashgate, 2005.

Matić, Milan B. *Ravnogorska ideja i štampi i propagandi četničkog pokreta u Srbiji 1941–1944*. Belgrade: Institut za savremenu istoriju, 1995.

Matijević, Zlatko. 'Pokušaj ustavopravnog definiranja položaja Katoličke crkve u Kraljevini Srba, Hrvata i Slovenaca: 1918–1921'. In *Liberalizam i Katolicizam u Hrvatkskoj*. II Dio, edited by Hans-Georg Fleck, 11–25. Zagreb: Zaklada Friedrich Naumann, 1999.

Mavrogordatos, George Th. 'Orthodoxy and Nationalism in the Greek Case'. In *Church and State in Contemporary Europe: The Chimera of Neutrality*, edited by John T. S. Madeley and Zsolt Enyedi, 117–36. London: Frank Cass, 2003.

Mazower, Mark. *The Balkans*. London: Weidenfeld and Nicolson, 2000.

McLeod, Hugh, and Werner Ustorf, eds. *The Decline of Christendom in Western Europe, 1750–2000*. Cambridge, Cambridge University Press, 2003.

Meininger, Thomas A. *The Formation of a Nationalist Bulgarian Intelligentsia, 1835–1878.* New York: Garland Publishing, 1987.

Melichárek, Maroš. 'Great Migration of the Serbs (1690) and Its Reflections in Modern Historiography'. *Serbian Studies Research* 8, no. 1 (2017): 87–102.

Metzger, Franziska. *Religion, Geschichte, Nation: Katholische Geschichtsschreibung in der Schweiz im 19. und 20. Jahrhundert – kommunikationstheoretische Perspektiven.* Stuttgart: Kohlhammer, 2010.

Michel, Patrick. *Politics and Religion in Eastern Europe: Catholicism in Hungary, Poland, and Czechoslovakia.* Oxford: Polity Press, 1991.

Milosavljevic, Olivera. *U tradiciji nacionalizma ili stereotipi srpskih intelektualaca XX veka o 'nama' i 'drugima'.* Belgrade: Helsinski odbor za ljudska prava u Srbiji, 2002.

Milošević, Zoran. *Crkva i politika: pravoslavlje i drustvene reforme.* Belgrade: Institut za politicke studije, 2002.

Mishkova, Diana. *Modernization and Political Elites in the Balkans before World War I.* Minneapolis: Center for Austrian Studies, University of Minnesota, 1994.

Mishkova, Diana. 'The Interesting Anomaly of Balkan Liberalism'. In *Liberty and the Search for Identity: Liberal Nationalisms and the Heritage of the Empires,* edited by Ivan Zoltan Denes, 399–456. Budapest: Central European University Press, 2006.

Mishkova, Diana. *Prisposobiavane na svobodata: modernost v Srbiia i Ruminiia prez XIX vek.* Sofia: Paradigma, 2001.

Mišović, Miloš. *Srpska Crkva i konkordatska kriza.* Belgrade: Sloboda, 1983.

Mitrović, Andrej. *Serbia's Great War, 1914–1918.* West Lafayette, IN: Purdue University Press, 2007.

Mitrović, Andrej, ed. *Srbi i Albanci u XX veku: Ciklus predavanja.* Belgrade: SANU, 1991.

Mojzes, Paul. *Yugoslavian Inferno: Ethnoreligious Warfare in the Balkans.* New York: Continuum, 1994.

Mommsen, Hans. 'The German Resistance against Hitler and the Restoration of Politics', *Journal of Modern History* 64 (December 1992): 112–27.

Moro, Renato. 'Religion and Politics in the Time of Secularization: The Sacralization of Politics and Politicization of Religion'. *Totalitarian Movements and Political Religions* 6, no.1 (June 2005): 71–86. https://doi.org/10.1080/14690760500099796.

Mosse, George L. *The Nationalization of the Masses: Political Symbolism and Mass Movements in Germany from the Napoleonic Wars through the Third Reich.* New York: Howard Fertig, 1975.

Mylonas, Christos. *Serbian Orthodox Fundamentals: The Quest for an Eternal Identity.* Budapest: Central European University Press, 2003.

Naimark, Norman M., and Holly Case, eds. *Yugoslavia and Its Historians: Understanding the Balkan Wars of the 1990s.* Stanford, CA: Stanford University Press, 2003.

Newman, John Paul. 'Forging a United Kingdom of Serbs, Croats and Slovenes: The Legacy of the First World War and the "Invalid Question"'. In *New Perspectives on*

Yugoslavia: Key Issues and Controversies, edited by Dejan Djokić and James Ker-Lindsay, 46–61. New York: Routledge, 2010.

Newman, John Paul. *Yugoslavia in the Shadow of War: Veterans and the Limits of State Building, 1903–1945*. Cambridge, Cambridge University Press, 2015.

Nielsen, Christian Axboe. *Making Yugoslavs: Identity in King Aleksandar's Yugoslavia*. Toronto, ON: University of Toronto Press, 2014.

Okey, Robin. *Taming Balkan Nationalism: The Habsburg 'Civilizing Mission' in Bosnia 1878–1914*. Oxford: Oxford University Press, 2007.

Parežanin, Ratko. *Drugi svetski rat i Dimitrije V. Ljotić*. Belgrade: A. Ž. Jelić, [1971] 2001.

Pavlowitch, Stevan K. *A History of the Balkans, 1804–1945*. London: Longman, 1999.

Pavlowitch, Stevan K. *Serbia: The History behind the Name*. London: Hurst, 2002.

Pelikan, Jaroslav. *Christian Doctrine and Modern Culture since 1700*. Chicago: University of Chicago Press, 1991.

Pelikan, Jaroslav. *The Spirit of Eastern Christendom, 600–1700*. Chicago: University of Chicago Press, 1993.

Perica, Vjekoslav. *Balkan Idols: Religion and Nationalism in Yugoslav States*. Oxford: Oxford University Press, 2002.

Perica, Vjekoslav. 'The Most Catholic Country in Europe? Church, State, and Society in Contemporary Croatia'. *Religion, State and Society* 34, no. 4 (December 2006): 311–46.

Perkins, Mary Anne. *Christendom and European Identity: The Legacy of a Grand Narrative since 1789*. Aldershot: Ashgate, 1999.

Perkins, Mary Anne. *Nation and Word, 1770–1850: Religious and Metaphysical Language in European National Consciousness*. Aldershot: Ashgate, 1999.

Perović, Latinka, ed. *Srbija u modernizacijskim procesima 19. i 20. Veka*. Belgrade: Authors, 2003.

Perović, Latinka. *Srpski socijalisti 19. veka: Prilog istroii socijalističke misli*. Belgrade: Službeni list SRJ, 1995.

Petrović, Ljubomir, 'Percepcije i Teorije Represije Kraljevine SHS 1918–1929'. *Istorija 20. veka* 2 (2006): 27–50.

Petrović, Ljubomir. 'U Potrazi za izmišljenom stvarnošću: Jugoslovenski identitet u casopisu "Jugosloven" 1931–1932'. *Istorija 20. veka* 1 (2007): 37–56.

Petrovic, Michael B. *A History of Modern Serbia: 1804–1918*. New York: Harcourt Brace Jovanovich, 1976.

Ploscariu, Iemima. A Dappled People: Jewish, Roma, and Romanian Evangelicals Challenging Nationalism in Interwar Romania. PhD diss., Dublin City University, 2021.

Pocock, J. G. A. 'The Concept of a Language and the Métier d' Historien: Some Considerations on Practice'. In *The Languages of Political Theory in Early-Modern Europe*, edited by Anthony Pagden, 19–38. Cambridge: Cambridge University Press, 1987.

Pollack, Detlef. 'Modifications in the Religious Field of Central and Eastern Europe'. *European Societies* 3, no. 2 (2001): 135–65. https://doi.org/10.1080/1461669012 0054302.
Pollack, Detlef, and Gert Pickel. *The Vitality of Religion-Church Integration and Politics in Eastern and Western Europe in Comparison*. Frankfurt(Oder): Frankfurter Institut für Transformationsstudien, 2000.
Popov, Nebojša, ed. *The Road to War in Serbia: Trauma and Catharsis*. Budapest: Central European University Press, 2000.
Popović, Nebojša A. *Slobodan Jovanović i Jugoslovenska država*. Belgrade: Institut za savremenu istoriju, 2003.
Pribichevich, Stoyan. 'Yugoslavia in the Balkans and Central Europe'. *International Affairs* 21, no. 4 (October 1945): 448–58.
Prlenda, Sandra. 'Young, Religious and Radical: The Croat Catholic Youth Organizations, 1922–1945'. In *Ideologies and National Identities: The Case of Twentieth-Century Southeastern Europe*, edited by John Lampe and Mark Mazower, 82–109. Budapest: Central European University Press, 2004.
Radić, Radmila. 'The Church and the "Serbian Question"'. In *The Road to War in Serbia: Trauma and Catharsis*, edited by Nebojša Popov, 247–73. Budapest: Central European University Press, 2000.
Radić, Radmila. *Država i verske zajednice: 1945–1970*. 2 Vols. Belgrade: Institut za noviju istoriju Srbije, 2002.
Radić, Radmila. *Hilandar u državnoj politici kraljevine Srbije i Jugoslavije 1896–1970*. Belgrade: Službeni list, 1998.
Radić, Radmila. *Narodna verovanja, religija i spiritizam u srpskom društvu 19. i u prvoj polovini 20. veka*. Belgrade: Institut za noviju istoriju Srbije, 2009.
Radić, Radmila. 'Religion in a Multinational State: The Case of Yugoslavia'. In *Yugoslavism: History of a Failed Idea: 1918–1992*, edited by Dejan Djokić, 196–207. London: C. Hurst, 2003.
Radić, Radmila. *Život u vremenima: Gavrilo Dožić, 1881–1950*. Belgrade: Institut za noviju istoriju Srbije, 2006.
Radosavljević, Jovan. *Život i stradanja Žiče i Studenice pod okupatorom, 1938–1945*. Sveta Gora: Manastir Hilandar, 1993.
Ramet, Pedro, ed. *Eastern Christianity and Politics in the Twentieth Century*. Durham, NC: Duke University Press, 1988.
Ramet, Pedro. 'From Strossmayer to Stepinac: Croatian National Ideology and Catholicism'. *Canadian Review of Studies in Nationalism* 12, no. 1 (1985): 123–39.
Ramet, Sabrina P. *Balkan Babel: Politics, Culture, and Religion in Yugoslavia*. Boulder, CO: Westview Press, 1992.
Ramet, Sabrina P., ed. *Orthodox Churches and Politics in Southeastern Europe: Nationalism, Conservativism, and Intolerance*. Cham, Switzerland: Palgrave Macmillan, 2020.

Ramet, Sabrina P., and Ola Listhaug, eds. *Serbia and the Serbs in World War Two*. New York: Palgrave Macmillan, 2011.
Reinhard, Wolfgang. 'Reformation, Counter-Reformation, and the Early Modern State: A Reassessment'. *Catholic Historical Review* 75, no. 3 (July 1989): 383–404.
Riis, Carsten. *Religion, Politics, and Historiography in Bulgaria*. Boulder, CO: East European Monographs, 2002.
Roudometof, Victor. *Nationalism, Globalization, and Orthodoxy: The Social Origins of Ethnic Conflict in the Balkans*. Contributions to the study of World History, no. 89. Westport, CT: Greenwood Press, 2001.
Ruff, Mark Edward. 'The Postmodern Challenge to the Secularization Thesis: A Critical Assessment'. *Schweizerische Zeitschrift für Religions-und Kulturgeschichte* 99 (2005): 385–401.
Samerski, Stefan, ed. *Die Renaissance der Nationalpatrone: Erinnerungskulturen in Ostmitteleuropa im 20./21. Jahrhundert*. Köln: Böhlau Verlag, 2007.
Schmitt, Carl. *Political Theology: Four Chapters on the Concept of Sovereignty*. Cambridge, MA: MIT Press, 1988.
Schulze Wessel, Martin, ed. *Nationalisierung der Religion und Sakralisierung der Nation im östlichen Europa*. Stuttgart: Steiner, 2006.
Schulze Wessel, Martin. 'Rechgläubigkeit und Gemeinschaft: Ekklesiologische und politische Bedeutungen des 'sobornost' Begriffs in Rußland'. In *Baupläne der sichtbaren Kirche: Sprachliche Konzepte religiöser Vergemeinschaftung in Europa*, edited by Lucian Hölscher, 196–211. Göttingen: Wallstein, 2007.
Seton-Watson, Hugh. *Eastern Europe between the Wars, 1918–1941*. Boulder, CO: Westview Press, 1986.
Seton-Watson, R. W. *The South Slav Question and the Habsburg Monarchy*. London: Constable, 1911.
Shemyakin, A. L. *Ideologiya Nikoly Pashitcha: Formirovaniye i evolyuciya, 1868–1981*. Moskva: Indrik, 1998.
Shkarovskiy, M. V. 'Sozdaniye i deyatel'nost Khorvatskoy Pravoslavnoy Tserkvi v gody Vtoroy mirovoy voyny'. *Vestnik Tserkovnoy Istorii* 3, no. 7 (2007): 221–62.
Šijaković, Bogoljub, ed. *Srspka teologija u dvadesetom veku: Istrazivacki problemi i rezultati*. Belgrade: Pravoslavni bogoslovski fakultet, 2007.
Šijaković, Bogoljub, and Akelksandar Raković. *Univerzitet i srpska teologija: Istroijski i prosvetni kontekst osnivanja Pravoslavnog bogoslovskog fakulteta u Beogradu*. Belgrade: Pravoslavni bogoslovski fakultet, 2010.
Simić, Bojan. 'Organizacija državne propagande na Balkanu tokom tridesetih godina XX veka: analiza slučaja Jugoslavije i Bugarske'. *Tokovi Istorije* 3 (2007): 132–46.
Slijepčević, Djoko. *Istorija Sprske Pravoslavne Crkve*, Vols 1–3. Belgrade: JRJ, 1991.
Smith, Anthony D. *Chosen Peoples: Sacred Sources of National Identity*. Oxford: Oxford University Press, 2008.
Smith, Helmut Walser. *German Nationalism and Religious Conflict: Culture, Ideology, Politics, 1870–1914*. Princeton, NJ: Princeton University Press, 1995.

Sotirović, Dragan, and Branko Jovanović, eds. *Srbija i Ravna Gora*. Belgrade: Institut za savremenu istoriju, 2004.

Stavrakakis, Yannis. 'Religious Populism and Political Culture'. *South European Society and Politics* 7, no. 3 (2003): 29–52.

Stephenson, Jill. 'Review Article: Resistance and the Third Reich'. *Journal of Contemporary History*, 36 no. 3 (July 2001): 507–16.

Stöckl, Kristina. 'The Lesson of the Revolution in Russian Émigré Theology and Contemporary Orthodox Thought'. *Religion, State and Society* 4 (2007): 285–300.

Stöckl, Kristina. 'Modernity and Its Critique in Twentieth-century Russian Orthodox Thought'.*Studies in East European Thought* 58, no. 4 (2007): 243–69. http://www.jstor.org/stable/23317542.

Stojanović, Dubravka. *Srbija i Demokratija, 1903–1914: Istorijska Studija o 'Zlatnom dobu srpske demokratije'*. Belgrade: Udruženje za društvenu istoriju, Čigoja, 2003.

Stokes, Gale. 'Church and Class in Early Balkan Nationalism'. *East European Quarterly* 13 (1979): 259–70.

Stokes, Gale. *Legitimacy through Liberalism: Vladimir Jovanovic and the Transformation of Serbian Politics*. Seattle: University of Washington Press, 1975.

Stokes, Gale. *Politics as Development: The Emergence of Political Parties in Nineteenth-century Serbia*. Durham, NC: Duke University Press, 1990.

Subotić, Dragan. *Episkop Nikolaj i Pravoslavni bogomoljački pokret*. Belgrade: Nova Iskra, 1996.

Subotić, Dragan. 'Kleronacionalizam i pravoslavlje'. *Marksistička misao* 1 (1987): 189–202.

Sugar, Peter F. *East European Nationalism, Politics and Religion*. Brookfield, VT: Ashgate, 1999.

Sugar, Peter F. *Nationalism and Religion in the Balkans since the Nineteenth Century*. Seattle: Henry M. Jackson School of International Studies. University of Washington, 1996.

Sugar, Peter F. *Nationality and Society in Habsburg and Ottoman Europe*. Aldershot: Variorum, 1997.

Suny, Ronald Grigor, *'They Can Live in the Desert but Nowhere Else': A History of the Armenian Genocide*. Princeton, NJ: Princeton University Press, 2015.

Suny, Ronald Grigor, and Michael D. Kennedy, eds. *Intellectuals and the Articulation of the Nation*. Ann Arbor: University of Michigan Press, 2002.

Šviker, Johan Hajinrih. *Politička istorija srba u Ugarskoj*. Trans. Tomislav Bekić. Novi Sad: Matica srpska, 1998.

Tal, Uriel. *Religion, Politics and Ideology in the Third Reich: Selected Essays*. London: Frank Cass, 2003.

Taylor, Charles. *A Secular Age*. Cambridge, MA: Belknap Press of Harvard University Press, 2007.

Tchurkina I. V., ed. *Rol' religii v formirovanii yuzhnoslavyanskikh naciy*. Moscow: URSS, 1999.

Todorova, Maria. *Imagining the Balkans*. New York: Oxford University Press, 1997.
Tomasevich, Jozo. *War and Revolution in Yugoslavia, 1941–1945: Occupation and Collaboration*. Stanford, CA: Stanford University Press 2001.
Trencsényi, Balázs, Maciej Janowski, Mónika Baár, Maria Falina and Michal Kopeček. *A History of Modern Political Thought in East Central Europe. Volume I: Negotiating Modernity in the 'Long Nineteenth Century'*. Oxford: Oxford University Press, 2016.
Trencsényi, Balázs, Dragos Petrescu, Christina Petrescu, Constantin Iordachi and Zoltán Kántor, eds. *Nation-Building and Contested Identities: Romanian and Hungarian Case Studies*. Budapest, Iasi, 2001.
Trgovčević, Ljubinka. 'The Enlightenment and the Beginnings of Modern Serbian Culture'. *Balcanica: Godišnjak instituta za balkanologiju* 37 (2006): 103–11.
Trgovčević, Ljubinka. *Naučnici Srbije i stvaranje jugoslovenske države: 1914–1920*. Belgrade: Narodna knjiga; Srpska književna zadruga, 1987.
Troch, Pieter. 'The Intertwining of Religion and Nationhood in Interwar Yugoslavia: The School Celebrations of St Sava's Day'. *Slavonic and East European Review* 91, no. 2 (2013): 235–61. https://doi.org/10.5699/slaveasteurorev2.91.2.0235.
Troch, Pieter. *Nationalism and Yugoslavia: Education, Yugoslavism and the Balkans before World War II*. London: I.B. Tauris, [2015] 2020.
Turnock, David. *Eastern Europe: An Historical Geography, 1815–1945*. London: Routledge, 1989.
Valtchinova, Galina. *Balkanski yasnovitki i prorotchitsi ot XX vek*. Sofia: Universitetsko izdatelstvo Sv. Kliment Ohridski, 2006.
Veer, Peter van der, and Hartmut Lehmann, ed. *Nation and Religion: Perspectives on Europe and Asia*. Princeton, NJ: Princeton University Press, 1999.
Velikonja, Mitja. *Religious Separation and Political Intolerance in Bosnia-Herzegovina*. College Station: Texas A&M University Press, 2003.
Verdery, Katherine. *The Political Lives of Dead Bodies: Reburial and Postsocialist Change*. New York: Columbia University Press, 1999.
Vladislav (Metropolitan), ed. *Sprska Pravoslavna Crkva 1920–1970: Spomenica o 50-godíšnjici vaspostavljanja Srpske Patriašije*. Belgrade: Sveti arhijerejski sinod Srpske pravoslavne crkve, 1971.
Voegelin, E. *Political Religions*. Lewiston, NY: Edwin Mellen Press, 1986.
Vucinich, Wayne. Review article of 'Istorija Srpske Pravoslavne Crkve' by Djoko Slijepčević, *Slavic Review* 48, no. 3 (Autumn 1989): 526.
Vukic, Neven. 'The Church in a Communist State: Justin Popovic (1894–1979) and the Struggle for Orthodoxy in Serbia/Yugoslavia'. *Journal of Church and State* 63, no. 2 (Spring 2021): 278–99. https://doi.org/10.1093/jcs/csaa033.
Vukic, Neven. 'Saintsavaism(s) and Nationalism: An Overview of the Development of the Serbian Orthodox Phenomenon of Saintsavaism, with a Special Focus on the Contribution of Justin Popovic (1894–1979)'. *Exchange* 50 (2021): 77–98. https://doi.org/10.1163/1572543X-12341586.

Vukomanović, Milan. *Homo viator: religija i novo doba*. Belgrade: Čigoja štampa, 2008.
Vukomanović, Milan. 'Religious Freedoms in Yugoslavia and the Relations between Religious Communities and the State'. *Religion in Eastern Europe* 22, no. 1 (February 2002): 38–44.
Vukomanović, Milan. 'Srpska pravoslavna crkva izmedju tradicionalizma, konzervatizma i fundamentalizma'. In *Istorija i sećanje*, edited by Olga Manojlović Pintar, 175–90. Belgrade: Institut za noviju istoriju Srbije, 2006.
Vulpius, Ricarda. *Nationalisierung der Religion. Russifizierungspolitik und ukrainische Nationsbildung: 1860–1920*. Wiesbaden: Harrassowitz, 2005.
Wachtel, Andrew B. *Making a Nation, Breaking a Nation: Literature and Cultural Politics in Yugoslavia*. Stanford, CA: Stanford University Press, 1998.
Warhola, James W. *Russian Orthodoxy and Political Culture Transformation*. Carl Beck papers in Russian and East European studies; no. 1006. Pittsburgh: Center for Russian & East European Studies, University of Pittsburgh, 1993.
Wheeler, Brett R. 'Modernist Reenchantments I: From Liberalism to Aestheticized Politics'. *German Quarterly* 74, no. 3 (Summer 2001): 223–36.
Wolff, R. J., and J. K. Hoensch, eds. *Catholics, the State and the European Radical Right 1919–1945*. Boudler, CO: Social Science Monographs, 1987.
Woods, Roger. 'The Radical Right: The "Conservative Revolutionaries" in Germany'. In *The Nature of the Right: European and American Politics and Political Thought since 1789*, edited by Roger Eatwell and Noël O'Sullivan, 124–45. London: Pinter, 1989.
Wortman, Richard S. *Scenarios of Power: Myth and Ceremony in Russian Monarchy*. Princeton, NJ: Princeton University Press, 1995.
Živojinović, Dragoljub R. *Varvarstvo u ime Hristovo: prilozi za Magnum Crimen*. Belgrade: Nova knjiga, 1988.
Žutić, Nikola. *Kraljevina Jugoslavija i Vatikan: odnos jugoslovenske države i rimske crkve, 1918–1935*. Belgrade: Arhiv Jugoslavije, 1994.
Žutić, Nikola. *Rimokatolička crkva i hrvatstvo od ilirske ideje do velikohrvatske realizacije, 1453–1941*. Belgrade: Institut za savremenu istoriju, 1997.

Index

Note: "Serbian Orthodox Church" is abbreviated as "SOC" and "East Orthodox Christianity" as "EOC".

Albania 48, 59, 67
  Albanian Golgotha 9, 59, 67, 68
Aleksandar Karadjordjević, (king) 53, 59,
    69–70, 77–8, 100, 107, 109, 167 n.61
  assassination and burial 76, 101, 104,
    105–6, 121
  and EOC 100, 106
  and integral Yugoslavism 69, 73,
    110, 126
  and religious equality 45
  SOC relationship with 53, 66, 76–7,
    100, 108, 130
Andjelković, Miloš 32, 36–7, 38–9, 59–
    60, 61, 62
Anglican Church 97, 138, 175 n.12
anti-Catholicism 48, 62, 64, 87, 90, 92–3,
    113, 114, 124, 144, 156 n.65, 169 n.82
anti-communism 98, 121–2, 137, 141,
    147–8, 149
  SOC and 83, 98, 113, 121–2, 128, 137
  See also communism
anti-Semitism 17, 65, 96, 145, 146
  See also Jews
anti-Western views 64
  East Orthodox 17, 120, 155 n.55
  Justin Popović 148, 149
  Serbian Orthodox 2–3, 39, 82, 98,
    148–9, 155 n.55
  and Serbian theology 16, 149
atheism 32, 33, 36, 72, 85–6, 98, 122
  and EOC 72, 83, 84, 98
  See also secularization
Austria 141
Austria-Hungary 20, 27, 28, 39, 47,
    57–8, 94
  Catholics in 47
  Muslims in 24–5, 49
  See also Habsburg Empire; Hungary
autocephaly 10, 13, 26, 48, 64, 97, 124

Axis Powers 117–18, 121, 135, 138, 142
  See also Tripartite Pact

Balkans, the 4, 25, 38, 41, 55, 87, 97–8,
    144
  Christianity in 13, 26
  EOC in 14, 22, 23, 96, 97–8
  Habsburg rule in 24, 25
  historiography of 4, 12, 19, 38
  Muslims in 14, 21, 24–5, 26
  nationalism in 2, 13, 22, 41
  Ottoman rule 13, 20–3
Balkan war (1912–1913) 25, 51, 67
Bauer, Antun (archbishop) 93, 112,
    175 n.19
Belgrade 1, 2, 15, 21, 26–7, 38, 48, 50, 52,
    53, 62, 66, 68, 76, 71, 87–8, 93, 100,
    106, 108–9, 112, 116, 17, 119, 129,
    137, 140, 141, 144, 146
  University of 44, 90, 116
Bern, University of 35–6, 65, 147
  See also Switzerland
Blaga, Lucian 102, 174 n.1
Bojović, Jevrem 35
Bolsheviks 83, 84, 85, 88, 92, 153 n.39
  See also communism; Russia
Bosnia
  Catholicism in 25, 79
  East Orthodox Church in 40, 52, 74,
    96–7, 116, 164 n.36
  East Orthodoxy community in 25, 27
  Islam in 24–5, 48–50, 67, 76, 91, 144
  national identity of 76, 136
  neo-Protestantism in 91, 95, 97
  Ottoman and Habsburg rule 24–6, 49
  religious diversity in 24, 79, 97
  See also Sarajevo
Božić, Nikola 31, 34
Bulgakov, Sergey 84

Index

Bulgaria 14, 45, 119
  clergy in 22, 26, 97, 131–2
  Good Samaritan movement in 131–2
Byzantine Empire
  architectural influence of 68, 100, 129–30
  as model of church and state 13, 55, 87
  theological influence of 1, 84, 119

calendars 64, 168 n.79
Cankov, Stefan 126
Catholicism, Roman 11, 22, 38, 43, 99, 123, 132
  Catholic Action 79, 112, 164 n.34, 175 n.19
  church–state relationship 50, 54–5, 60–1, 85, 93, 107, 175 n.16
  conversion to 35, 96
  Croatian identity and 47, 70, 109, 124, 156 n.65, 175 n.19
  Croatian nationalism and 47, 92–3, 132
  East Orthodox Christian relations with 27, 61, 93
  and education policies 46, 54–5, 70, 80, 93–4
  in the Habsburg Empire 22–3, 24, 25, 82
  in the Independent State of Croatia 142
  missionary activities 111, 132
  and modernity 47, 72, 78–9, 84
  political action in Yugoslavia 66, 92–3, 100, 102, 103, 111, 164 n.34
  relationship with the Yugoslav state 47, 48, 78, 112
  religious education and 36, 46, 107–8
  and secularization 80, 84, 85, 87
  Serbian identity and 34–5, 41
  as SOC threat 62, 79, 82, 87, 91–3
  as SOC threat, Concordat 72, 108, 111, 113, 124
  theological education 35, 36, 64–5, 147
  youth organizations 78–9, 81, 112, 132
  and Yugoslavism 42, 44, 48, 62–3, 66, 87, 92, 111
  and Yugoslav state policies 45–6, 74, 80, 81, 85, 108
  See also anti-Catholicism; Concordat crisis; Vatican, the
Chetniks 137, 138, 139, 144–5, 147
  See also Mihajlović, Draža
churches, national 10, 14, 23, 53, 97, 98
  SOC as 26, 62, 112–13, 123, 124
church–state relationship 7, 14, 15, 29, 46, 55, 65, 115, 118, 125, 144, 167 n.68
  EOC and 27, 29, 35, 50, 60–1, 87, 92, 98, 118, 122–3, 125
  in independent Serbia 27–8, 29–34, 38, 39, 40, 52, 60, 91
  in nation-states 26, 35, 60, 118, 124, 125
  Roman Catholicism and 50, 54–5, 60–1, 85, 93, 107, 175 n.16
  in Serbian history 16, 27, 87
  SOC conception of 55, 56, 87, 115, 120, 125
  in Yugoslavia 28, 45–7, 48, 52, 53, 55, 58, 65–6, 72, 74–8, 81, 84–5, 104, 107, 128, 144, 165 n.45
  See also Concordat crisis
communism 2, 16, 83, 139, 142
  Communist party of Yugoslavia 108, 175 n.16
  and EOC 17, 83, 98, 143
  and religion in general 13, 85, 122, 137
  and Yugoslavia post-war 136–7
  See also anti-communism; atheism; Marxism; Partisans
Concordat crisis 4, 15–16, 47–8, 76, 101, 103, 107–15, 120, 124, 175 n.16
Congress of Berlin 21, 24, 28
Constantinople (Istanbul) 13, 21, 24, 26, 49, 87
  See also Islam; Ottoman Empire; Patriarchate of Constantinople
constitutions
  independent Serbia 29, 31
  SOC 52, 75–6
  Yugoslavia 1921 45, 46, 47, 48, 50, 51, 56, 73
  Yugoslavia 1931 45, 46, 73, 104–5, 108, 111
conversion 63, 72, 91, 95, 96, 97
Ćorović, Vladimir 44, 60, 116
coups d'état
  1903 41
  1941 3, 118, 135, 137–8, 145
Crainic, Nichifor 98, 102, 148, 174 n.1
Crnjanski, Miloš 127
Croatia 25, 57, 116, 140
  Bosnian Muslims in 49
  Catholic clergy of 48, 51, 92–3, 112

Catholic identity in 47, 70, 109, 124, 156 n.65, 175 n.19
Catholicism in, general 62, 63, 78–9, 110, 112, 142
Croatian Peasant Party 73, 92, 112, 172 n.68
nationalism in 47, 92–3, 109, 117, 132, 142
Second World War legacy of 136, 139
and Yugoslavism 44, 47, 117, 133
See also Concordat crisis; Jelačić, Ban Josip; Independent State of Croatia, Maček, Vlatko; Protulipac, Ivan; Radić, Stjepan; Ribar, Ivan; Smodlaka, Josip; Ustaša
Cvetković, Dragiša (prime minister) 75, 104, 109, 118, 128, 145
Cvetković–Maček agreement 107, 116
relationship with SOC 106–7, 115
Cvijović, Josif 140–1

democracy 98, 105, 109, 156 n.65, 167 n.68
in Croatia 42, 162 n.6, 175 n.16
in Serbia 30, 31, 38
and the SOC 2, 76, 83, 93, 108, 111, 114–15
social democracy 20, 36, 38, 103
Devrnja, Milutin 127
diversity, ethnic 3, 25, 120
demographics 45, 46, 91
and Serbian nationalism 24, 57, 66
and Yugoslavism 2, 41, 60, 66
See also multinationalism
diversity, religious 12
in Bosnia 24, 79, 97
Habsburg Empire 22, 24
SOC and 91–100, 110, 111, 120, 121
in Yugoslavia pre-dictatorship 3, 25, 45, 66
in Yugoslavia during dictatorship 78–80, 84, 93–4
in Yugoslavia post-dictatorship 106–7, 110, 115, 120
See also equality, religious
Djaja, Jovan 43
Djordjević, Irinej 90, 116, 118, 138, 172 n.61
Djurić, Milan (archpriest) 33–4
Dostoevsky, Fyodor 37, 88, 128, 148

Dožić, Gavrilo (patriarch) 75, 105, 138, 144
after the Second World War 141, 147
and the dictatorship 71–2, 74, 165 n.45, 170 n.24
and Yugoslavism 69, 77, 115, 121
Dubrovnik 2, 96
Dučić, Jovan 41
Durham, Mary Edith 19

Ecumenical Patriarchate 13–14, 22, 26, 118
ecumenism 44, 148
EOC and 63–4, 80, 97, 119
SOC and 63–4, 65, 80, 97, 175 n.12
education 30, 57, 90, 98, 171 n.35
and the Concordat crisis 107–8, 112
curricula, schools 14, 36, 46–7, 54, 79–80, 81, 89, 100–1
of East Orthodox clergy 37
history of 15, 171 n.35
in independent Serbia 30, 31, 36–7
Čedomir Marjanović's theory of 36, 40
modernism and reform in 19, 23
and modern state- and nation-building 10, 11, 19
and nationalism 36, 37, 92, 117, 124, 128
under Ottoman and Habsburg rule 23–4, 26
and the peasantry 26, 95–6
and religious pluralism 79–80, 81, 93–4
and secularization 38–9
and the Serbian Cultural Club 116–17
of Serbian Orthodox clergy 30, 31, 37, 39, 72, 88, 90, 102
social 36, 40
SOC policies 81, 90, 91, 100, 117
and svetosavlje 125–6
teachers, clergy as 15, 23, 54–5, 79, 80, 81, 88
teachers, public roles of 31, 33, 37, 46
and Yugoslavism 79, 81
Yugoslav state policies of 54–5, 70, 79–81, 93–4, 123
Education, Ministry of 75, 81, 93–4, 104
England 36, 138, 147, 148, 172 n.61, 175 n.12
Nikolaj Velimirović in 65, 168 n.81
See also Anglican Church

Enlightenment, the 6, 8, 24, 44
equality, religious 22, 50, 86, 91
   and the SOC 86, 91, 108, 114
   and Yugoslavism 44, 120
   Yugoslav state policies and 45, 59, 84, 91, 108
   See also diversity, religious

fascism 2, 102, 113, 128, 142, 153 n.39
   anti-fascism 142, 146
   Romanian 98, 174 n.1
   Serbian 65, 96, 98, 130, 146
   in Yugoslavia 136, 137, 141

Gaj, Ljudevit 43, 63
Germogen (Maksimov, archbishop) 140, 144
Glasnik Srpske (Pravoslavne) Patrijršije 85, 87, 92, 114, 115, 129
God Worshipper movement 94–6, 97, 98, 132, 173 n.76
   and Dimitrije Ljotić 96, 130
   SOC and 94–6, 127, 130–1
   social work of 4, 115
Greece 22, 68, 120, 127, 141, 148–9, 166 n.61
   and the Ecumenical Patriarchate 13–14, 22, 26
   in the First World War 59, 68, 166 n.61
   Greek language 26, 60
   nationalism in 13–14
   Orthodox Church of 13, 22, 64, 97–8, 148–9

Habsburg Empire 22–5, 80
   Bosnians in 24–5, 26, 49–50
   Catholicism in 22–3, 82
   church–state relationship in 23, 25
   EOC in 13, 15, 20, 23–4, 26, 52, 165 n.37
   Islam in 24–5, 49–50, 76
   Serbs in 15, 20–1, 23–4, 25, 26, 117
   See also Austria-Hungary
Herzegovina 50, 52, 164 n.36
Hrišćanska misao 105, 106, 121–2, 127
   See also Slijepčević, Djoko
Hungary 14, 91, 156 n.65, 164 n.36
   in the Habsburg Empire 23, 24, 26
   See also Austria-Hungary

Ilić, Aleksa 27, 161 n.63
Ilić, V. J. 68
Independent State of Croatia (NDH) 136, 139–40, 141, 142
Islam
   anti-Muslim sentiment 13, 21, 26, 49, 50, 76, 144
   Balkan, in general 17, 21
   in Bosnia 24–5, 48–50, 67, 76, 91, 144
   conversion to 35, 96
   and the Habsburg Empire 24, 50
   in Montenegro 50, 76
   muftis 24, 49, 50, 76
   reis-ul-ulemas 49, 50, 76
   and secularization 80, 84
   in Serbia 25, 50, 76
   in Yugoslavia 45–7, 50, 66, 70, 74, 76, 80, 91, 93–4, 169 n.82
   Yugoslav political parties 49–50, 76
   See also Ottoman Empire; Spaho, Mehmed
Istanbul. *See* Constantinople
IVZ (Islamska Zajednica Vjerska) 49–50, 76

Jelačić, Ban Josip 43
Jews 22, 23, 46, 142
   See also anti-Semitism
Joseph II (emperor) 22, 24
   See also Habsburg Empire
Jovanović, Slobodan 116, 117
Justice, Ministry of 46, 50, 51, 75, 76, 121
   under German occupation 37, 144

Karadjordjević dynasty 76, 77
Kešeljević, Nikola 85
Kirilović, Dimitrije 80, 171 n.35
Korošec, Anton 51, 105
Kosovo 22, 59, 67
   martyrdom epic 9, 29–30, 34, 67, 68, 128–9
   modern 13, 20, 24
   Muslims of 49
   Serbian nationalism and 128, 132

language
   Greek 26, 60
   liturgical 48, 62–3, 107, 124
   Russian 61, 63
   Serbo-Croatian 43, 63, 116

and Yugoslavism 43
  See also nationalism, linguistic
Lazar (prince) 29, 106, 128
  See also Kosovo: martyrdom epic
Leopold I (emperor) 23
Leroy-Beaulieu, Anatole 38, 162 n.65
liberalism 14, 38, 82, 103
  as threat 79, 82, 87, 92
Liberal Party, Serbian 20, 28
  See also Mihailo
'liberation and unification' 52–3, 57–8, 59, 78, 106, 123
Ljotić, Dimitrije 108, 131, 138, 139, 143, 145–7
  and God Worshipper movement 96
  and Nikolaj Velimirović 138, 141, 145, 146
  See also Zbor

Macedonia 22, 40, 45, 143, 164 n.36, 176 n.24
  Muslims in 48–9
Maček, Vlatko 104, 105, 109, 112
  Cvetković–Maček agreement 107, 116
Maria Theresa (empress) 22
  See also Habsburg Empire
Marinković, Živan 130–1, 132
Marjanović, Čedomir 35–6, 37, 40, 144, 161 n.63
martyrdom 9
  and King Aleksandar 106
  Kosovo epic and 9, 29–30, 34, 67, 68, 128–9
  Serb national narrative of 59, 68, 99, 118, 123, 136, 139
  of the SOC 99, 123, 139
  and Nikolaj Velimirović 16
Marxism 83, 103
  See also communism
materialism 38, 79, 83, 130
  and atheism 36, 72, 83–4, 85, 98
  and communism 92, 122
  as modern 32, 82, 83
  and nationalism 118
Medan, Danilo R. 125–6
Merz, Ivan 79
Meštrović, Ivan 41, 69–70, 100, 166 n.61
Mihailo (metropolitan) 27, 28, 30, 165 n.43
Mihajlović, Draža 137, 140, 145

  See also Chetniks
Milentije (bishop) 34–5
Millet system 13, 22, 23, 25, 26, 49
Mišović, Miloš 15–16
modernity
  and EOC 25, 63, 72, 82, 83
  SOC challenges 72, 82–4, 102, 120, 132–3, 135, 147 (*see also* atheism; communism; democracy; materialism; secularization; socialism)
  SOC svetosavlje response 101, 123, 132
modernization 6, 19, 21, 44, 63, 79, 84–5
Mojsej, Archbishop 27
Moljević, Stevan 144–5
Montenegro 26, 59, 74, 140, 176 n.24
  Christian clergy of 52, 115, 164 n.36 (*see also* Dožić, Gavrilo; Njegoš, Petar Petrović)
  and concordats 47, 112–13
  Islam in 48, 50, 76
monuments and memorials 67–8, 69, 166 n.61
Moscow 2, 88
  See also Russia
multinationalism 2, 3, 41, 57, 60, 120
  See also diversity, ethnic
Muslims. *See* Islam
myths 8–9, 13, 41, 67, 88, 123, 174 n.1
  and the Battle of Kosovo 29–30, 67, 106
  and German nationalism 11, 125
  and Nikolaj Velimirović 16–17

Najdanović, Dimitrije 15, 98–100, 102–4, 119, 135, 149
  Chetnik critique 138, 145
  and the God Worshipper movement 96
  and Dimitrije Ljotić 138, 145, 146, 147
  and political Orthodoxism 103, 131
  Svetosavlje involvement 90, 127–8
nationalism 61, 67, 123, 131, 142
  Croatian 92, 107, 109, 112, 117, 142, 156 n.65
  German 10, 11, 125
  Macedonian 143
  Montenegrin 74, 77
  Serbian 19–20, 25, 35, 124
  Slovenian 73, 77, 117
  Yugoslav 81, 86, 100, 132
nationalism, linguistic 8, 43, 63, 78

National Socialism 125, 146, 153 n.39
  See also Nazi Germany
Nazarenes 27, 62, 94, 95, 97
Nazi Germany 17, 115, 117
  invasion of Yugoslavia 137, 140
  public rituals of 125, 153 n.39
  Nikolaj Velimirović and 125, 139, 146
Nedić, Milan 37, 137, 139, 141, 143, 144, 145
Neo-Patristic movement 84, 119–20
neo-Protestantism 27, 62, 94, 95, 97
Njegoš, Petar Petrović (archbishop) 68–70, 169 n.90
Novi Sad 24, 171 n.35

Obradović, Dositej 24
Obrenović dynasty
  Alexander (king) 30
  Milan (king) 27, 28, 165 n.43
  Miloš (prince) 26
  See also Serbia, independent
Orthodoxism, political 17, 98, 102–4, 131, 132, 147, 174 n.1
Orthodox public. *See* public, Orthodox
Ottoman Empire 20–2, 23, 24–5, 29, 49, 112
  Balkan Christian independence from 13, 15
  EOC in 13–14, 20, 22
  millet system in 13, 21, 25, 26, 49
  Patriarchate of Peć, abolition 15, 24, 52, 53
  Serbian identity under 19–20, 21, 22, 25, 26

Pantelić, Miloš 39
Parenta, Miloš 72, 77, 78, 79, 87, 97, 98
Partisans 136, 137, 139, 143
Pašić, Nikola 31, 32, 58, 69, 78, 92, 167 n.68
Patriarchate, Serbian. *See* Serbian Patriarchate
Patriarchate of Constantinople 13, 53, 64, 118, 164 n.36, 168 n.79
Patriarchate of Peć 15, 24, 52, 53
  See also Serbian Patriarchate
Paul (Karadjordjević), prince regent 104–5, 107, 109, 115–16, 118, 138
Pavlović, Dimitrije (patriarch) 37, 76, 121, 161 n.63, 165 n.43
  election to patriarch 53–4, 57, 59
  and the God Worshipper movement 94, 95
  and Yugoslavism 56, 59
Petar I Karadjordjević (king) 30, 58
Petar II Karadjordjević (king) 104, 117, 118, 137–8
Poland 9, 164 n.34
political Orthodoxism. *See* Orthodoxism, political
Popović, Justin 16, 90, 117, 148–9, 172 n.61
  See also svetosavlje (ideology); Velimirović, Nikolaj
post-communism 13, 14, 17, 142
Pribićević, Svetozar 77
Protestantism 11, 23, 55, 61, 99, 132, 168 n.81
  See also neo-Protestantism
Protulipac, Ivan 78–9
public, Orthodox 82, 83–4, 89, 91, 98–9, 119, 129

questions, national 109, 125
  Serbian 103, 117, 120, 133
  Yugoslav 17, 72, 133

Radić, Stjepan 73, 92, 107
Radical Party, Serbian 31, 32, 33, 34, 43, 93
reforms
  agrarian 51, 107
  Habsburg 22–4
  Ottoman (Tanzimat) 21–2
  SOC 62–5, 71, 72, 75–6, 83, 85
religion, definition of 4–5
Religions, Ministry of 46–7, 51, 52, 53, 75, 92
  See also Cvetković, Dragiša
Ribar, Ivan 111–12, 175 n.16
Ristić, Jovan 28
Romania 45, 64, 97, 148, 164 n.36
  EOC in 97–8, 174 n.1
  fascism in 98, 174 n.1
  political Orthodoxism and 102
  theology in 119, 120, 132, 174 n.1
Russia 65, 68, 85
  Bolshevik Revolution of 83, 84, 88, 122
  émigrés from 84, 87–8, 119–20, 122
  Empire of 25, 36, 38, 88
  and independent Serbia 25, 28

Orthodox Church of 25, 37, 88, 140, 147, 168 n.79
  religious thought of 16, 84, 88, 119–20, 167 n.68
  theological seminaries in 37, 88, 90, 148

sacralization 9, 11, 30, 128
  of the nation 9, 10, 30, 128
  of politics 10–11, 153 n.39 (*see also* Orthodoxism, political)
saints
  East Orthodox 29
  Serbian Orthodox 29, 69
  See also Popović, Justin; Sava, Saint; Velimirović, Nikolaj
Sarajevo 47, 48, 50, 76, 96, 97, 117, 140
  See also Bosnia
Sava, Saint 33, 34, 58, 70, 97, 122, 123–4, 125–7
  cathedral of (Belgrade) 129
  celebration of 1935 4, 93–4, 122–3, 126
  Serbian nationalism and 122, 123–4, 125–7, 146
  SOC and 113, 121, 122, 126–7
  Yugoslav state policies and 70, 93, 100
sects and sectarian movements 6, 46, 62, 64, 72, 95
  East Orthodox 23, 94–5
  East Orthodox relations with 63, 72, 99, 130
  neo-Protestant 27, 62, 91, 94, 95, 97
  Protestant 132
secularization 5–6, 79, 80, 123
  as Enlightenment doctrine 6, 8, 24, 44
  and EOC 14, 63, 84, 87, 88
  as modernity 14, 38–9, 44, 62, 63, 84–5, 125
  nationalism and 9, 43, 118
  of politics 38–9, 51, 111–12
  svetosavlje as response to 123
  thesis of 6–7, 10
  as threat to Christianity 103, 127, 132
  as threat to the SOC 2, 12, 59, 85, 101, 133
  as Western 24, 37, 82–3
  Yugoslavism and 59–60, 85–6, 89, 100
Serbia 15, 20, 21, 24, 25–34, 36–40, 52, 58–9, 67, 80, 164 n.36
  church–state relationship in 27–8, 29–34, 38, 39, 40, 52, 60, 91

constitution of 29, 31
  EOC in 19, 27, 29, 32, 33, 91
Serbian Cultural Club 116–17
Serbian Patriarchate 51–6, 58, 71–2, 121
  and anti-Catholic sentiment 91–2
  library of 17, 88
  Second World War and 139–40
  and Serbian nationalism 58, 77, 166 n.55
  as SOC centralization 52, 74, 75–6, 164 n.36, 166 n.50
  See also Patriarchate of Peć
Skerlić, Jovan 43
Slavs, southern 17, 42, 43, 65, 68, 162 n.6
Slijepčević, Djoko 15, 90, 156 n.64, 164 n.36
  God Worshipper membership 96
  Hrišćanska misao editorship 105, 127
  Zbor membership 96, 147
Slovenia 47, 93, 141
  Catholicism in 91, 111
  and liberation rhetoric 67
  nationalism of 73, 77, 117
  and Yugoslavism 73, 99–100, 117
Smodlaka, Josip 42, 162 n.6
sobornost 61, 167 n.68
socialism 32, 38, 83
  SOC and 38, 83, 137
  Yugoslavist 136, 137, 141–2, 148
social work 38, 40, 91, 98, 128, 132
  God Worshipper movement and 4, 96, 115
Sokol movement 78, 112, 128
Spaho, Mehmed 49, 76, 105
Sremski Karlovci 23, 24, 27, 43, 52, 53, 84, 88, 164 n.36, 165 n.37
Stadler, Josip (archbishop) 47
state-building
  Serbian 3, 26, 27, 40
  Yugoslav 41, 60, 138
Stepinac, Alojzije (archbishop) 132, 137, 142
Stojadinović, Milan 34, 72, 104–5, 107, 108, 109
Strossmayer, Josip Juraj (archbishop) 44, 47, 92
svetosavlje (ideology) 4, 101, 126, 128, 130, 132
  Danilo R. Medan and 125–6
  Justin Popović and 148–9

Nikolaj Velimirović and 113, 123, 125, 128, 138, 148-9
Svetosavlje (journal) 90-1, 105, 127-8
Switzerland 12, 36, 65, 141, 147
   See also Bern, University of
symphonia 55, 87, 119
   See also Byzantine Empire
synods
   East Orthodox 97, 168 n.79
   SOC 66, 81, 140-1, 144

theology 5, 11, 16, 37, 81, 84, 88, 97, 102, 119-20, 161 n.63, 167 n.68
   Belgrade Theological Seminary 35, 90, 165 n.43
   Church doctrine and 60, 61, 87
   and ecumenism 64-5
   and modernity 32, 82
   and nationalism 12, 34, 61, 99, 105, 132
   publications 71, 90, 105
   University of Bern 35-6, 65-6
   See also Najdanović, Dimitrije; Pašić, Nikola; Pavlović, Dimitrije; Popović, Justin; Slijepčević, Djoko
Tito, Josip Broz 136, 137, 147
Tripartite Pact 117-18, 138
   See also Axis Powers
Trumbić, Ante 50
Tsankov, Stefan 119
Turić, Jure 80

unification
   and liberation rhetoric 52-3, 57-8, 59, 78, 106, 123
   political 51, 56, 67, 70, 73, 77
   of the SOC 51-6, 57, 58, 65, 90, 164 n.36 (*see also* Serbian Patriarchate)
Ustaša 139, 140, 142
   See also Croatia
Uzunović, Nikola 104

Varnava (patriarch) 15, 74, 76-7, 88, 92, 96, 102, 108, 109, 113
Vasić, D. J. 71, 99
Vatican, the 27, 109, 124, 142, 156 n.65
   and the Concordat 15, 47-8, 76, 107-8, 110, 111, 120
   See also Catholicism, Roman; Concordat crisis

Velimirović, Nikolaj 4, 15, 16-17, 34, 74, 95, 113, 116, 123-6, 138, 146-7, 148, 149
   and the 1941 coup d'état 138, 146
   anti-Semitism of 17, 65, 146
   canonization of 16, 147
   and Dimitrije Ljotić 138, 141, 145, 146
   and Djoko Slijepčević 105
   and ecumenism 65, 97, 148, 168 n.81, 169 n.82
   education 35, 65
   during the Second World War 16, 118, 135, 138, 139, 140, 141, 146
   and the God Worshipper movement 95-6
   influence on *Svetosavlje* 90, 127-8
   and Justin Popović 16, 148
   support for Adolf Hitler 125, 139, 146
Vesnik Srpske Crkve 31, 33, 38, 39, 162 n.65
Vienna 23, 24, 141, 159 n.16
   See also Austria-Hungary
Vojvodina 15, 23, 62, 66, 84, 94-5, 128-9, 164 n.36

World War, First 9, 21, 59, 67-8, 94, 135, 138
World War, Second 133, 135, 136-7, 142-3
   collaboration during 135, 137, 138, 141, 142-3, 144 (*see also* Germogen; Ljotić, Dimitrije; Marjanović, Čedomir; Nedić, Milan; Velimirović, Nikolaj)
   EOC during 140, 144, 147
   German invasion and occupation 135, 137, 138-41
   God Worshipper movement during 96
   nation-building and 2, 41, 46
   resistance during 135, 142-3
   Serbian nationalism during 138, 139, 144
   SOC during 137, 138-42, 143
   SOC after 137, 147-9
   Yugoslavia after 147-9

youth movements and organizations 72, 79, 81, 89, 132
   Catholic 78-9, 112
Yugoslavism 17, 42, 43, 58, 82

Catholicism and 44, 92
and the dictatorship 73–4, 76–7, 78, 81–2
and East Orthodox culture 99–100
and education 79, 81 (*see also* education)
integral 57, 105, 111, 122, 126
and King Aleksandar 69, 73, 126
Milan Stojadinović and 105
national diversity and 2, 60, 74, 81, 117
Petar Petrović Njegoš and 68–70
religious diversity and 41–5, 60, 78, 81, 100, 123
secularization and 43–4, 86, 89–90, 123, 126
Serbian identity/nationalism and 57, 77, 110, 117, 126
as supranational 41, 86, 126

Zbor 96, 130, 137, 145, 147
 See also Ljotić, Dimitrije
Zeitinlik cemetery 68
Živanović, Aleksandar 80
Živković, Petar (prime minister) 74, 77, 78, 104, 108, 165 n.45
and church–state relations 71–2, 75

www.ingramcontent.com/pod-product-compliance
Lightning Source LLC
Chambersburg PA
CBHW062227300426
44115CB00012BA/2248